Geomorphology, Hydrology, and Ecology of Great Basin Meadow Complexes—Implications for Management and Restoration

United States Department of Agriculture / Forest Service
Rocky Mountain Research Station
General Technical Report RMRS-GTR-258
August 2011

ABSTRACT

This report contains the results of a 6-year project conducted by the U.S. Department of Agriculture, Forest Service, Rocky Mountain Research Station and U.S. Environmental Protection Agency, Office of Research and Development on stream incision and meadow ecosystem degradation in the central Great Basin. The project included a coarse-scale assessment of 56 different meadows systems coupled with more detailed, fine-scale analyses of six of those meadows. This report presents basic information on the linked geomorphic, hydrologic, and vegetation characteristics of the meadow systems. Then, the causes of degradation; the underlying geomorphic, hydrologic, and biotic processes operating within the meadows; and the factors required to evaluate the sensitivity or, conversely, resistance of streams and their associated meadow complexes to stream incision are described. Finally, management and treatment options are provided based on our current understanding of both the causes of degradation and the underlying processes.

Keywords: riparian areas, wetlands, semi-arid ecosystems, degradation, stream incision, stabilization

EDITORS

Jeanne C. Chambers is a Research Ecologist with the U.S. Department of Agriculture, Forest Service, Rocky Mountain Research Station in Reno, Nevada, and an Adjunct Professor at the University of Nevada, Reno. Her primary research focus is on the restoration of disturbed or degraded ecosystems in the western United States. She served as the Team Leader of the Great Basin Ecosystem Management Project for Restoring and Maintaining Sustainable Riparian Ecosystems from 1993 until its completion in 2009.

Jerry R. Miller holds the Blanton J. Whitmire Distinguished Professorship of Environmental Sciences at Western Carolina University. He has worked extensively in the United States and South America on the geomorphic responses of river systems to natural and anthropogenic disturbance and is coauthor of the third and fourth editions of the textbook *Process Geomorphology* (McGraw-Hill).

Cover photo: View of three Kingston Canyon meadows taken from Big Creek Peak. *Photo by Mark Lord.*

ACKNOWLEDGMENTS

Financial and technical support for this project was provided by the U.S. Environmental Protection Agency and U.S. Department of Agriculture, Forest Service, Rocky Mountain Research Station. The U.S. Department of Agriculture, Humboldt-Toiyabe National Forest provided logistic support and funded the stream stabilization project in Kingston Canyon.

Kate Dwire, Dave Weixelman, Peter Weisberg, Sharon Lawlor, John Sandberg, Scott Baggett, and Erin Goergen provided review comments.

AUTHORS

Jeanne C. Chambers
U.S. Department of Agriculture, Forest Service
Rocky Mountain Research Station
Reno, Nevada
jchambers@fs.fed.us

Sudeep Chandra
Department of Natural Resources and Environmental Science
University of Nevada, Reno
sudeep@cabnr.unr.edu

Tom Dudley
Marine Science Institute, University of California at Santa Barbara
tdudley@msi.ucsb.edu

Dru Germanoski
Department of Geology and Environmental Sciences
Lafayette College
Lafayette, Pennsylvania
germanod@lafayette.edu

Chris A. Jannusch
Department of Natural Resources and Environmental Science
University of Nevada, Reno
cjannusch@ucdavis.alumni.com

David G. Jewett
U.S. Environmental Protection Agency
Office of Research and Development
Ada, Oklahoma
Jewett.david@epamail.epa.gov

Mark L. Lord
Department of Geosciences and Natural Resources
Western Carolina University
Cullowhee, North Carolina
mlord@wcu.edu

Jerry R. Miller
Department of Geosciences and Natural Resources
Western Carolina University
Cullowhee, North Carolina
jmiller@wcu.edu

Wendy Trowbridge
Department of Natural Resources and Environmental Science
University of Nevada, Reno
wtrowbridge@cabnr.unr.edu

Contents

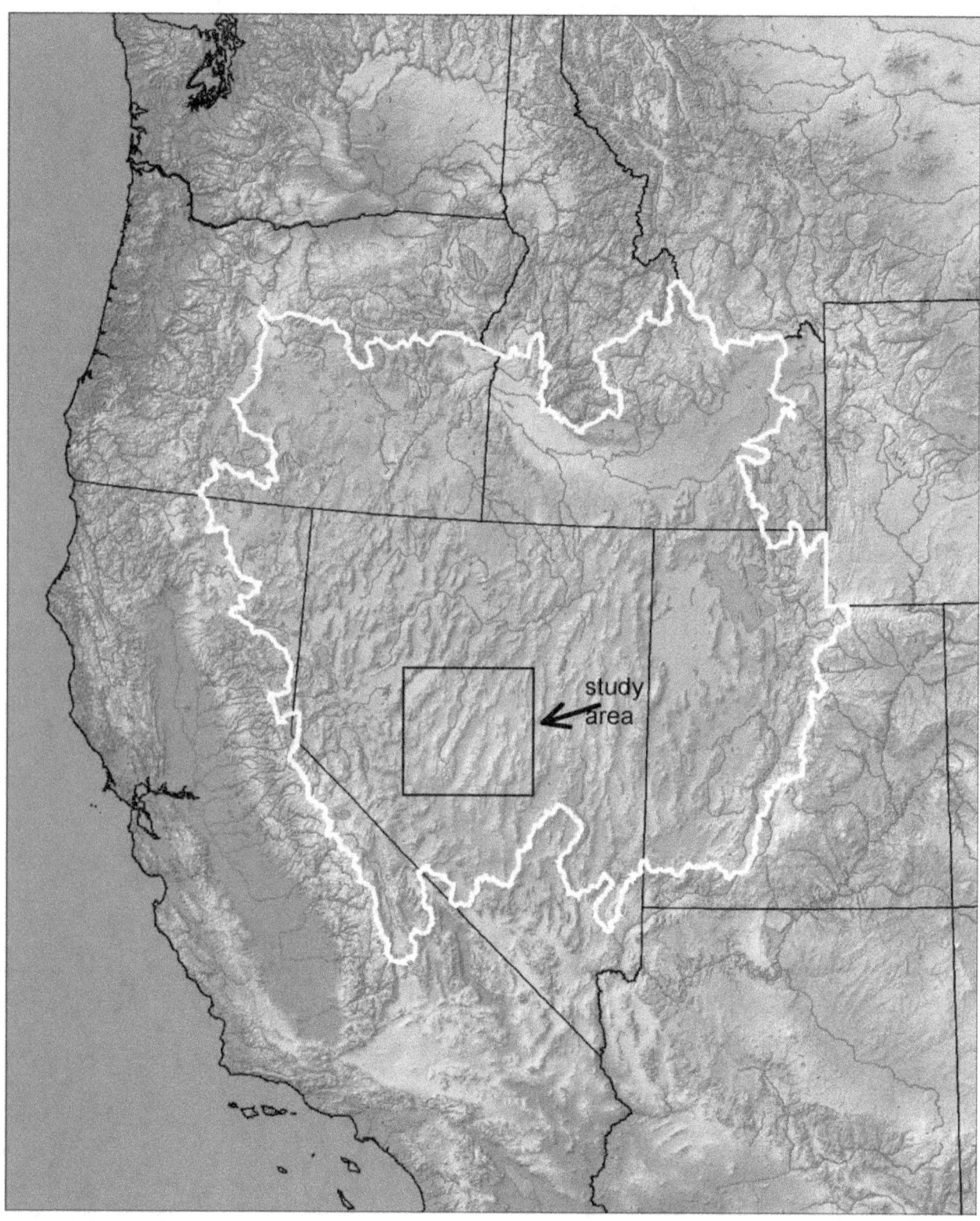

Figure 1.1. Map of the floristic Great Basin, outlined in white with the study area inset.

Chapter 1:   Introduction and Overview

Jeanne C. Chambers, Jerry R. Miller, and Dru Germanoski

The Problem—Stream Incision and Meadow Degradation

Streams and riparian ecosystems are a particularly valuable resource in the arid to semi-arid Great Basin, supplying water for agriculture and domestic uses, forage for livestock, and habitat for diverse aquatic and terrestrial organisms. In upland watersheds of the central Great Basin, many of the streams and riparian ecosystems have been severely degraded (Chambers and Miller 2004b; Chambers and others 2004a). A primary cause of this degradation is ongoing stream incision (downcutting) that occurs during episodic high flow events (Miller and others 2001, 2004). Meadow complexes (areas with shallow water tables that are dominated largely by grasses and carices) are at especially high risk of degradation because they often occur in hydrologic and geomorphic settings that are susceptible to stream incision (Chambers and others 2004a, 2004b; Germanoski and Miller 2004; Jewett and others 2004). In many cases, streams have been isolated from their original floodplains, and there have been significant changes in channel pattern and form. As the channels have incised, the base level for groundwater discharge has been lowered, resulting in deeper water tables. Because riparian vegetation depends on groundwater availability, there have been changes in the structure and composition of meadow ecosystems (Wright and Chambers 2002; Chambers and others 2004a, 2004b). The net effect has been a decrease in the aerial extent of the riparian corridor and a loss of meadow ecosystems.

In this chapter, we briefly review the major causes of, and controls on, channel incision and meadow degradation in the central Great Basin and discuss a conceptual basis for meadow restoration and management. In subsequent chapters, we focus on our current understanding of meadow ecosystems and the development of management strategies. We begin with an overview of the geologic, climatic, and hydrologic setting of the central Great Basin.

Geological, Geographical, and Hydrologic Setting

Great Basin Physiography

The hydrologic Great Basin encompasses an area of over 500,000 km² and includes most of the state of Nevada and portions of California, Oregon, Idaho, Utah, and Arizona (fig. 1.1). Despite rugged topography and prominent topographic relief, the region has no significant external surface drainage (Mifflin 1988). The Great Basin is part of the Basin and Range physiographic province that consists of over 400 discrete mountain ranges that are separated by intermontane basins (Dohrenwend 1987). The mountain ranges and basins are oriented in a north-south direction, vary in length from tens to hundreds of kilometers and are typically 15 to 25 km wide (fig. 1.2; Dohrenwend 1987). Basin elevations are about 1300 to 1600 m above sea level, while mountain ranges have elevations that exceed 3500 m (Stewart 1978).

The topography of the Basin and Range was produced by regional ongoing uplift and extensional tectonism that began in the Miocene (approximately 17 million years before present [BP]) (Stewart 1978; Thatcher and others 1999). Horizontal extension produced horst and graben structures. Horsts are up-thrown blocks of crustal material that are bounded by normal faults on either side. Basin-forming grabens are down-dropped crustal blocks, again bound by normal faults. Mountain ranges and basins also are formed by extension-driven rotation of crustal blocks (Stewart 1978). The high relief between mountain ranges and adjacent basins produces steep potential energy gradients that drive stream incision in the mountains and sediment transfer to the intermontane basins. As a result, the mountains are deeply incised, and mountain fronts are fringed by coalescing alluvial fans that grade into basin-fill alluvium and lacustrine deposits (fig. 1.3).

Great Basin Geology

Lithology and Structure. Bedrock within the Great Basin of central Nevada ranges from Late Precambrian to Tertiary in age and is composed of the full spectrum of rock types, including intrusive (plutonic) and extrusive (volcanic) igneous rocks, chemical and clastic sedimentary rocks and metamorphic rocks. From Late Precambrian through the Paleozoic, the area that is now the Great Basin consisted of a continental margin that was characterized by deposition of sediment from the western continental landscape. Clastic (primarily shale and sandstone) and chemical (primarily limestone) sedimentary rocks were produced in a marine sedimentary basin throughout the Paleozoic (Stewart 1978). The continental margin evolved into an active subduction zone that produced igneous plutons that intruded and metamorphosed the Paleozoic sedimentary rocks and generated explosive volcanic eruptions that mantled the landscape with ashflow tuffs, ignimbrites, rhyolite flows and, later, localized basaltic lavas.

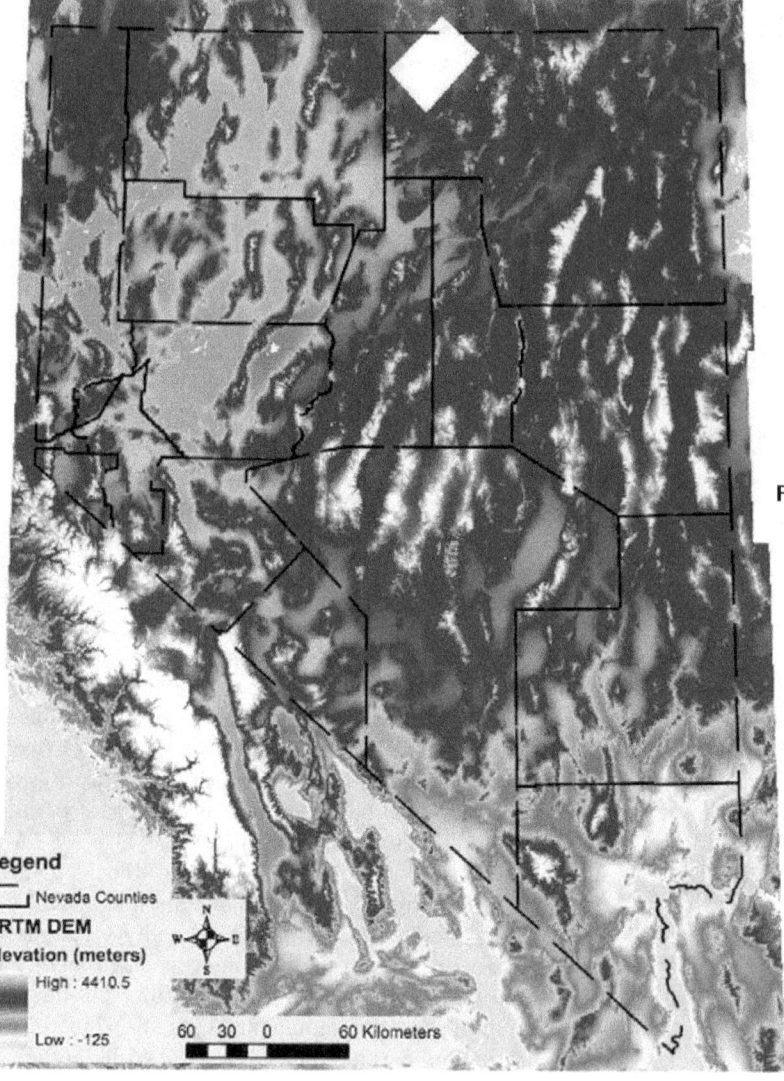

Figure 1.2. Digital elevation map for the Great Basin. White rectangle in top center reflects a gap in the elevation data. Map based on U.S. Geological Survey data files.

Legend
Nevada Counties
SRTM DEM
Elevation (meters)
High : 4410.5
Low : -125

60 30 0   60 Kilometers

Figure 1.3. Alfalfa fields at the base of the alluvial apron on the east side of the Toiyabe Range that are irrigated by shallow groundwater.

The Lower Paleozoic units in the study area consist of sedimentary, low-grade metamorphic and volcanogenic rocks. In the northern portion of the study area, two distinct groups of Lower Paleozoic rocks are present: (1) a carbonate assemblage with minor shale and quartzite, and (2) an assemblage that consists of siliceous chert-rich sedimentary rocks, volcanic flows, and pyroclastic rocks (Stewart and McKee 1977). The siliceous rocks were deposited in the western portion of the depositional basin and then thrust over the carbonate rocks during the Antler Orogeny (Stewart and McKee 1977). In the southern portion of the study area, siliciclastics, including sandstones, siltstones, and shales, are more common than carbonates and have been metamorphosed to quartzites, phyllitic schists, phyllite, and slate (Kleinhampl and Ziony 1985).

During the Late Paleozoic, clastic sediment that was derived from the Antler orogenic belt was deposited across the deformed lower Paleozoic rocks. Pyroclastic volcanic rocks and clastic sedimentary rocks that were deposited in a marine back-arc basin to the west were subsequently thrust eastward during the Permian along the Golconda Fault over the coarse clastic units (Stewart and McKee 1977). Thus, Paleozoic rocks consist of a complex assemblage of rock types deposited in diverse depositional settings and thrust faulted and deformed during the Late Paleozoic Antler Orogeny.

The Paleozoic rocks were intruded by igneous plutons during the Mesozoic (primarily the Jurassic and Cretaceous), including the Austin pluton, which is the largest in the region. The Austin pluton is exposed at the surface in three areas near Austin in the Toiyabe Range. Petrologic characteristics suggest that the three exposures are part of a single large batholith that is separated by inliers of Paleozoic sedimentary rocks (Stewart and McKee 1977). The intrusive rocks primarily range from quartz monzonites to granodiorites in composition and are characterized by a platy sheet structure that makes some of the large plutons appear to be bedded (Stewart and McKee 1977).

Cenozoic age rocks are dominated by volcanic materials following the emplacement of scattered intrusive quartz monzonite and quartz diorite plutons in the Late Eocene to Early Miocene. The earliest phase of Tertiary volcanism was dominated by andesitic and dacitic lavas that were extruded during the early Oligocene. These extrusions were followed by a shift to rhyolite and quartz-latite ash-flow tuffs in the late Oligocene. These rocks are capped by Miocene and Pliocene volcanics that range in composition from andesite to basalt with basaltic eruptions occurring into the Pleistocene (Stewart and McKee 1977).

Paleozoic rocks were folded, metamorphosed, and cut by low angle thrust faults from west to east during the Late Paleozoic Antler and Sonoma Orogenies and, to a lesser extent, during the Mesozoic Laramide Orogeny. Recent work in the Toiyabe Range in the center of the study area (fig. 1.1) indicates that the structural history of the Basin and Range is more complex than previously recognized and that there were elements of structural extension and transpression in the Late Paleozoic that produced normal faults perpendicular and tangential to the Toiyabe Range (Smith and Miller

1990). In the Miocene, the tectonic regime changed from compressional to an extensional regime that led to episodes of uplift and crustal extension that were responsible for development of the modern topography.

River incision into rising, fault-bounded horsts and rotationally uplifted mountain ranges coevolved with uplift and both processes continued throughout the Cenozoic. As a result, mountain uplands are deeply dissected by rivers that drain both east and west from the axis of each range into intermontane basins. Although the mountains are erosional landscapes with streams that flow directly on bedrock in many locations, valleys are locally floored by Holocene age alluvium to depths exceeding 50 m. Axial valley-fill sediment interfingers with alluvial fan sediment from side-valley tributaries. In many cases, fans prograde into the axial valleys as pronounced landforms. Hillslopes are mantled locally with a thin veneer of alluvium with scree chutes formed in zero-order tributaries. Soils are typically thin and poorly developed owing to the arid climate, steep slopes, and erosion.

Great Basin Hydrology

Distribution of Precipitation and Evapotranspiration. The Great Basin is a semi-arid to arid region. Average annual precipitation varies from less than 150 to approximately 700 mm/yr (6 to 27.5 inches/yr; fig. 1.4) with the majority of the precipitation falling as snow during winter months. Precipitation varies significantly between individual mountain ranges and intervening basins and from mountain range to mountain range due to orographic effects (Mifflin 1988). The highest precipitation occurs in higher, broader mountain ranges because of the ability of high mountains to influence moist air masses moving across the basin from west to east.

In the Great Basin, evaporation potential exceeds annual precipitation because of the combination of low precipitation and high average temperatures. Similar to the spatial distribution of precipitation, the evaporation potential varies from range to range and between a mountain range and its adjacent basins. However, the trends are opposite of precipitation patterns; average annual temperature and evaporation potential is higher in intermontane basins than in mountain ranges, and annual average temperature varies inversely with elevation in the mountains. Therefore, the water supply is decidedly asymmetric with mountains serving as water sources and basins serving as "sinks."

Major Rivers and Mountain Streams. The Basin and Range topography exerts tremendous control on the regional hydrology (fig. 1.5). The down-dropped grabens and intermontane basins create regionally significant depressions that capture surface water drainage for hundreds of square kilometers. In the most extreme case, basin elevation extends below sea level in Death Valley in the southwestern portion of the Basin and Range. Thus, the Great Basin is a unique region in North America because all major rivers in the region drain into lakes or sinks in intermontane basins, and no major rivers leave the region and drain to the ocean.

The longest river in the Great Basin is the Humboldt River, which drains from east to west across northern Nevada from

USDA Forest Service Gen. Tech. Rep. RMRS-GTR-258. 2011.

3

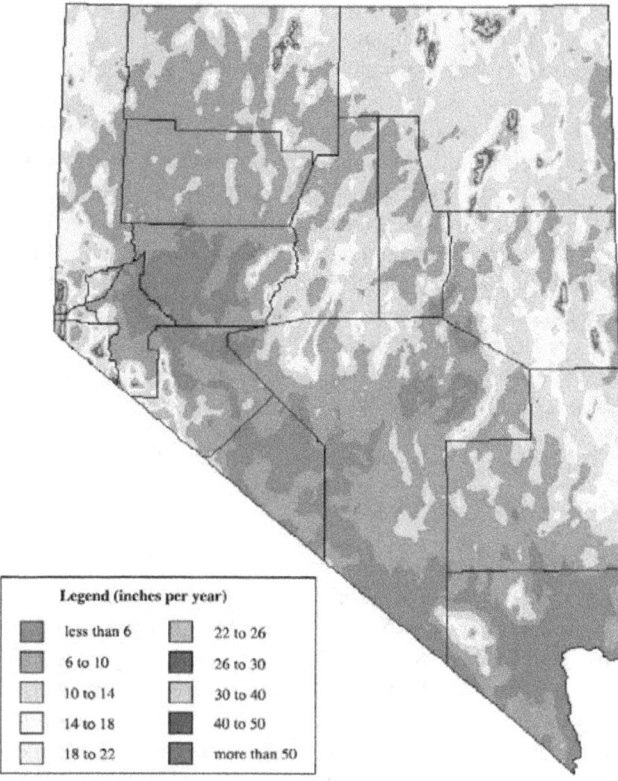

Average Annual Precipitation
Nevada
Period: 1961-1990   Unit: inches

Legend (inches per year)

less than 6		22 to 26	
6 to 10		26 to 30	
10 to 14		30 to 40	
14 to 18		40 to 50	
18 to 22		more than 50	

Figure 1.4. Average annual precipitation for the State of Nevada.

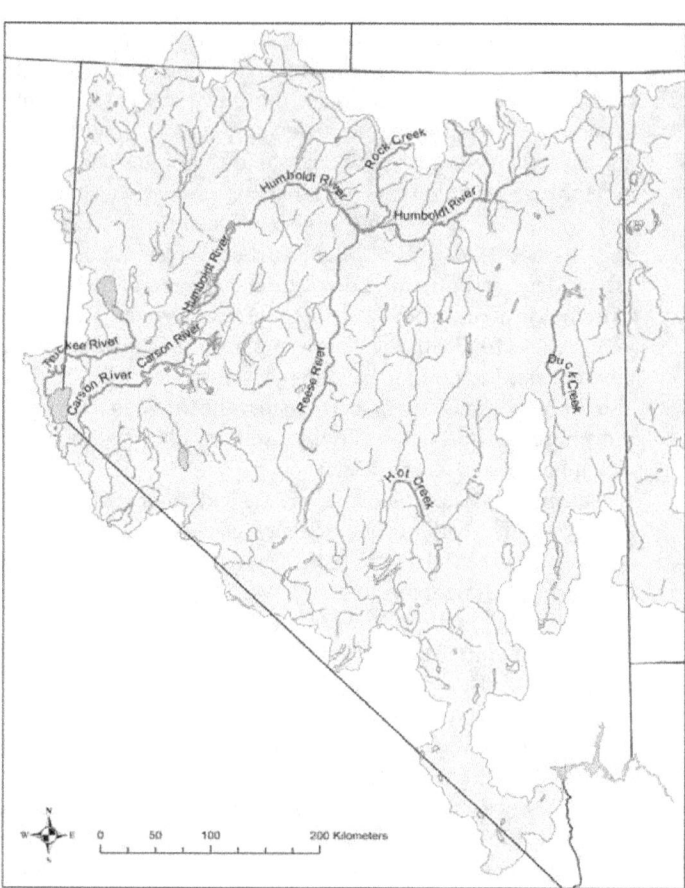

Figure 1.5. River systems in the hydrologic Great Basin of Nevada.

its headwaters in the East Humboldt Range, through Rye Patch Reservoir, to its terminus at Humboldt sink almost 500 km away. The Reese River rises in the study area in the southern portion of the Toiyabe Range and flows north to its junction with the Humboldt River at Battle Mountain. It is the second longest river in Nevada but, despite its regional prominence, the Reese River is intermittent and consists of alternating gaining and losing reaches. In fact, along many segments the valley floor lacks well-defined surface channels, and down-valley flow of water primarily occurs in the subsurface. The Reese River has flowed as a continuous surface water body from head to mouth only three times in the Twentieth Century. Other major rivers in the Great Basin are the Carson River, which drains into Carson Sink, and the Truckee River, which rises in the eastern Sierra and drains into Pyramid Lake. Many intermontane basins in the region do not have major streams or rivers and instead are occupied by playa lakes that capture all of the local drainage from the surrounding mountains.

The highest density of surface water streams occurs in the mountains because most precipitation in the region falls in the mountains, where evapotranspiration is relatively low. Mountain streams are fed by rainfall, snowmelt, and springs

that are distributed throughout the drainage basins particularly at mid to high elevations.

Discharge from mountain watersheds varies with drainage basin area, local mean annual precipitation, and percentage of the drainage basin that is at high altitude (Hess 2002). Because evapotranspiration potential increases from mountains to intermontane basins and because alluvial fan sediments at mountain fronts tend to be thick and permeable, most mountain streams are rarely integrated with the intermontane basin drainage system. Most of the time a significant percentage of water that is delivered to the mountain front from small mountain streams infiltrates into the alluvial-fill sediments. High evapotranspiration rates further deplete this surface water discharge as streams transition form cooler, more shaded confines of mountain valleys onto the apex of the mountain-front alluvial fans (fig. 1.3). Large watersheds that drain higher mountain systems like Big Creek and Kingston Canyon in the Toiyabe Range and Barley Creek in the Monitor Range are able to collect sufficient discharge to flow into the axes of intermontane basins more frequently. Surface water drainage networks are typically integrated as continuous surface water flow systems with a frequency of about several times per century under the current climatic regime. However, mountain watersheds may feed playa lakes and master drainage networks far out into the main basins as subsurface groundwater flow.

Causes of Degradation—Climate Change and Other Natural and Anthropogenic Disturbance

The causes of degradation of riparian corridors and meadow complexes in the central Great Basin are the result of complex and interrelated responses of geomorphic, hydrologic, and vegetation processes to natural and anthropogenic disturbances as well as changes in climate. Anthropogenic disturbances include all human activities that affect physical and biological processes within a watershed, and natural disturbances include phenomena such as floods, landslides, and wildfires. Climate change operates over longer temporal scales and larger spatial scales than natural disturbances and exerts a major control on watershed processes in arid and semi-arid ecosystems. Restoration and management activities must therefore take into account the significant effects of both past and present climate on geomorphic and fluvial processes in the Great Basin and, consequently, on riparian and aquatic ecosystems. In upland watersheds of the central Great Basin, climate-driven changes in hillslope and fluvial processes that occurred during the mid-to-late Holocene still influence the composition and pattern of riparian ecosystems over a broad range of scales (Miller and others 2001, 2004; Chambers and others 2004a). Paleoecological and stratigraphic data collected in the central Great Basin indicate that a major drought occurred in the Region from approximately 2580 to 1900 years BP (Miller and others 2001; Tausch and others 2004). During this drought, most of the available fine-grained sediments were stripped from hillslopes and deposited on valley floors and side-valley alluvial fans (Miller and others 2001, 2004). As a consequence of this hillslope erosion, streams are currently sediment limited and exhibit a natural tendency to incise. Available geomorphic data indicate that over the past 2000 years, the dominant response of streams to both natural and anthropogenic disturbance has been incision. The most recent episode of incision began about 450 years BP before Anglo-American settlement of the region in 1860. However, incision has been more intense and pervasive during the past 150 years. Most of this recent incision occurs during episodic, high flow events that are highly variable both among and within years in these semi-arid ecosystems. In recent decades, high flow events capable of producing significant incision occurred in the mid-1970s, 1983, 1995, 1998, and 2005 due to high precipitation and rapid runoff (Chambers and others 1998; Germanoski and others 2001).

The rate and magnitude of steam incision in central Great Basin watersheds have been increased by anthropogenic disturbances. Roads that are located in valley bottoms are perhaps the major human-related cause of recent stream incision and riparian area degradation in the central Great Basin. The effects of roads on stream systems have been clearly documented for other locations (USDA Forest Service 1997; Jones and others 2000; Trombulak and Frissel 2000). In the central Great Basin, several cases of "road captures" have been documented and many other cases have been observed where streams were diverted onto road surfaces during high flows (Lahde 2003). These diversions result in increased shear stress and stream power and, ultimately, localized stream incision (Lahde 2003). Once initiated, knickpoint migration often results in stream incision along the channel.

There is no direct evidence linking regional stream incision to overgrazing by livestock in the central Great Basin, but overgrazing has undoubtedly had localized effects on stream channels. Effects similar to those for road captures have been documented for livestock trails elsewhere in the western United States (Trimble and Mendel 1995) and likely occur for off-road vehicle trails. Also, overgrazing by livestock has been shown to negatively affect stream bank and channel stability and often has been associated with localized changes in stream morphology (see reviews in Trimble and Mendel 1995; Belsky and others 1999; National Research Council 2002). Generalized effects of overgrazing by livestock on riparian ecosystems include undesirable changes in species composition and structure, soil properties, biogeochemical cycling, and water quality. These effects are well documented elsewhere (see reviews in Kauffman and Krueger 1984; Skovlin 1984; Clary and Webster 1989; National Research Council 1992, 2002; Fleischner 1994; Ohmart 1996; Belsky and others 1999).

Processes That Influence Stream Incision and Meadow Ecosystems

Stream and restoration ecologists have recognized for some time that effective management and restoration approaches must not only address the appropriate scales but also must be process based (Frissell and others 1986; Goodwin and others 1997). Recent research in the central Great Basin illustrates the close linkages among watershed, valley segment, and reach-level controls and geomorphic, hydrologic, and vegetation processes (Lord and others 2009). Watersheds differ in sensitivity to both natural and anthropogenic disturbance and, thus, in the likelihood of stream incision (Germanoski and Miller 2004). Ecologists use the terms "resistance" and "resilience" to evaluate the sensitivity of ecosystems to disturbance. Resistance refers to the ability of an ecosystem to maintain characteristic processes despite various stressors or disturbances, while resilience refers to the capacity to regain the same processes over time following stress or disturbance (Society for Ecological Restoration International 2002). Major disturbances can result in threshold crossings and new ecological states characterized by different ecological processes. Similarly, geomorphologists describe the sensitivity of landforms to disturbance as the propensity for a change in the environment to result in a new equilibrium state (Schumm and Brackenridge 1987; Germanoski and Miller 2004). Watershed sensitivity to disturbance is influenced by factors such as the erosional resistance of the underlying bedrock and channel-forming materials and watershed relief, morphometry, and hydrology. In the central Great Basin, watershed sensitivity to disturbance and, thus, stream incision is related to watershed characteristics such as geology, size, relief, and morphometry and valley segment attributes such as gradient, width, and substrate size (Germanoski and Miller 2004). Watersheds that are highly sensitive to disturbance exhibit a greater response to more frequent, lower magnitude runoff events than watersheds that are less sensitive to disturbance.

The combined geomorphic and hydrologic characteristics of the watersheds determine the pattern and composition of riparian vegetation at watershed to valley segment scales (Chambers and others 2004a, 2004b). Thus, watershed, valley-segment, and stream reach attributes, such as those that characterize basin sensitivity to disturbance, also have good predictive value for riparian ecosystems, including the presence, characteristics, and ecological condition of meadow complexes. For example, flood-dominated watersheds that are characterized by tertiary volcanic rock, high-relief, narrow valleys, bedrock control, minimal sediment storage, and multiple discontinuous terraces rarely have the geomorphic or hydrologic conditions to support meadow ecosystems (Chambers and others 2004b; Germanoski and Miller 2004). In contrast, fan-dominated watersheds that are characterized by prominent side-valley alluvial fans or side-valley tributary deposits (graded fans) often have the geomorphic and hydrologic conditions necessary to support meadow complexes.

Watersheds with prominent side-valley alluvial fans have been well-studied in the central Great Basin (Germanoski and Miller 2004; Jewett and others 2004; Miller and others 2001, 2004) and provide an excellent example of how watershed characteristics influence the occurrence of meadows and processes that cause meadow degradation over time. The most recent period of fan aggradation in the region occurred during the first half of the drought that occurred from about 2500 to 1300 years BP. In some cases, the fans extended across the entire width of the valley floor and impinged on opposing hillslopes, blocking down-valley transport of water and sediment along the axial stream channel. Significant quantities of sediment were deposited upstream of these fans, resulting in a reduction in valley floor gradient and an increase in valley floor width. The toes of the fans were subsequently breached, and fan sediments were carried down valley, causing several meters of aggradation along the riparian corridor. Today, watersheds with well-developed fans often are characterized by stepped-valley profiles and riparian corridors that exhibit abrupt changes in local geomorphic, hydrologic, and vegetation attributes. Meadow ecosystems typically occur upstream of side-valley alluvial fans where necessary conditions (bedrock highs, finer textured sediments, and/or springs) exist to maintain shallow water tables. Woody vegetation (willows, rose, aspen, and cottonwood) typically occurs at the fan and above the meadow complex. Many fans serve as local base-level controls that determine the rate and magnitude of upstream incision. These fans are subject to stream incision due to high shear stress associated with high flow events. Consequently, meadow ecosystems that are located immediately upstream of alluvial fans often are at risk of degradation due to stream incision through fan deposits.

Regardless of the watershed characteristics and cause of disturbance, stream incision lowers the base level for groundwater discharge and may result in deeper water tables. Meadow complexes occur along hydrologic gradients (Weixelman and others 1996; Castelli and others 2000) that are influenced by the rates and magnitudes of incision along the axial channels and development and entrenchment of surface channels within meadows (Wright and Chambers 2002; Chambers and others 2004a, 2004b; Jewett and others 2004). At one end of the hydrologic gradient, wet meadow ecological types exist with water tables at or near the ground surface and limited, shallow, and discontinuous surface channels. Prior to incision, shallow overland flow typically predominates during spring snowmelt and periods of high runoff. At the other end of the hydrologic gradient, dry meadow and sagebrush ecological types exist that have water tables from 150 to 250 cm below the ground surface and that seldom experience overland flows. As stream incision progresses and water tables drop, wetter meadow ecological types are progressively converted to drier meadow types. In the worst case scenario, the hydrologic regime and riparian vegetation are so severely affected that meadow complexes are replaced by drier plant communities that are dominated by sagebrush and wetter meadow plant communities exist only within the stratigraphic record.

Conceptual Basis for Restoration and Management

Restoring and maintaining riparian ecosystems in the Great Basin is a management priority but has proven difficult because of ongoing and widespread stream incision and failure of standard stream stabilization measures such as livestock management or instream structures to prevent or reverse this degradation (Clary 1995; Kondolf 1995; Kaufman and others 1997; Clary and Kinney 2002; Wohl 2004). Many streams and riparian ecosystems in upland watersheds of the central Great Basin are currently functioning as nonequilibrium systems due to depletion of hillslope sediments during the mid-to-late Holocene drought and the tendency for stream incision (Chambers and others 2004b; Germanoski and Miller 2004; Miller and others 2004). Some streams have adjusted to the current geomorphic conditions and have reached their maximum depth of incision under the current sediment and hydrologic regime. Others are still adjusting and will continue to incise because of channel heterogeneity and lack of hillslope sediments. In many cases, incised streams have crossed geomorphic thresholds and, because of the changes in stream processes and groundwater regimes, riparian ecosystems also have crossed thresholds. Threshold crossings occur when a system does not return to the original state following disturbance, and can be defined based on the limits of natural variability within systems (Ritter and others 1999).

For stream systems and riparian ecosystems in the central Great Basin that have crossed geomorphic and hydrologic thresholds, return to the predisturbance state is not an ecologically or economically viable goal. The restoration and management potential of a stream system or riparian ecosystem must be based on current, not historic, conditions.

Chambers and others (2004b) defined the goal of restoration and management activities as reestablishing and maintaining sustainable fluvial systems and riparian ecosystems that exhibit both characteristic processes and related biological, chemical, and physical linkages among system components (modified from Natural Research Council 1992). In this context, sustainable stream systems and riparian ecosystems exhibit natural variability, yet maintain characteristic processes, including rates and magnitudes of geomorphic activity, hydrologic flux and storage, biogeochemical cycling and storage, and biological activity and production (Christensen and others 1996; Wohl and others 2005). Sustainable ecosystems provide valuable ecosystem services, including high quality water, habitat for aquatic and terrestrial organisms, forage and browse, and recreational opportunities.

Reestablishing and maintaining riparian ecosystems in the central Great Basin and elsewhere requires an integrated and interdisciplinary approach that addresses the geomorphic, hydrologic and biological components of the system (Chambers and others 2004b; Wohl and others 2005). As illustrated above, and as has been advocated elsewhere, a critical first step is to develop an understanding of the causes of degradation and of the underlying physical and biotic processes (Goodwin and others 1997; Wissmar and Beschta 1998; Wohl and others 2005). Once developed, this integrated understanding of riparian ecosystems can be used for prioritizing restoration and management activities and for determining appropriate techniques.

Developing the necessary understanding for effective management/restoration of riparian areas requires addressing appropriate spatial and temporal scales. A watershed can be viewed as a hierarchical system containing different spatial and temporal scales that are nested within one another (Schumm and Lichty 1965; Frissell and others 1986; Newbury and Gaboury 1993). Scales can range from an entire watershed (10^1 to 10^6 years, km^2) to individual events or particles (<10 years, <0.10 cm^2). A watershed perspective and the historical evaluation of different scales provide a more complete understanding of riparian ecosystems and their interactions with the geomorphic and hydrologic regime (Wissmar and Beschta 1998). Scales that are addressed here are the watershed, riparian corridor, valley segment, and stream reach (fig. 1.6). The riparian corridor is the integrated network of stream channels and adjacent geomorphic

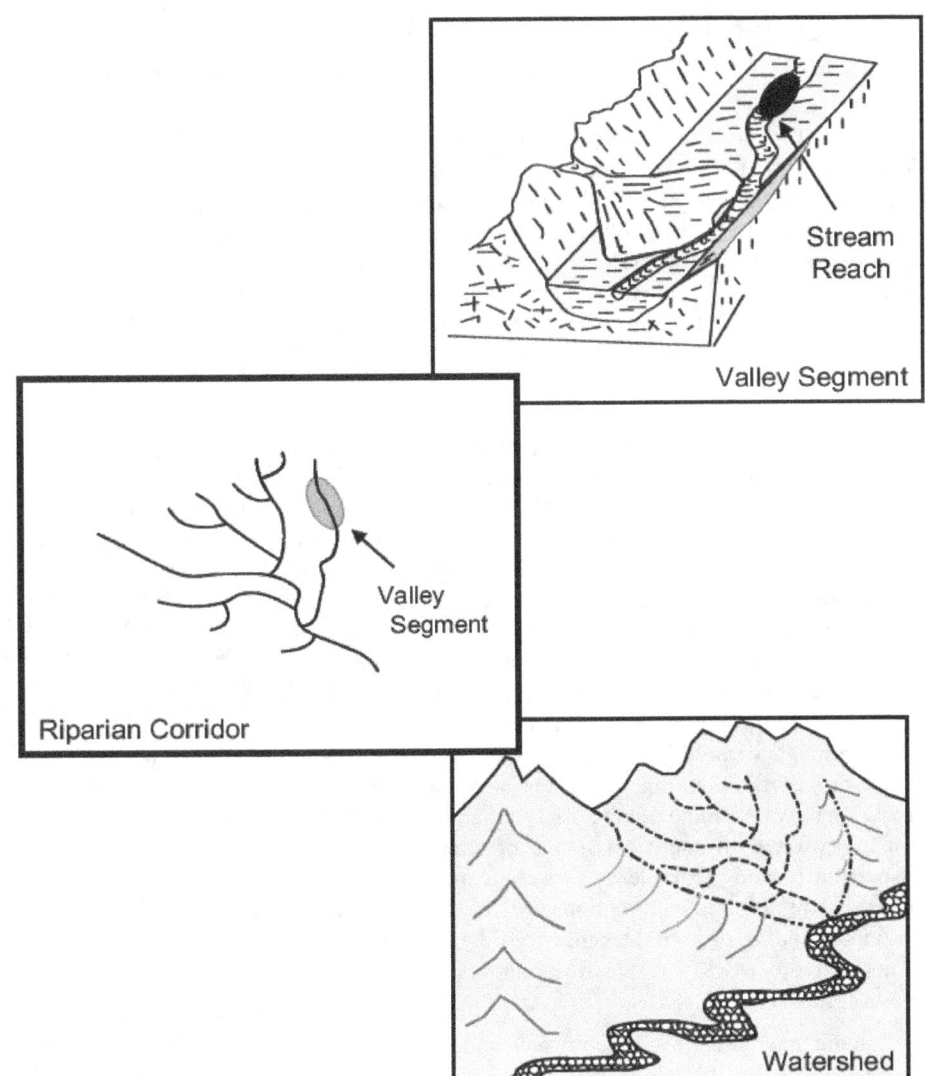

Figure 1.6. Spatial scales of study.

USDA Forest Service Gen. Tech. Rep. RMRS-GTR-258. 2011.

7

surfaces (in other words, floodplain and terraces) that are located primarily on alluvial deposits in valley bottoms. The riparian corridor receives water and sediment from surrounding hillslopes and represents a pivotal interface between surface and groundwater flow systems. Characteristics of watersheds and riparian corridors are often closely related to sensitivity of watersheds to disturbance, likelihood of stream incision (Germanoski and Miller 2004), and dominant vegetation types within the watershed (Chambers and others 2004b). Nested within riparian corridors are valley segments that have semi-uniform valley characteristics (slopes, widths, and geologic materials) and similar climatic conditions. The smallest components in our hierarchy are stream reaches or sections of the valley segments with relatively uniform channel morphology, bed material composition, bank conditions, and woody debris. Characteristics of valley segments and stream reaches determine the geomorphic setting and hydrologic regime of riparian ecosystems and, thus, site-specific geomorphic, hydrologic, and vegetation processes that influence resistance and resilience of riparian ecosystems to high flow events and other perturbations (Chambers and others 2004b; Jewett and others 2004).

Objectives and Contents of This Report

In 1992, a USDA Forest Service, Rocky Mountain Research Station ecosystem management project on restoring and maintaining sustainable riparian ecosystems was initiated to address the problems associated with stream incision and riparian ecosystem degradation in the central Great Basin (see Chambers and Miller 2004b). A collaborative project was developed with the U.S. Environmental Protection Agency's (USEPA) Office of Research and Development in 2002 to build on the results of the ecosystem management project and to develop management options for addressing the current effects of stream incision on meadow complexes. This report contains the results of the collaborative Forest Service and EPA project, which was based on a coarse-scale assessment of 56 individual meadow systems coupled with more detailed, fine-scale analyses of 6 of those meadows (fig. 1.7). It provides the necessary understanding and tools to develop effective restoration and management programs for meadow complexes in the central Great Basin. The approach used by the collaborative project is reflected in the report's contents. First, the causes of degradation and underlying geomorphic, hydrologic, and biotic processes operating within the meadows are examined. Then, we examine the factors required to evaluate the sensitivity or, conversely, resistance of streams and their associated meadow complexes to stream incision. Finally, management and treatment options are developed based on an understanding of both the causes of degradation and the underlying processes. The specific components of this report are as follows:

- An understanding of the geomorphic and hydrologic controls on Great Basin meadow complexes;

- An understanding of the geomorphic, hydrologic, and vegetation processes that affect watershed and meadow sustainability;

- Information on the factors needed to evaluate sensitivity to disturbance for both watersheds and meadow complexes;

- Information on the value of biodiversity indicators for aquatic and terrestrial macro-invertebrates for evaluating restoration outcomes and ecological conditions of meadows and their associated stream systems;

- A characterization of meadow complexes that exist within central Great Basin watersheds based on watershed and valley segment/reach-scale attributes; and

- Methods for maintaining or restoring the stream systems and vegetation communities associated with riparian meadows.

References

Belsky, A.J.; Matzke, A.; Uselman, S. 1999. Survey of livestock influences on stream and riparian ecosystems in the western United States. Journal of Soil and Water Conservation. 51: 419-431.

Castelli, R.M.; Chambers, J.C.; Tausch, R.J. 2000. Soil-plant relations along a soil-water gradient in Great Basin riparian meadows. Wetlands. 20: 251-266.

Chambers, J.C.; Farleigh, K.; Tausch, R.J.; Miller, J.R.; Germanoski, D.; Martin, D.; Nowak, C. 1998. Understanding long- and short-term changes in vegetation and geomorphic processes: the key to riparian restoration. In: Potts, D.F., ed. Rangeland management and water resources. Herndon, VA: American Water Resources Association and Society for Range Management: 101-110.

Chambers, J.C.; Miller, J.R. eds. 2004a. Great Basin Riparian Ecosystems—Ecology, Management and Restoration. Covelo, CA: Island Press. 303 p.

Chambers, J.C.; Miller, J.R. 2004b. Restoring and maintaining sustainable riparian ecosystems–the Great Basin Ecosystem Management Project. In: Chambers, J.C.; Miller, J.R., eds. Great Basin Riparian Ecosystems—Ecology, Management, and Restoration. Covelo, CA: Island Press: 1-24.

Chambers, J.C.; Miller, J.R.; Germanoski, D.; Weixelman, D.A. 2004a. Process based approaches for managing and restoring riparian ecosystems. In: Chambers, J.C.; Miller, J.R., eds. Great Basin Riparian Ecosystems—Ecology, Management, and Restoration. Covelo, CA: Island Press: 261-292.

Chambers, J.C.; Tausch, R.J.; Korfmacher, J.L.; Miller, J.R.; Jewett, D.G. 2004b. Effects of geomorphic processes and hydrologic regimes on riparian vegetation. In: Chambers, J.C.; Miller, J.R., eds. Great Basin Riparian Ecosystems—Ecology, Management, and Restoration. Covelo, CA: Island Press: 196-231.

Clary, W.P.; Webster, B.F. 1989. Managing grazing of riparian areas in the Intermountain Region. Gen. Tech. Rep. INT-263. Ogden, UT: U.S. Department of Agriculture, Forest Service, Intermountain Forest and Range Experiment Station. 11 p.

Clary, W.P. 1995. Vegetation and soil responses to grazing simulation on riparian meadows. Journal of Range Management. 48: 18-25.

Clary, W.P.; Kinney, J.W. 2002. Streambank and vegetation response to simulated cattle grazing. Wetlands. 22: 139-148.

Christensen, N.L.; Bartuska, A.M.; Brown, J.H.; Carpenter, S.; D'Antonio, C.; Francis, R.; Franklin, J.F.; MacMahon, J.A.; Noss, R.F.; Parsons, D.J.; Peterson, C.H.; Turner, M.G.; Woodmansee,

8

USDA Forest Service Gen. Tech. Rep. RMRS-GTR-258. 2011.

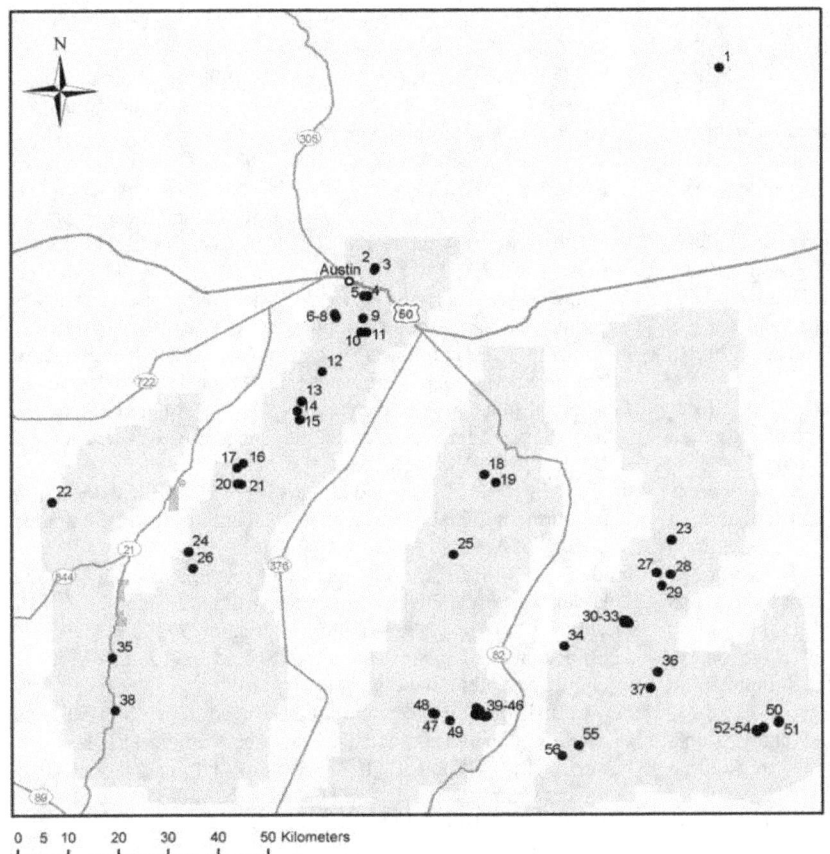

Figure 1.7. Locations of the meadow complexes evaluated by the project and discussed in this report. Land owernship designations: Forest Service = green; Bureau of Land Management = tan; Bureau of Indian Affairs = brown; nonfederal = white.

1.	Red Canyon	20.	San Juan 1	39.	Corcoran main 3
2.	Emigrant 1	21.	San Juan 2	40.	Corcoran main 2
3.	Emigrant 2	22.	Lebeau	41.	Corcoran main 1
4.	Cahill 2	23.	Willow	42.	Corcoran 5
5.	Cahill 3	24.	Mohawk	43.	Corcoran 4
6.	Johnson 1	25.	West Northumberland	44.	Corcoran 3
7.	Johnson 2	26.	South Crane	45.	Corcoran 2
8.	Johnson 3	27.	West Dobbin	46.	Corcoran 1
9.	Birch Tributary	28.	Stargo	47.	Meadow 2
10.	Birch 1	29.	East Dobbin	48.	Meadow 1
11.	Birch 2	30.	Wadsworth 1	49.	Round Mountain
12.	Big Creek	31.	Wadsworth 3	50.	Six Mile 1
13.	Kingston 3	32.	Wadsworth 2	51.	Six Mile 2
14.	Kingston 1	33.	Wadsworth 4	52.	Little Cow
15.	Kingston 0	34.	Mosquito	53.	Fandango 1
16.	Washington	35.	Indian Valley	54.	Fandango 2
17.	Cottonwood	36.	Danville	55.	Barley 1
18.	Corral 2	37.	Green Monster	56.	Barley Tributary
19.	Corral 1	38.	Cloverdale		

R.G. 1996. The report of the Ecological Society of America Committee on the scientific basis for ecosystem management. Ecological Applications. 6: 665-691.

Dohrenwend, J.C. 1987. Basin and Range. In: Graf, W.L., ed. Geomorphic Systems of North America: Boulder, CO: Geological Society of America, Centennial Special Volume 2: 303-342.

Fleischner, T.L. 1994. Ecological costs of livestock grazing in western North America. Conservation Biology. 8: 629-644.

Frissel, C.A.; Liss, W.J.; Warren, C.E.; Hurley, M.D. 1986. A hierarchical framework for stream habitat classification: viewing streams in a watershed context. Environmental Management. 10: 199-214.

Germanoski, D.; Ryder, C.; Miller, J.R. 2001. Spatial variation of incision and deposition within a rapidly incised upland watershed, central Nevada. Proceedings of the 7th Interagency Sedimentation Conference; 25-29 March 2001; Reno, NV: Subcomittee on Sedimentation. v. 2: 141-148.

Germanoski, D.; Miller, J.R. 2004. Basin sensitivity to channel incision in response to natural and anthropogenic disturbance. In: Chambers, J.C.; Miller, J.R., eds. Great Basin Riparian Ecosystems—Ecology, Management, and Restoration. Covelo, CA: Island Press: 88-123.

Goodwin, C.N.; Hawkins, C.P.; Kershner, J.L. 1997. Riparian restoration in the western United States: overview and perspective. Restoration Ecology. 5: 4-14.

Hess, G.W.; Bohman, L.R. 1996. Techniques for estimating monthly mean streamflow at gaged sites and monthly streamflow duration characteristics at ungaged sites in central Nevada. U.S. Geological Survey Open-File Report 96-559. 15 p.

Hess, G.W. 2002. Updated techniques for estimating monthly streamflow duration characteristics at ungaged and partial-record sites in central Nevada. U.S. Geological Survey Open-File Report 02-168. 16 p.

Jewett, D.G.; Lord, M.; Miller, J.R.; Chambers, J.C. 2004. Geomorphic and hydrologic controls on surface and subsurface flow regimes in riparian meadow ecosystems. In: Chambers, J.C.; Miller, J.R., eds. Great Basin Riparian Ecosystems—Ecology, Management, and Restoration. Covelo, CA: Island Press: 124-161.

Jones, J.A.; Swanson, F.J.; Wernpie, B.C.; Sjyder, K.U. 2000. Effects of roads on hydrology, geomorphology, and disturbance patches in stream networks. Conservation Biology. 14: 76-85.

Kauffman, J.B.; Krueger, W.C. 1984. Livestock impacts on riparian ecosystems and streamside management implications...a review. Journal of Range Management. 37: 430-438.

Kauffman, J.B.; Beschta, R.L.; Otting, N.; Lytjen, D. 1997. An ecological perspective of riparian and stream restoration in the western United States. Fisheries. 22: 12-24.

Kleinhampl, F.J.; Ziony, J.I. 1985. Geology of northern Nye County, Nevada. Nevada Bureau of Mines and Geology. Bulletin 99A. 172 p.

Kondolf, G.M.; Larson, M. 1995. Historical channel analysis and its application to riparian and aquatic habitat restoration. Aquatic Conservation. 5: 108-126.

Lahde, D. 2003. The influence of secondary roads on stream incision in watersheds of the central Great Basin. Department of Natural Resources and Environmental Sciences, University of Nevada, Reno. Thesis. 106 p.

Meizer, O.E. 1916. Groundwater in Big Smoky Valley, Nevada. U.S. Geological Survey, Water Supply Paper 375: 85-116.

Lord, M.; Miller, J.; Germanoski, D.; Jewett, D.; Villarroel, L.; Tury, R.; Walsh, D.; Chambers, J. 2009. Do reach-scale geomorphically defined process zones predict sensitivity of channel systems and hydrologic processes in the mountains of the central Great Basin? Geological Society of America Abstracts with Programs. 41: 624.

Mifflin, M.D. 1988. Region 5, Great Basin. In: Back, W.; Rosenshein, J.S.; Seaber, P.R., eds. Hydrogeology: Boulder, CO: Geological Society of America, The Geology of North America. O-2: 69-86.

Miller, J.; Germanoski, D.; Waltman, K.; Tausch, R.; Chambers, J. 2001. Influence of late Holocene processes and landforms on modern channel dynamics in upland watersheds of central Nevada. Geomorphology. 38: 373-391.

Miller, J.R.; House, K.; Germanoski, D.; Tausch, R.J.; Chambers, J.C. 2004. Fluvial geomorphic responses to Holocene climate change. In: Chambers, J.C.; Miller, J.R., eds. Great Basin Riparian Ecosystems—Ecology, Management, and Restoration. Covelo, CA: Island Press: 49-87.

National Research Council. 1992. Restoration of aquatic ecosystems: science, technology, and public policy. Washington, DC: National Academy Press. 552 p.

National Research Council. 2002. Riparian areas: functions and strategies for management. Washington, DC: National Academy Press. 428 p.

Newbury, R.; Gaboury, M. 1993. Exploration and rehabilitation of hydraulic habitats in steams using principles of fluvial behaviour. Freshwater Biology. 29: 195-210.

Ohmart, R.D. 1996. Historical and present impacts of livestock grazing on fish and wildlife resources in western riparian habitats.

In: Krausman, P.R., ed. Rangeland Wildlife. Denver, CO: Society for Range Management: 245-279.

Ritter, D.F.; Kochel, R.C.; Miller, J.R. 1999. The disruption of Grassy Creek: implications concerning catastrophic events and thresholds. Geomorphology. 29: 323-338.

Schumm, S.A.; Brackenridge, G.R. 1987. River response. In: Ruddiman, W.F.; Wright, H.E., Jr., eds. North America and adjacent oceans during the last deglaciation, the geology of North America, volume K-3. Boulder, CO: Geological Society of America: 221-240.

Schumm, S.A.; Lichty, R.W. 1965. Time, space, and causality in geomorphology. American Journal of Science. 263: 110-119.

Skovlin, J.M. 1984. Impacts of grazing on wetlands and riparian habitat: a review of our knowledge. In: National Research Council; National Academy of Sciences, corp. eds. Developing Strategies for Range Management. Society for Range Management. Boulder, CO: Westview Press: 1001-1103.

Smith, D.L. 1992. History and kinematics of Cenozoic extension in the northern Toiyabe Range, Lander County, Nevada. Geological Society of America Bulletin. 104: 789-801.

Smith, D.L.; Miller, E.L. 1990. Late Paleozoic Extension in the Great Basin, western United States. Geology.18: 712-715.

Society for Ecological Restoration International. 2002. The SERI Primer on Ecological Restoration. Science and Policy Working Group. Available: www.seri.org.

Stewart, J.H. 1978. Basin-range structure in western North America: a review. Geological Society of America Memoir. 152: 1-31.

Stewart, J.H.; McKee, E.H. 1977. Geology and mineral deposits of Lander County, Nevada. Part I Geology. Nevada Bureau of Mines and Geology. Bulletin 88.

Tausch, R.J.; Nowak, C.L.; Mensing, S.W. 2004. Climate change and associated vegetation dynamics during the Holocene: the paleoecological record. In: Chambers, J.C.; Miller, J.R., eds. Great Basin Riparian Ecosystems—Ecology, Management, and Restoration. Covelo, CA: Island Press: 24-48.

Thatcher, W.; Foulger, G.R.; Julian, B.R.; Svarc, J.; Quilty, E.; Bawden, G.W. 1999. Present-day deformation across the Basin and Range Province, western United States. Science. 283: 1714-1718.

Trimble, S.W.; Mendel, A.C. 1995. The cow as a geomorphic agent—a critical review. Geomorphology. 13: 233-253.

Trombulak, S.C.; Frissell, C.A. 2000. Review of ecological effects of roads on terrestrial and aquatic communities. Conservation Biology. 14: 18-30.

USDA Forest Service. 1997. The water/road interaction technology series: an introduction. San Dimas, CA: Technology and Development Program.

Weixelman, D.A.; Zamudio, D.C.; Zamudio, K.A. 1996. Central Nevada riparian field guide. R6-ECOL-TP. Ogden, UT: U.S. Department of Agriculture, Forest Service, Intermountain Region.

Wissmar, R.C.; Beschta, R.L. 1998. Restoration and management of riparian ecosystems: a catchment perspective. Freshwater Biology. 40: 571-585.

Wohl, E. 2004. Disconnected rivers: linking rivers to landscapes. New Haven, CT: Yale University Press. 301 pages.

Wohl, E.; Angermeier, P.L.; Bledsoe, B.; Kondolf, G.M.; MacDonnell, L.; Merritt, D.M.; Palmer, M.A.; Poff, N.L.; Tarboton, D. 2005. River restoration. Water Resources Research. 41:10301.

Wright, M.J.; Chambers, J.C. 2002. Restoring riparian meadows currently dominated by Artemisia using threshold and alternative state concepts—aboveground vegetation response. Applied Vegetation Science. 5: 237-246.

Chapter 2: Controls on Meadow Distribution and Characteristics

Dru Germanoski, Jerry R. Miller, and Mark L. Lord

Introduction

Meadow complexes are located in distinct geomorphic and hydrologic settings that allow groundwater to be at or near the ground surface during at least part of the year. Meadows are manifestations of the subsurface flow system, and their distribution is controlled by factors that cause localized zones of groundwater discharge. Knowledge of the factors that serve as controls on groundwater discharge and formation of meadow complexes is necessary to understand why meadows occur where they do and how anthropogenic activities might affect their persistence and ecological condition. In this chapter, we examine physical factors that lead to the formation of meadow complexes in upland watersheds of the central Great Basin. We then describe variations in meadow characteristics across the region and parameters that produce differences in the nature of meadow complexes at basin scales. In subsequent chapters, we examine the geomorphic, hydrologic, and vegetation processes that operate within individual wet meadow complexes.

Factors Affecting Meadow Distribution and Development

Precipitation

Wet meadows require a reliable supply of groundwater that supports high water tables year after year and that sustains the phreatophytic vegetation characteristic of these discrete ecosystems (Castelli and others 2000). The ultimate supply of this water is precipitation. Annual precipitation varies from 150 mm/year to approximately 700 mm/year in the study area (Oregon Climate Service 2009) and falls mostly as snow in winter. Observed spatial variations in precipitation closely parallel changes in elevation (figs.1.2 and 1.4). Watersheds that have a significant portion of their drainage area located at high elevations should be able to capture more rain and snow and, therefore, have more available water. In fact, it has been demonstrated that stream discharge and flow duration are proportional to and can be estimated by the size of the drainage basin and the percentage of the drainage basin that is located at elevations above 3050 m (Hess 2002).

The highest elevations within the six mountain ranges in the study area (Shoshone, Toiyabe, Toquima, Monitor, Roberts, and Hot Creek Ranges) occur in the central and southern portions of the Toiyabe, southern Toquima, and central Monitor Ranges (fig. 1.2). The highest annual precipitation values are recorded in the central and southern Toiyabe and southern Toquima Mountains (fig. 1.4) and, as expected, meadow complexes are abundant in those areas. In contrast, basins located in sections of mountain ranges that do not have significant area at high elevation (greater than approximately 2500 m) and that are characterized by limited annual precipitation contain relatively few meadows. For example, much of the Shoshone Range and the northern and southernmost portions of the Toiyabe, Toquima, and Monitor Ranges are lower in elevation and receive less precipitation. Therefore, meadow complexes are uncommon in these regions. Analyses of color-enhanced satellite images of the region reveal that meadow complexes also are uncommon in low-elevation mountain ranges in the surrounding area, including the Pancake Range, Antelope Range, the Park Range, and Simpson Park Mountains.

Geologic, Stratigraphic, and Hydrologic Controls

Groundwater along riparian corridors of most basins is typically located well below the ground surface (usually greater than 3 to 5 m), even when an ample supply of groundwater would be expected based on the watershed's elevation and precipitation. Thus, meadow complexes represent an anomalous condition where groundwater levels are elevated compared to adjacent upstream and downstream reaches of the riparian corridor. These spatial changes in subsurface water levels raise two important, interrelated questions: (1) Is the water that is found within meadows entirely derived from its down-valley movement through valley fill? and (2) Are other factors causing groundwater levels to rise locally? The meadows may be products of localized inputs of water to the valley that raise water levels, of changes in hydrologic flow conditions that produce upwelling, or of some combination of the two. The answers to these questions require an understanding of the geologic, stratigraphic, and geomorphic settings of meadow complexes.

History and Timing of Sedimentation Events. The geomorphic characteristics of the valley bottoms, including those in the vicinity of meadow complexes, largely reflect erosional and depositional events that occurred during the late Holocene (approximately 4500 years BP to the present). The geomorphic history of the basins was documented primarily by examining and dating alluvial stratigraphic deposits in approximately 30 upland watersheds spread across the central Great Basin (Miller and others 2001, 2004). The most detailed studies occurred in the Big Creek, Barley,

USDA Forest Service Gen. Tech. Rep. RMRS-GTR-258. 2011.

11

Kingston, San Juan, Cottonwood, and Indian Valley basins (fig 1.7). Results indicated that while sediment was always being produced, transported, stored, and exported from the upland basins, significant temporal variations in sediment production and transport dynamics occurred during the late Holocene often in response to discrete changes in climate. During the Neoglacial (4500 to 2500 years BP), a period of cooler, moister conditions and relatively high vegetation abundance, the landscape was relatively stable and little sediment was transported to alluvial fans located at the mouth of tributaries (called side-valley alluvial fans) or to the alluvial valley floor (Chambers and others 1998; Miller and others 2001). As a result, soils formed in the stable valley fill and alluvial fan deposits (Miller and others 2001). Landscape stability changed, however, with the onset of the post-Neoglacial drought that began in this area approximately 2600 years BP. The post-Neoglacial drought was a time of relative aridity, during which upland vegetation changed substantially toward dryland assemblages. Available paleoecological data (primarily from woodrat middens) indicate that the number of plant taxa present decreased from a relatively high level to the lowest levels observed during the Holocene (Miller and others 2001; Tausch and others 2004). The decrease in vegetation cover apparently led to erosional stripping of hillslope sediment when infrequent but intense rainfall events occurred. The eroded sediment was redeposited on side-valley alluvial fans and throughout the valley network from approximately 2580±70 to 1980±60 years BP. A high frequency of wildfires also may have accompanied the drought, as indicated by a large amount of charcoal in alluvial deposits that were created during the time period. Presumably, destruction of vegetation by wildfires facilitated soil erosion and sediment accumulation in the valleys.

The sediment that was generated during the post-Neoglacial drought buried the soils that had developed in earlier deposits. Thus, a paleosol dated to approximately 3500 years BP can be found at the base of most post-Neoglacial deposits throughout the region and marks the beginning of widespread sedimentation. Stratigraphic data from stream-cut exposures and sediment cores indicate that deposition within the valley and on the fans usually resulted

in deposits 0.5 to 2 m thick. In addition, stratigraphic profiles revealed that sediment that was eroded from the hillslopes was routed through low-order tributaries to the side-valley fans causing fan progradation. Fan sediments were then eroded and routed down higher-order channels and axial valleys resulting in contemporaneous deposition along major trunk streams. The process created an interfingering relationship between fan and axial valley deposits (fig. 2.1) (Miller and others 2001). This alternating sequence of deposition and erosion allowed much of the coarser sediment (cobbles and boulders) to be stored in side-valley fans and more of the finer-grained materials (pebbles, sand, silt, and clay) to be redeposited along the axial drainage system.

A product of fan progradation into the axial valleys was a reduction of channel gradients immediately upstream. The reduced gradients appear to have further promoted accumulation of sediment along the axial valley (fig. 2.2). In some cases, radial fan profiles indicate that fan deposits traversed the entire width of the valley, effectively blocking down-valley movement of water and sediment. Although these blockages were probably breached rapidly, they may have promoted sediment aggradation temporarily by reducing downstream flow velocities.

Since about 1980 years BP, the stream systems throughout the region have undergone periods of stability that were separated by episodes of channel incision. Interestingly, incision appears to have begun prior to the end of more typical moisture conditions during the Holocene (Tausch and others 2004). Miller and others (2001, 2004) argue that the onset of incision was related to depletion of fine-grained sediment on hillslopes and reduced sediment loading to the axial valley, an argument that is supported by a general increase in grain size of the valley-fill deposits through time. The inability of the current hydrologic regime to move sediment from the hillslopes likely produced the current tendency for modern channels to incise in response to natural or anthropogenic disturbances.

The depositional history of the upland basins led to a rather simple stratigraphic sequence throughout most of the valley bottoms (fig. 2.1). However, detailed studies have revealed that the stratigraphy upstream of prograding fans

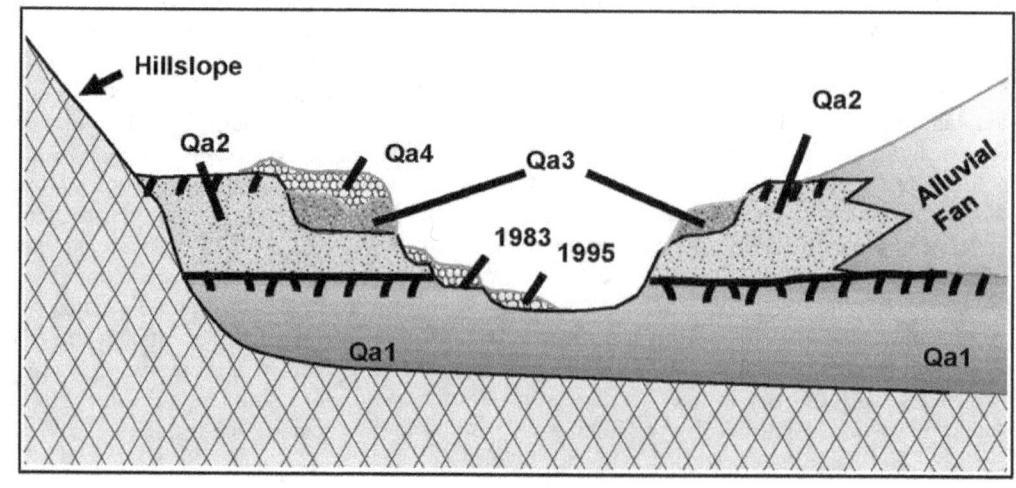

Figure 2.1. Generalized valley fill stratigraphy found between wet meadow complexes. The different Quaternary alluvial units (Qa1 to Qa4) show the ages of the valley fill.

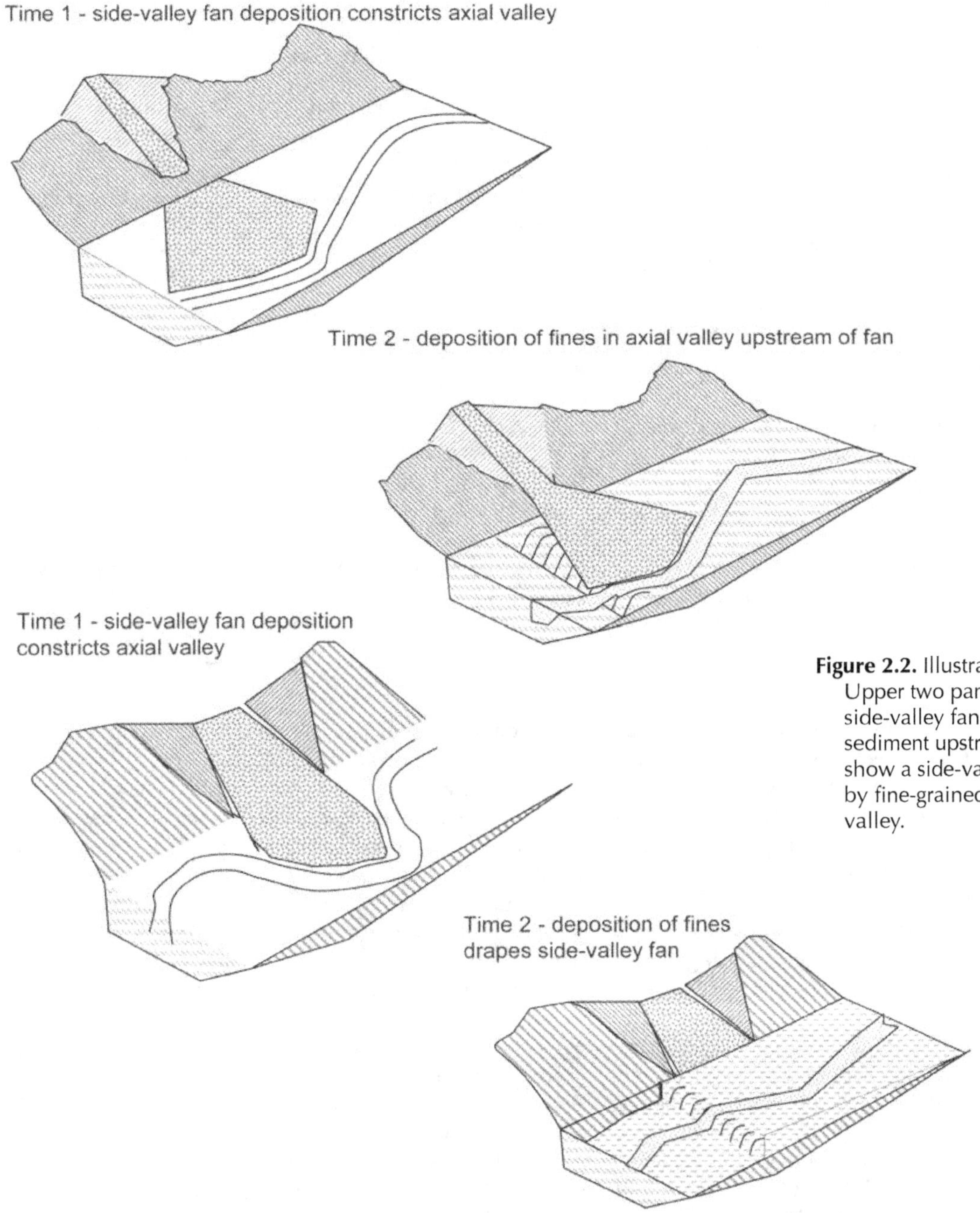

Time 1 - side-valley fan deposition constricts axial valley

Time 2 - deposition of fines in axial valley upstream of fan

Time 1 - side-valley fan deposition constricts axial valley

Time 2 - deposition of fines drapes side-valley fan

Figure 2.2. Illustration of fan controls. Upper two panels show a prograding side-valley fan trapping fine-grained sediment upstream. Lower two panels show a side-valley fan that is buried by fine-grained sediment in the axial valley.

and of other areas with dramatically reduced valley width is enormously complex. This complexity results from several factors: (1) interfingering of axial valley and fan deposits; (2) abrupt downstream variations in stream sediment transport capacity upstream of the fans as a result of reduced channel gradients and the damming effect of the fans; and (3) geologically frequent episodes of channel avulsion associated with localized aggradation of the axial channel. Although localized aggradation and avulsion might seem to contradict the fact that most channels are currently incising, investigations of the avulsion process show that it is associated with the temporary influx of coarse sediment to the reach during high-magnitude runoff events. Avulsion is significant in that it produces discontinuous lenses of coarse-grained

sediment that are surrounded by finer-grained materials, creating deposits that are sedimentologically variable.

Data from sediment cores collected in Barley, Birch, and Kingston indicate that the greatest volume of Holocene sedimentation occurred from approximately 5250 to 8650 years BP (unpublished radiocarbon data). Sediment dated through this time period ranges from 2.40 to 12.75 m below the surface of the valley fill and pre-dates the Neoglacial. The character of these deposits is similar to that found in younger materials, suggesting that the processes responsible for formation of deposits during the past 2580 years have been repeated many times, creating the stratigraphic architecture that comprises valley fill in these drainage basins.

USDA Forest Service Gen. Tech. Rep. RMRS-GTR-258. 2011.

13

Table 2.1. Watershed groups derived from an analysis of basin sensitivity to disturbance.

Category	Geology	Relief characteristics	Basin shape	Fan influence and longitudinal profile	Incision and terraces
Group 1 Flood-dominated	Volcanic rocks	Rugged, high stream power, high hypsometric integrals	Equant, low shape factor	Low fan influence	Localized incision, discontinuous terraces
Group 2 Deeply incised	Volcanic rocks	Rugged, high stream power, high hypsometric integrals	Elongated, high shape factor	Low fan influence, smoothed longitudinal profile	Deeply incised, many continuous terraces
Group 3 Fan-dominated	Sedimentary and metasedimentary rocks	Low stream power, low hypsometric integrals	Elongated, high shape factor	High fan influence, stepped longitudinal profile	Localized incision, discontinuous terraces
Group 4 Pseudo-stable	Intrusive igneous and siliciclastic rocks	Moderate to high stream power, high hypsometric integrals	Equant, low shape factor	Low fan influence, stepped longitudinal profile	Localized deep incision, discontinuous terraces

Field observations revealed that incision not only varied along a given channel but between basins, despite the fact that timing of deposition and observed stratigraphic relationships within the valley fill were similar. This indicated that different watersheds differed in sensitivity to natural and anthropogenic disturbance (Germanoski and Miller 2004). Landscape sensitivity can be defined in many ways (Allison and Thomas 1993), but it is defined here after Brunsden and Thornes (1979) as "the likelihood that a given change in the controls of the system will produce a sensible, recognizable, and persistent response [in the landform of interest]." The concept of sensitivity arises from the recognition that many fluvial systems are subjected to similar types and magnitudes of perturbation but often respond differently (Schumm 1991). In the central Great Basin, study watersheds were subdivided into four groups with respect to style of geomorphic adjustments during the late Holocene and to sensitivity of the axial channel to change (table 2.1; Germanoski and Miller 2004). The causes for observed differences in landscape sensitivity among basins cannot be explained entirely using watershed-scale parameters (such as basin relief, area, shape, drainage density, etc.) but are partly explained by differences in basin geology. For example, basins that developed in volcanic rocks were found to be relatively sensitive, probably because volcanic assemblages produce small bed-material sediment (which can be more easily transported than larger debris) and significant runoff.

Detailed mapping of incision depths along the axial valley of basins with continuous channels revealed that the amount of entrenchment is highly variable along the riparian corridor and is controlled in many cases by bedrock and coarse-grained fan deposits. These deposits often form steps in the longitudinal valley profiles and serve as local base level controls that dictate the amount of erosion that occurs upstream of the side-valley fans.

The region's geomorphic history has had several significant influences on both the nature and distribution of meadow complexes. First, the stratigraphic units that resulted from various erosional and depositional events vary dramatically in their ability to store and transmit water. Because meadow complexes are groundwater-dependent, variations in the units' permeability have profound influences on subsurface flow along the valley bottom, in general, and meadows, in particular. There is some evidence that fine-grained stratigraphic units at or near the ground surface are required in order for meadows to form. Second, the localized, stratigraphic complexity of the valley fill that is often more pronounced beneath meadows complicates the observed hydrologic responses of meadows to external disturbances like stream incision. Third, the geomorphic development of the basins has led to sites along the valley bottom where valley width and, presumably, depth to bedrock are abruptly constricted, thereby decreasing the area through which subsurface waters can flow. Not one of these factors necessarily results in meadow complexes, but in combination they can result in groundwater levels near or at the Earth's surface.

Down-Valley Constrictions of the Unconsolidated Flow Field. Groundwater levels along the valley bottom of most basins are located several meters below the surface, except beneath meadows. A reduction in the cross-sectional area of the valley fill can reduce the area through which water that is moving down-valley through unconsolidated sediments can flow. This mechanism is similar to the effect of a funnel; the constriction at the neck of the funnel causes water to pool above it. Constriction of a valley's cross-sectional area has

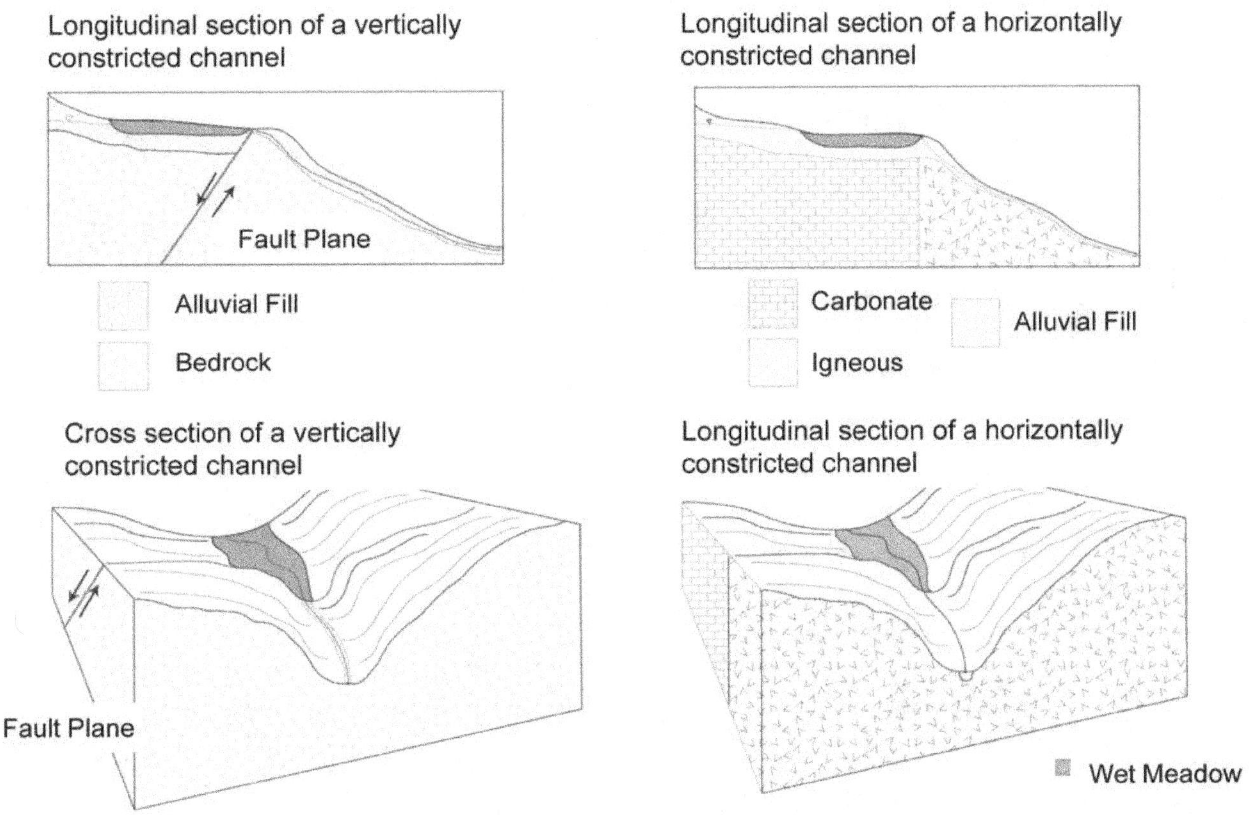

Figure 2.3. Lateral and vertical constriction formed by resistant bedrock.

the potential to cause localized pooling, significantly raising subsurface water levels. Most meadows are located immediately upstream of valley constrictions that are created either singularly or in conjunction with: (1) bedrock protrusions from the valley sides; (2) bedrock highs beneath the valley fill; and/or (3) accumulation of sediment associated with side-valley alluvial fans.

Bedrock Constrictions. The hydrologic damming effect of a bedrock constriction is straightforward because permeability of bedrock is generally less than that of unconsolidated alluvial valley fill. Thus, the rate at which water can move down-valley is greatly reduced by bedrock constrictions. Horizontal protrusions of bedrock into valley fill occur primarily at three distinct locations: (1) where the geology changes, from upstream to downstream, from a less to more erosionally resistant rock unit (fig. 2.3); (2) where the channel locally follows the trace of a fracture or fault and remains in the same location though time rather than migrating laterally and widening the valley floor as in other areas (fig. 2.3); and (3) near the mouth of a tributary where bedrock drainage divides project from the hillslope into the axial valley and constrict valley width (fig. 2.4). Valley width changes that are associated with faults may or may not be associated with regional tectonic structures.

While horizontal protrusion of bedrock into a valley can be easily observed in the field and on aerial photographs, upward (vertical) protrusion of bedrock into the valley fill cannot be directly observed. Seismic analyses were used to determine if upward protrusions represented a viable mechanism for reducing the cross-sectional area of the valley fill (Sturtevant 2007). More specifically, bedrock offsets associated with thrust and normal faults that were known to cross upland valleys were evaluated to determine if they created bedrock highs and caused decreased thickness of the alluvial fill. Meadow complexes often occur at sites where faults align with tributary channels and obliquely traverse upland valleys. Bedrock highs could be produced by differences in erosional resistance of bedrock units and different rates of stream channel incision during valley development.

Seismic (geophysical) analyses of six meadows within the Barley, Big Creek, Birch, Corcoran, Kingston, and Indian Valley basins determined that both topographic highs and faults were present within some but not all of the rock units beneath meadows (fig. 2.5) (Sturtevant 2007). Four different structural combinations were found: rock units that contained both faults and topographic bedrock highs, rock units that contained only faults, rock units that contained only topographic highs, and rock units that contained neither (table 2.2). Importantly, where bedrock highs were found, they often occurred immediately downstream of meadows in locations where they could exert strong control on groundwater level. Also, topographic highs along the bedrock-valley fill contact that were observed in the geophysical surveys were collocated (overlain by) with side-valley alluvial fan

Longitudinal Section of a Horizontally Constricted Channel

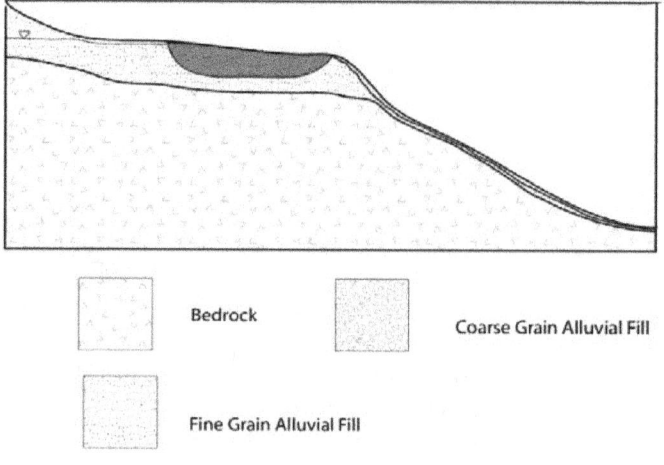

Bedrock

Coarse Grain Alluvial Fill

Fine Grain Alluvial Fill

Figure 2.4. Lateral constriction formed by a drainage divide.

Cross Section of a Horizontally Constricted Channel

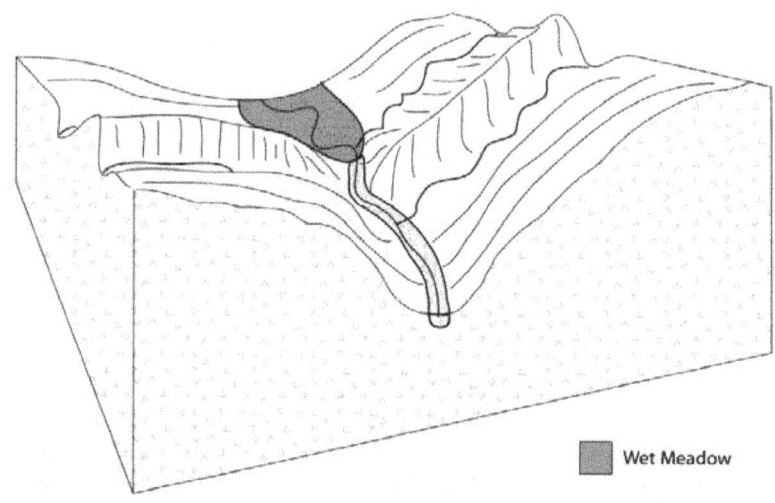

Wet Meadow

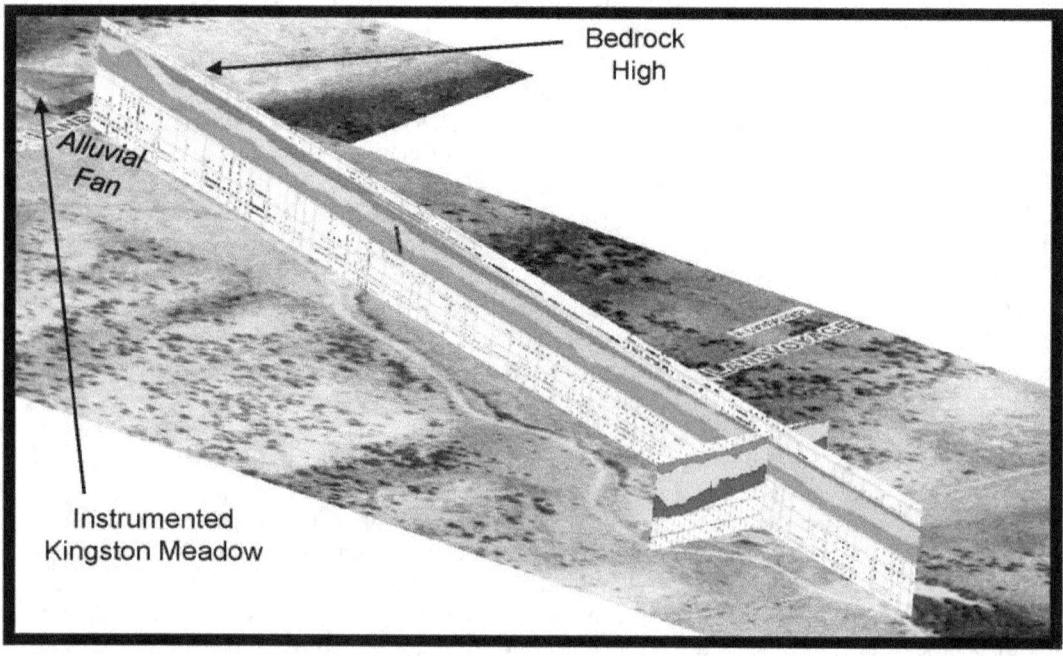

Bedrock
High

Alluvial
Fan

Instrumented
Kingston Meadow

Figure 2.5. Seismic refraction tomography profiles in Kingston Canyon. The vertical panels that represent the seismic stratigraphy are superimposed on an aerial photo of the meadow to show the location. The bedrock layer is shown in the blue/dark green layer. Light green and magenta layers are unconsolidated sediment. The fault (black line) from the reflection data is superimposed onto the refraction tomography. Note the bedrock high in the upper left corner of the image, which is the end of the wet meadow complex.

USDA Forest Service Gen. Tech. Rep. RMRS-GTR-258. 2011.

Table 2.2. Summary of types and extent of bedrock control on meadow ecosystems (modified from Sturtevant 2007).

Skematic Diagram	Geologic Control
	None
	Fault(s) Present
	Bedrock High Beneath Alluvium or Constricting Valley Width
	Fault(s) Present Bedrock High Beneath Alluvium or Constricting Valley Width

deposits (fig. 2.6). The joint occurrence of fans and topographic highs may result from protection of the bedrock from erosion by side-valley fan deposits as the axial channel eroded rock units during valley development. Deposition on the fans would tend to confine the channel to the opposing side of the valley, thereby limiting the amount of bedrock erosion that could occur beneath the fans. Regardless of the mechanisms responsible for fan formation, the geophysical data suggest that, in some cases, bedrock protrusions likely play a role in meadow development.

Constrictions Created by Side-Valley Alluvial Fans. As many as 39 of the wet meadows that were studied are located immediately upstream of side-valley alluvial fans. Where side-valley tributaries have delivered large quantities of sediment to the axial valley, alluvial fans prograde into, or even entirely across, the axial valley floor. Thus, fan deposits and the landforms that they create can be viewed as forming another type of valley constriction in the central Great Basin. Side-valley fans occur as two distinctly different morphological types: (1) fans that have distinct alluvial fan morphology and that prograde onto the valley floor (fig. 2.7a); and (2) fans that lack a distinct fan-morphology but that grade smoothly onto the valley floor (fig. 2.7b). The classic prograding fan morphology is easy to recognize and the valley constriction is self-evident (fig. 2.7a). Effects of graded fans on valley morphology are less obvious to the untrained eye, but the physical effects of fan deposits on the mainstem axial valley are no less significant (fig. 2.7b).

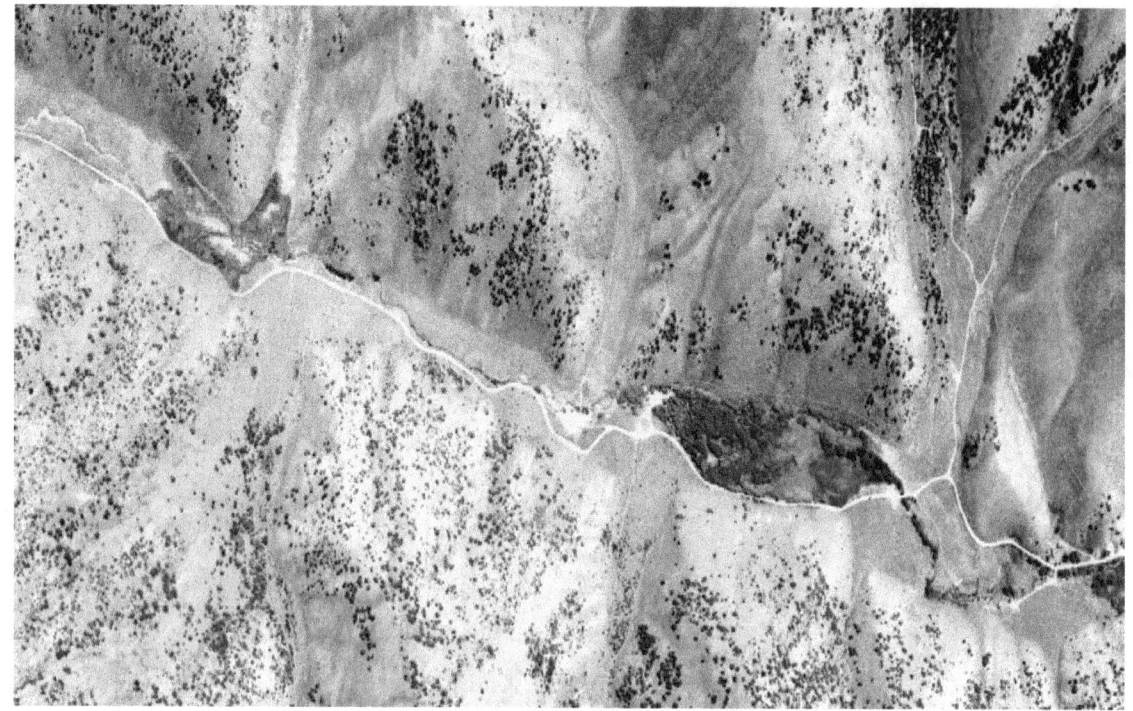

Figure 2.6. Wet meadows upstream of side-valley fans in Kingston Canyon, Toiyabe Range.

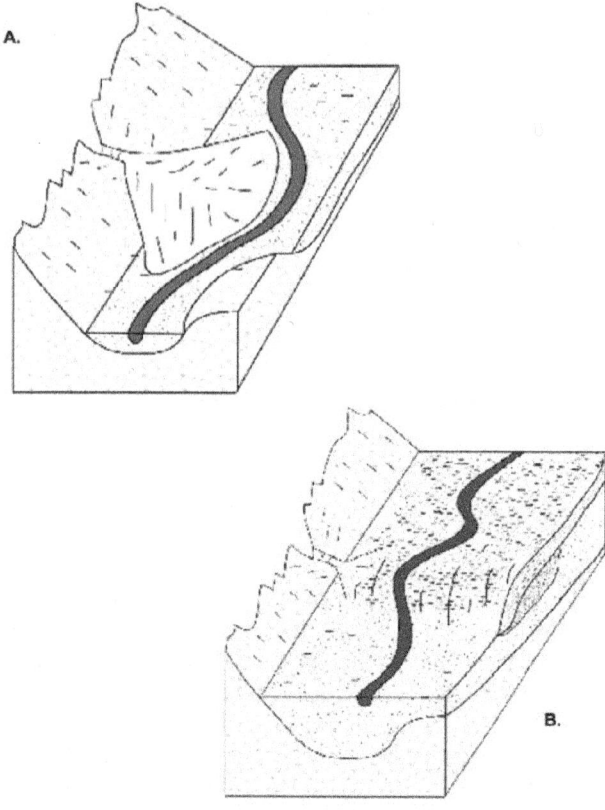

Figure 2.7. A. Meadow upstream of a prograding side-valley fan. B. Meadow upstream of a plunging side-valley alluvial fan.

The development of prograded versus graded fans is determined primarily by the morphology of the tributary valley, which in turn is influenced by the overall geomorphology of the drainage basin (Germanoski and Miller 2004). Where tributary drainage basins are long and have gentle gradients, the tributary valleys have more accommodation space for sediment to be stored and, thus, greater sediment accumulation. In such circumstances, side-valley fans are more likely to grade into the axial valley fill or to be buried by axial valley fill sediments. Where tributary drainage basins are short and have steep gradients, tributary valleys have little space to accommodate sediment storage and more sediment is delivered to the axial valley. In this case, side-valley fans are more likely to prograde into the axial valley. Short tributaries and prograding fans are most common in elongate drainage basins.

Some prograding fans can be found in basins that do not, at first glance, possess an elongate form. For example, Big Creek possesses a much more equant morphology than Kingston. However, it is clear from evaluating satellite images and aerial photos that the Big Creek drainage basin's morphology appears equant in plan view because it consists of two major tributary channels. The Big Creek drainage basin is bisected by a drainage divide rather than by the trunk channel of a dendritic drainage network as drainage basin morphometric analysis assumes. Thus, the elongation ratio (3.6) underpredicts the likelihood that tributary channels will be short and steep and that side-valley fans will be significant landforms. Corcoran basin, located in the southeastern section of the Toquima Range (fig. 1.7), is

Table 2.3. List of meadows and the geomorphic controls on each meadow's development. BR = bed rock; DD = drainage divide; Fan = alluvial fan; TC = tributary confluence.

Meadow	Control	Meadow	Control	Meadow	Control
Lebeau	Fan	Mohawk	BR	Willow (Monitor Range)	DD
Emmigrant 1	DD	South Crane	Fan	West Dobbin	DD
Emmigrant 2	Fan	Indian Valley	Fan/TC	Stargo	Fan
Cahill 2	Fan	Cloverdale	Fan	East Dobbin	Fan
Cahill 3	Fan	Corral 1	Fan/BR	Wadsworth 1	TC
Johnson 1	Fan	Corral 2	BR/Fan	Wadsworth 2	Fan
Johnson 2	Fan	West Northumberland	DD	Wadsworth 3	Fan
Johnson 3	Fan	Corcoran Main 1	DD	Wadsworth 4	DD
Birch Tributary	Fan/DD	Corcoran Main 2	Fan	Mosquito	Fan
Birch 1	DD	Corcoran Main 3	Fan	Danville	BR
Birch 2	Fan	Corcoran 1	Fan	Green Monster	BR
Big Creek	Fan	Corcoran 2	Fan	Barley	Fan
Kingston 0	Fan	Corcoran 3	Fan	Barley Trib.	DD
Kingston 1	Fan	Corcoran 4	Fan/TC	Fandango 1	Fan
Kingston 3	Fan	Corcoran 5	Fan	Fandango 2	Fan
Washington	Fan	Meadow 1	Fan	Little Cow	DD/BR
Cottonwood	Fan	Meadow 2	Fan	Six Mile 1	Fan
San Juan 1	TC	Round Mountain	TC	Six Mile 2	Fan
San Juan 2	Fan	Red Canyon	DD		

another example of a basin with an equant shape overall. However, the basin is composed of two major tributaries that drain from the north (North Fork) and east (Corral Canyon), and it has a morphology that facilitates side-valley tributary control because individual sub-basins have elongate geometries that favor the influence of side-valley fans. Although the elongation ratio of a drainage basin is a good indicator that side-valley fan constrictions will be common, these examples illustrate that some drainage basins that are equant in shape may have two elongate sub-basins that facilitate side-valley fan development.

Hydrologic Effects of Side-Valley Alluvial Fans. Unlike bedrock protrusions, the effects of side-valley alluvial fans on groundwater are more indirect because fan sediments are unlikely to reduce the rate of groundwater flow. Field observations and sediment cores taken from five drainage basins in the study area indicate that most fan deposits are coarser-grained than axial valley fill sediments. Thus, fan deposits are likely to possess higher permeabilities and hydraulic conductivities than valley fill. However, fan progradation often results in deposition of fine-grained sediments immediately upstream. Observations of 56 meadows in the central Great Basin indicate that sedimentation upstream of side-valley alluvial fans and tributary junctions is the most common factor influencing development of meadows, followed by sedimentation upstream of bedrock-related geomorphic constrictions (table 2.3). The importance of these fine-grained units, which possess low permeabilities, is that they are likely to reduce down-valley groundwater flow rates, resulting in a rise in water levels. Slug test data showed that deposits beneath the meadows locally possessed relatively low hydraulic conductivities, on the order of 10^{-5} cm/s (unpublished data from Lord and Jewett). Our observations also indicated that the formation of wet meadows, in general, requires accumulation of relatively impermeable fine-grained sediment near

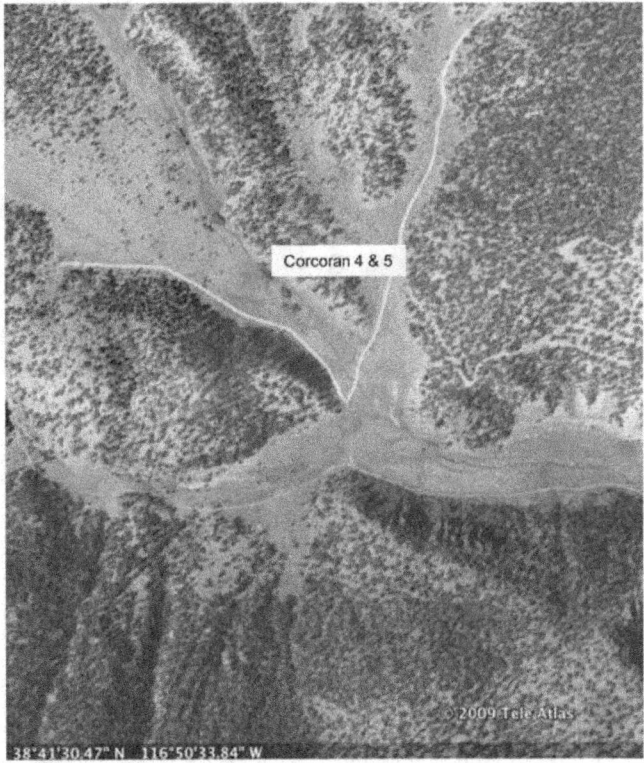

Figure 2.8. Meadow upstream of the junction of two high-order tributaries.

the ground surface that: (1) retards the ability of the water to rapidly discharge at the surface and drain the underlying aquifer; (2) creates artesian flow conditions, which allow the meadows to remain saturated over long periods of time; and (3) forces the water to flow through underlying deposits that are finer-grained within the meadow than upstream and downstream and that reduce the rate of groundwater flow.

USDA Forest Service Gen. Tech. Rep. RMRS-GTR-258. 2011.

19

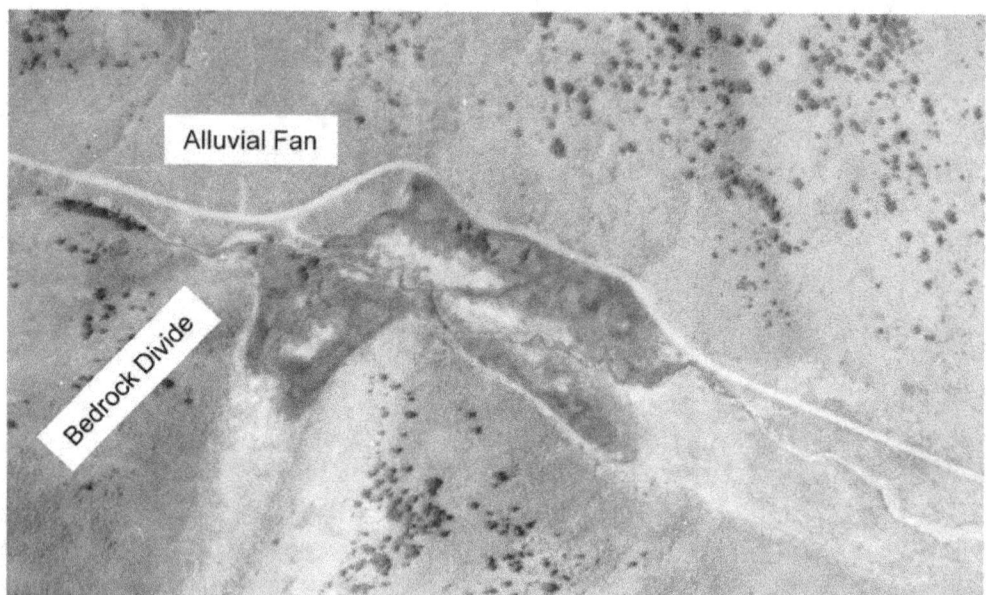

Figure 2.9. Valley constrictions downstream of the Kingston 3 meadow in Kingston Canyon.

A few meadows are located where fine-grained sediment has accumulated above tributary junctions (fig. 2.8). However, in this case, enhanced fine-grained sediment accumulated as a result of temporary sediment damming upstream of a tributary valley without the formation of side-valley fan deposits. This process appears to be most prevalent in systems where tributaries are underlain by poorly welded volcanic tuffs that produce disproportionately large volumes of fine-grained sediment in comparison to basins underlain by sedimentary rocks, crystalline rocks, massive welded tuffs, or crystalline rhyolite. In addition, the characteristics of sediment deposition from side valley sources appear to be related to tributary size. Prograding fans tend to form where sediment producing tributaries are steep first- or second-order channels, while graded fans form when side-valley channels are lower gradient, perhaps third-order channels, and tributary junction sedimentation occurs where two higher-order tributaries join.

Fine-grained sediment deposition also may be an important component of meadow development upstream of bedrock constrictions. Fine-grained sediment often is produced upstream of bedrock drainage divides that are associated with tributary channels that project into the axial valley, a situation that is commonly observed in the headwater areas of a drainage basin. Also, more than one type of fan and/or valley constriction may be present, all of which contribute to the development of a meadow (fig. 2.9). An excellent example occurs in Kingston Canyon, located on the east side of the Toiyabe Range (fig. 1.7), which is underlain primarily by a complex set of sedimentary and metasedimentary rocks of Cambrian and Ordovician age and exhibits an elongated morphology with a shape factor of 5.1. As previously noted, elongate basin shapes increase the probability that prominent side-valley fans will form by prograding into the axial valley. A meadow in Kingston Canyon (Kingston 3) is located immediately upstream of a prominent, prograding side-valley fan. However, the axial valley is further

constricted by protrusion of a bedrock hillslope that the fan deposits abut against and a graded side-valley fan from a tributary on the east (fig. 2.9). These features cause a significant decrease in the gradient of the longitudinal profiles of the axial channel and valley floor upstream of the constrictions. The decrease in slope facilitates the accumulation of fine-grained sediment, which reduces groundwater flow rates through the valley fill.

Although the type of valley constriction that occurs in a basin depends on its plan view morphology, every meadow is unique, and the causative factors of meadow formation are likely to vary even within individual watersheds. For example, Corcoran Canyon is located on the east side of the southern Toquima Range, is underlain by volcanic tuffs of Tertiary age, and has two major tributaries. The main branch has an elongation ratio of 5.2, whereas the west branch has an elongation ratio of 4.1. The elongated geometry of these basins facilitates development of side-valley fans that have the potential to prograde into the axial valley. The eight well-developed meadows in Corcoran Canyon are found in similar, but slightly different geomorphic settings (fig. 2.10). Meadows within the main branch of Corcoran Canyon (labeled Main 1, 2, and 3) all terminate downstream at graded, side-valley alluvial fans with some of the fans partially buried by axial valley-fill sediment. However, the geomorphic setting of meadow 1 differs in that it is perched upstream of a fan that grades onto the valley floor just upstream of a bedrock constriction. The position of this meadow likely reflects the combined effects of a bedrock constriction and graded alluvial fan on sediment deposited upstream of the constriction (fig. 2.11). Similarly, five meadows occur in the west branch of Corcoran Canyon, but only the first three meadows (labeled 1, 2, and 3) are positioned upstream of side-valley alluvial fans that are graded to the axial valley floor. Meadows 4 and 5 differ somewhat and are located in a northern tributary of the West Fork of Corcoran Canyon just upstream of tributary confluences (fig. 2.11). Although

Figure 2.10. Eight meadows in Corcoran Canyon.

Figure 2.11. Corcoran Meadow-fan and bedrock control.

detailed stratigraphic data are lacking, geomorphic architecture of the valleys suggests that fine-grained sedimentation within the valley of the West Fork of Corcoran Canyon reduced the rate of groundwater flow moving down-valley along its tributary channels, creating meadows immediately upstream of the confluence. In other words, sediment deposition in the axial valley blocked sediment from entering from the northern tributary, thereby allowing fine-grained deposits with low hydraulic conductivity to accumulate in the tributary above the channel junctions. The net effect is that meadows 4 and 5 are in a geomorphic setting different from those elsewhere, although the basic factors contributing to meadow formation (water supply, fine-grained sediment accumulation, and constrictions on flow rates) are present.

USDA Forest Service Gen. Tech. Rep. RMRS-GTR-258. 2011.

21

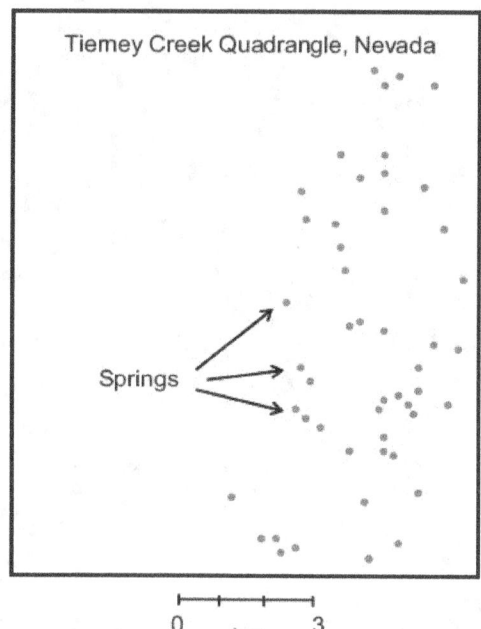

Figure 2.12. Location of springs mapped on 7.5 minute USGS Topographic Sheets. Note linear alignment of springs.

Source of Meadow Waters

The general assumption has been that the primary source of water to the meadows is precipitation in upstream portions of the basin that flows down-valley through unconsolidated fill to the meadow complex. While flow through valley fill is undoubtedly an important groundwater source, two other sources can be important. First, where meadows exist immediately upstream of side-valley alluvial fans, some subsurface water is derived from movement of water through the tributary valley fill that forms the fan. The importance of this source is detailed in Chapter 3. Second, groundwater may be supplied to some meadows as it emerges from faults and fractures in the underlying bedrock that traverses the axial valleys, as observed in Kingston 3 and Big Creek. Faults were found within the bedrock at a number of sites (Sturtevant 2007), and it is possible that the water at these locations originated in other, adjacent basins. Movement and discharge of water along bedrock faults and fractures is supported by maps of spring locations on 1:24,000 scale topographic sheets (fig. 2.12). Although springs are present in most meadows, springs often occur without meadows and, more importantly, frequently align along linear trends (fig. 2.12) indicative of structural features such as fractures and faults.

Summary

Local and regional analyses show that meadows are located in specific geomorphic and hydrologic settings. However, each meadow complex is a unique feature and cannot be unequivocally described by any single set of causative factors without geomorphologic investigation. Most meadows result from a combination of factors, the most important of which are an adequate water supply and some mechanism that retards down-valley movement of groundwater and causes a rise in groundwater levels. The reduction in goundwater flow may be produced by several different factors, including the vertical or lateral constriction of the valley fill by bedrock and/or a change in grain size of the valley-fill deposits. Reductions in grain size, and permeability of the resulting deposits, are commonly associated with deposition upstream of side-valley alluvial fans and bedrock protrusions. Meadows usually exhibit relatively impermeable, fine-grained sediment near the ground surface that: (1) slows the water and prevents it from rapidly discharging at the surface and draining the underlying aquifer; (2) creates artesian flow conditions that allow meadows to remain saturated over long periods of time; and (3) forces water to flow through underlying deposits that are finer-grained in the meadow than upstream and that reduce the rate of groundwater flow. These factors are discussed in more detail in Chapter 3.

Given that meadow complexes are supported by groundwater and that an adequate water supply is needed for their continued existence, it is important to determine the source of groundwater to the meadows. Several sources, occurring either individually or in combination, have been identified, the most important of which are: (1) water that is derived primarily from precipitation that flows down-valley through unconsolidated valley fill; (2) water that moves through alluvial fill and fan deposits within adjacent tributaries; and (3) water that is discharged from bedrock faults and springs and that may be derived from other watersheds. Any activity that reduces the supply of groundwater to the meadow risks negatively affecting the meadow's ecological condition.

References

Allison, R.J.; Thomas D.S.G. 1993. The sensitivity of landscapes. In: Thomas, D.S.G.; Allison, R.J., eds. Landscape Sensitivity. Chichester, UK: John Wiley and Sons.

Castelli, R.M.; Chambers, J.C.; Tausch, R.J. 2000. Soil-plant relations along a soil-water gradient in Great Basin riparian meadows. Wetlands. 20: 251-266.

Chambers, J.C.; Farleigh, K.; Tausch, R.J.; Miller, J.R.; Germanoski, D.; Martin, D.; Nowak, C. 1998. Understanding long- and short-term changes in vegetation and geomorphic processes: the key to riparian restoration. In: Potts, D.F., ed. Rangeland management and water resources. Herndon, VA: American Water Resources Association and Society for Range Management: 101-110.

Hess, G.W. 2002. Updated techniques for estimating monthly streamflow duration characteristics at ungaged and partial-record sites in Central Nevada. U.S. Geological Survey Open-File Report 02-168. 16 p.

Germanoski, D.; Miller, J.R. 2004. Basin sensitivity to channel incision in response to natural and anthropogenic disturbance. In: Chambers, J.C.; Miller, J.R., eds. Great Basin Riparian Ecosystems—Ecology, Management, and Restoration. Covelo, CA: Island Press: 88-123.

Miller, J.R.; Germanoski, D.; Waltman, K.; Tausch, R.; Chambers, J. 2001. Influence of late Holocene hillslope processes and landforms on modern channel dynamics in upland watersheds of central Nevada. Geomorphology. 38: 373-391.

Miller, J.R.; House, K.; Germanoski, D.; Tausch, R.J.; Chambers, J.C. 2004. Fluvial geomorphic responses to Holocene climate change. In: Chambers, J.C.; Miller, J.R., eds. Great Basin Riparian Ecosystems—Ecology, Management, and Restoration. Covelo, CA: Island Press: 49-87.

Oregon Climate Service. 2009. Oregon State University. Available: http://www.ocs.oregonstate.edu/index html. [29 Dec 2010].

Schumm, S.A. 1991. To Interpret the Earth: Ten Ways to be Wrong. Cambridge, UK: Cambridge University Press. 134 p.

Sturtevant, K.A. 2007. Integrating multiple geophysical methods to analyze geologic controls of riparian meadow complexes, central Great Basin, NV. Thesis, Department of Geology, State University of New York at Buffalo. 378 p.

Tausch, R.J.; Nowak, C.L.; Mensing, S.W. 2004. Climate change and associated vegetation dynamics during the Holocene: the paleoecological record. In: Chambers, J.C.; Miller, J.R., eds. Great Basin Riparian Ecosystems—Ecology, Management, and Restoration. Covelo, CA: Island Press: 24-48.

USDA Forest Service Gen. Tech. Rep. RMRS-GTR-258. 2011.

23

Chapter 3: Geomorphic Processes Affecting Meadow Ecosystems

Jerry R. Miller, Dru Germanoski, and Mark L. Lord

Introduction

Three geomorphic processes are of primary concern with respect to the current and future state of wet meadow ecosystems: channel incision, avulsion (the abrupt movement of the channel to a new location on the valley floor), and gully formation. Gully formation often is accompanied by upvalley headcut migration and a phenomenon referred to as "groundwater sapping" that is defined as erosion of bank materials by groundwater flow. In this chapter, we examine the effects of each of these processes on meadow complexes. Although these processes are discussed separately, they are often interconnected and the rates at which they proceed depend on their interactions. Therefore, the potential to stabilize or rehabilitate a specific meadow must not only include an evaluation of the individual processes but also their combined effects.

Channel and Valley Incision

Our interest in channel incision stems largely from the potential of a lowered streambed to result in a drop of the adjacent water table and a subsequent change in riparian meadow vegetation and aquatic habitat. Incision also may lead to other detrimental geomorphic effects, including: (1) an increase in bank heights, which can decrease the frequency and magnitude of overbank flooding and increase rates of bank erosion; (2) a change in cross-sectional channel morphology; and (3) a loss in complexity of the streambed and an overall decline in aquatic habitat. In general, incision occurs anywhere that sediment removed from the reach exceeds the amount entering the reach, provided that the stream's power is capable of moving the bed material (substrate). Both sediment supply and stream power vary through time and space. Thus, the magnitude and rate of incision vary along the channel at any given time, and through time at any given location. In addition, the means through which the bed is actually lowered can involve several different processes, depending on the nature of the bed and bank materials, the stream's capacity to transport sediment, and the pre-existing channel morphology. The most important of these processes are erosion of the channel bed through entrainment of individual particles and the formation and subsequent migration of knickpoints.

Channel Incision by Particle Entrainment

Where an integrated stream network exists, the most ubiquitous process through which channels in the upland basins incise is through the grain-by-grain entrainment of sediment from the channel bed and its subsequent downstream transport at a rate that exceeds its replenishment. This grain-by-grain transport process can occur anywhere that unconsolidated sediment forms the channel floor but, in these study sites, it is most prevalent along stream segments that are located between meadow complexes. The tendency for incision to occur is driven largely by the region's history of intense hillslope stripping of fine sediment between approximately 2580 and 1980 years BP, a process that has reduced sediment input to the axial drainage systems. Specifically, the inability of material to be transported off of hillslopes and into the drainage network has resulted in a general lack of bedload and has contributed to the tendency for channels to incise.

Given that bedload transport rates are likely to increase with increasing discharge, most incision occurs during periods of relatively high runoff. For example, repeated measurements of cross-sectional channel geometry along eight incising reaches in five watersheds (Big Creek, Kingston, San Juan, Cottonwood, and Washington; fig. 1.7) showed that while bed degradation during the low runoff years of the early 1990s was limited, incision during the relatively high runoff period of 1995 was significant and ranged from 5 to 36 cm (fig. 3.1a; Chambers and others 1998). Incision was accompanied by significant bank undercutting (up to 18 cm; fig. 3.1c) as well as by bank loss and/or deposition (-6 to +38 cm; fig. 3.1b). Deposition along the banks was primarily associated with growth of pre-existing gravel bars. Variations in the degree of channel incision and bank modification were related to size of the bed material, cover of bank vegetation, and age and stem density of willows growing on terrace surfaces along the channel margins.

The correlation between rapid rates of incision with years of relatively high runoff also is supported by dendrogeomorphic data. Terraces located along the eight surveyed reaches described above were dated by determining the maximum age of willows that colonized their surface (fig. 3.2) using dendrochronological methods (after Sigafoos 1964; Phipps 1985). The presumption is that extensive willow colonization occurred shortly after the geomorphic surface was formed, and the sediments were no longer being transported during low to moderate runoff events (Sigafoos 1964). The results show that willow age correlates with height of gravel terraces located along the channel. Maximum willow ages

24

USDA Forest Service Gen. Tech. Rep. RMRS-GTR-258. 2011.

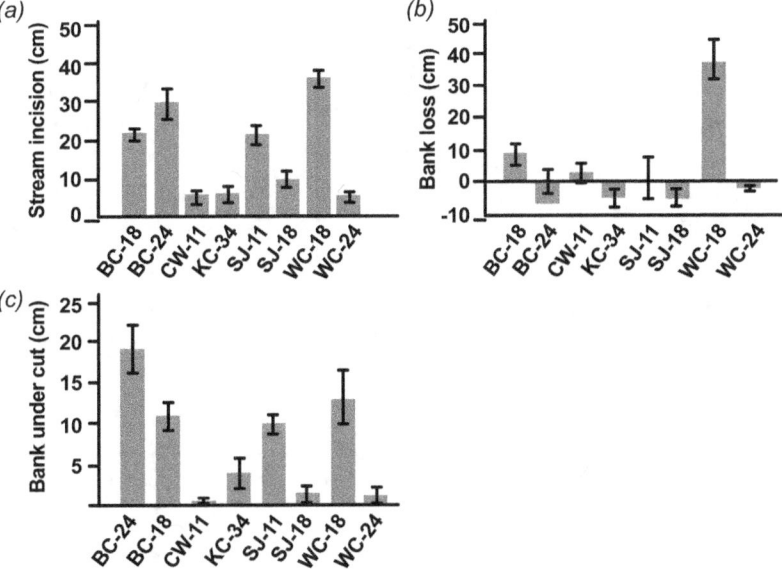

(a)

Stream incision (cm)

(b)

Bank loss (cm)

Figure 3.1. (a) Amount of stream incision, (b) bank erosion, and (c) bank undercutting measured at monitoring cross sections during the high runoff year of 1995; SJ = San Juan Creek; BC = Big Creek; WC = Washington Creek; KC = Kingston Creek; and CW = Cottonwood Creek.

(c)

Bank under cut (cm)

Figure 3.2. Willow covered terrace surface located along Big Creek. Colonization of the surface is assumed to occur following incision and the cessation of annual particle entrainment.

for the most recent terrace at the time of data collection (in 1997) were 11 to 12 years, corresponding to high runoff events in 1983-1984. The maximum ages of other willows clustered around 18 to 20 and 24 years, as measured in 1997. These willows presumably colonized new terrace surfaces created by channel incision during high flows and overbank flooding in the 1970s (1973, 1975, and 1978; fig. 3.3). Older stands of willows could not be accurately dated because individual willow stems survive less than 50 years (Chambers and others 1998). However, older stands were found on terraces above the geomorphic surfaces that were created in the 1970s. Thus, the stands were likely to have established either before the recent episodes of channel incision or along a limited number of stream reaches that had not incised.

Most watersheds within the study area exhibit convexities in the longitudinal profile of the axial channel, which represent zones of inherent instability that are prone to entrenchment. Once incised, base level is lowered and

upstream reaches must adjust. Importantly, spatial variations in the rate and magnitude of incision are closely related to the degree to which erosion has lowered local base level along concaved upstream reaches, most of which are produced by side-valley alluvial fans. Where incision occurs, a proportional amount of upstream incision is likely to follow, either by means of individual particle transport or through knickpoint processes.

Incision by Knickpoint Processes

While channel incision by means of particle entrainment and transport is wide-spread, much of the observed incision is associated with the localized development and migration of knickpoints. Knickpoints, broadly defined as abrupt changes in channel gradient, are generally associated with episodes of entrenchment in response to a lowering of base level. Detailed mapping of knickpoint distribution along the

USDA Forest Service Gen. Tech. Rep. RMRS-GTR-258. 2011.

25

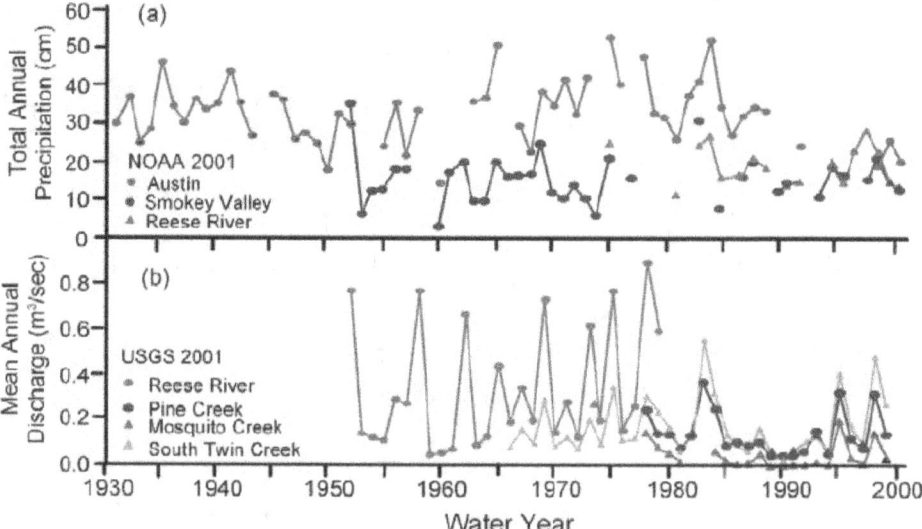

Figure 3.3. (a) Total annual precipitation measured for Smokey Valley, Reese River, and Austin, Nevada; (b) mean annual discharge for selected stream systems in central Nevada.

downstream reaches of 10 basins, combined with field observations from more than 20 additional watersheds in central Nevada, demonstrate that knickpoints can be found throughout the drainage network, with the exception of zero- and first-order streams (Germanoski and Miller 2004). However, knickpoints are concentrated at or immediately upstream of convexities in the valley floor. Knickpoints are particularly prevalent at and upstream of side-valley alluvial fans that influence valley/channel gradients (fig. 3.4). Where these fans occur with meadow complexes, knickpoints play a critical role in channel incision through the meadows.

Experimental and field studies conducted over the past three decades have shown that the nature of knickpoint migration and evolution can be highly variable from site to site (fig. 3.5) and is dependent on the composition of the bed material, variations in the material's resistance to erosion (particularly the presence of stratification), and the relationship between channel bed shear stress and the critical tractive force required to initiate particle motion (Gilbert 1896; Pickup 1975; Gardner 1983; Cosby and Whipple 2007). Knickpoints found at the toe of side-valley alluvial fans are composed primarily of cobble or boulder-sized clasts, which are significantly larger than bed material located either up- or downstream of the knickpoint face. The height of the knickpoint face is equivalent to the diameter of the clasts that form the knickpoint. Thus, the knickpoint represents the cross-channel alignment of several large, interlocking boulders that require relatively

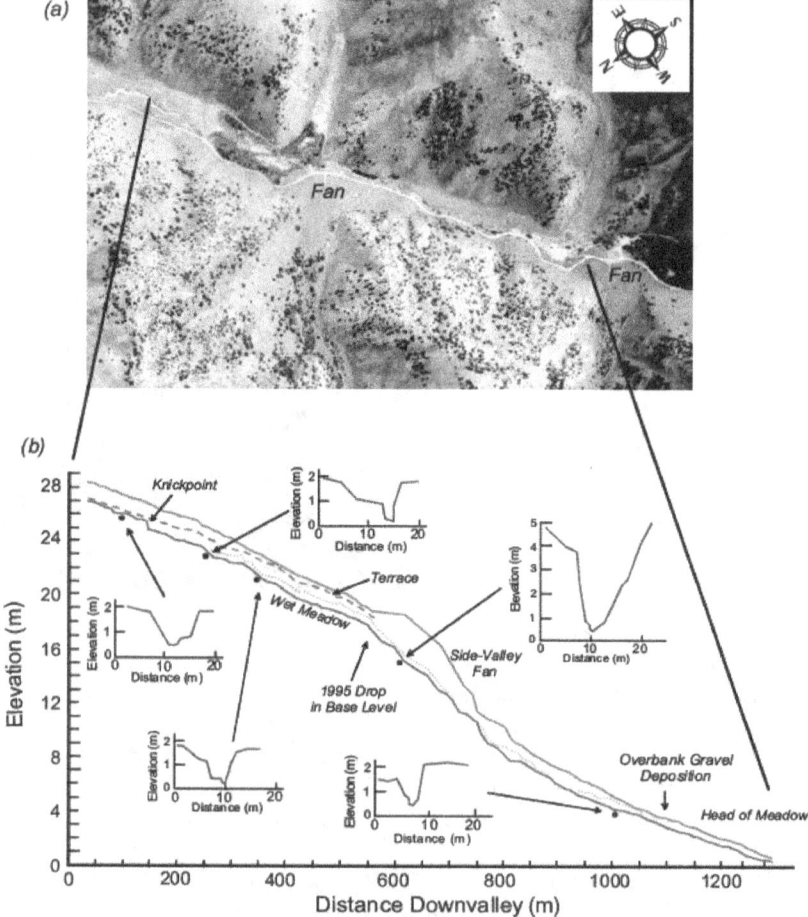

Figure 3.4. Longitudinal profile showing changes in channel gradients across a large side-valley alluvial fan in Kingston Canyon. Note the drop in elevation of the valley floor across the fan, a feature that creates a local zone of channel instability. Incision through the fan is limited by course fan sediments within the channel bed.

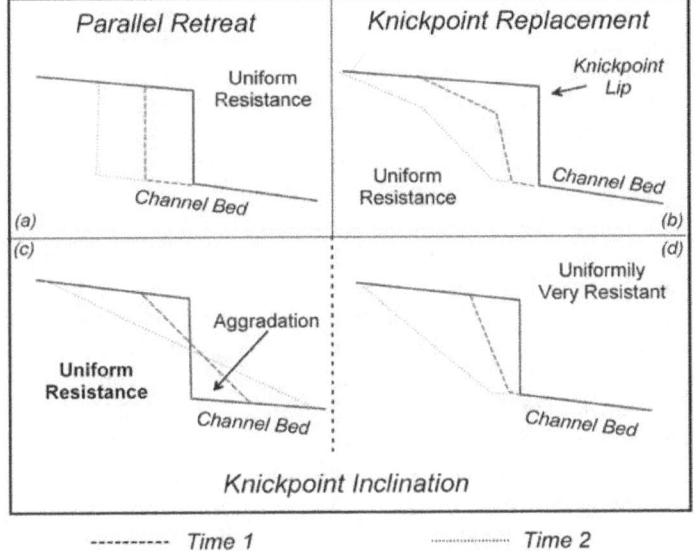

Parallel Retreat | Knickpoint Replacement

(a) Uniform Resistance — Channel Bed

(b) Knickpoint Lip — Uniform Resistance — Channel Bed

(c) Uniform Resistance — Aggradation — Channel Bed

(d) Uniformily Very Resistant — Channel Bed

Knickpoint Inclination

---------- Time 1   ················· Time 2
————— Initial Channel Bed Profile

Figure 3.5. Three models of knickpoint evolution described by Gardner (1983). Knickpoints in central Nevada primarily evolve by (a) parallel retreat when formed in fine-grained sediment, and by (c) knickpoint inclination when developed in non-cohesive, coarse-grained sediment. In the latter case, knickpoint advancement is limited, but the process of knickpoint inclination results in a lowering of local base level, which is subsequently translated upstream.

high values of shear stress to be moved (figs. 3.6a and b). It is not entirely clear if the boulder-sized material that forms the knickpoints is transported into place, or if knickpoints represent more resistant zones in the channel bed that are exposed as finer materials are entrained and transported out of the reach. It is likely that both mechanisms occur depending on the local bed material composition and flow conditions.

What is significant about these knickpoints is that once one or more of the lip-forming boulders are moved downstream, finer material immediately upstream of the knickpoint face can be transported through the breach. This allows the slope of the channel bed upstream of the knickpoint to decline. In most cases, the finer material is not redeposited immediately downstream of the knickpoint but is transported out of the area, resulting in a drop in base level and the evolution of knickpoint morphology by means of knickpoint inclination (fig. 3.5c). The erosional resistance of these knickpoints is important because it largely dictates the rate at which the channel bed, composed predominantly of fan sediment, can be incised.

Knickpoints along stream reaches that traverse meadows and that are located upstream of the side-valley fans (fig. 3.6a) are different from those found within the non-cohesive gravels of the over-steepened fan reach. Here, the knickpoints are formed in fine-grained cohesive sediments that typically underlie a thin veneer of gravel in the channel bed of the meadow complex. These types of knickpoints usually migrate upstream through the meadow complex for considerable distances and eventually disappear where the composition of the channel bed becomes dominated by gravel rather than fine-grained alluvium (i.e., silts, clays, and fine sand). During upstream migration of the knickpoint, an inset terrace is commonly formed that extends upstream from the side-valley fan through the meadow complex and beyond (e.g., fig. 3.4b, dashed line). The occurrence of the terrace upstream of the meadow (and the known upstream extent of knickpoint migration) suggests that the effects of the base-level drop at the fan are realized over a significant portion of the axial drainage.

The style of knickpoint migration and evolution that is observed within the meadows is referred to as parallel retreat (fig. 3.5a) because the knickpoint face remains roughly vertical as it migrates upstream (fig. 3.6a). Gardner (1983) argues that three factors are needed for parallel knickpoint retreat:

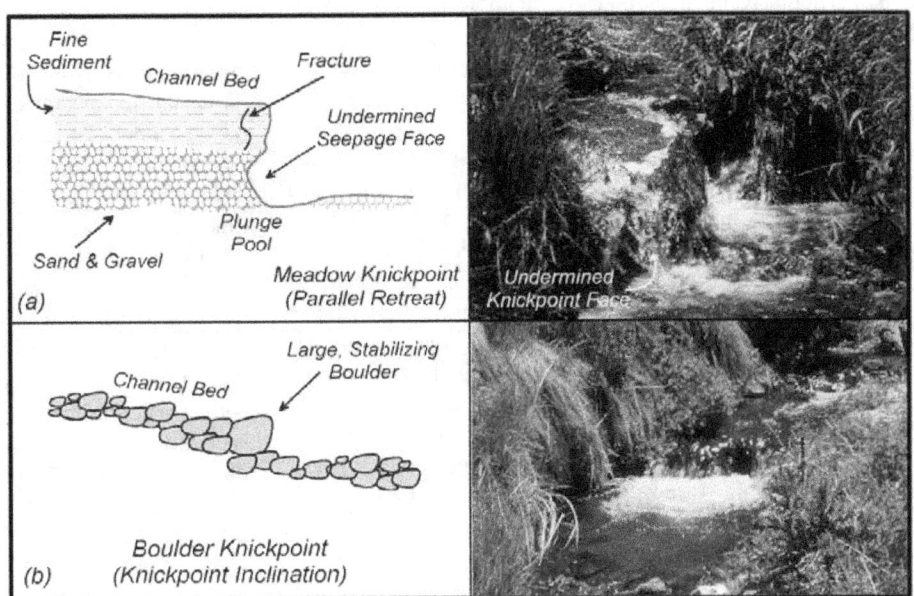

Figure 3.6. Morphology of knickpoints commonly observed along incised channels. (a) Knickpoint developed in fine-grained sediment; (b) knickpoint developed in coarse-grained sediment. Knickpoints formed in fine-grained, cohesive sediments migrate upstream by means of parallel retreat, whereas upstream advancement of knickpoints formed in coarse sediment is limited. Both photographs were taken along Kingston Canyon in 1997.

Fine Sediment — Channel Bed — Fracture — Undermined Seepage Face — Plunge Pool — Sand & Gravel — Meadow Knickpoint (Parallel Retreat) (a) — Undermined Knickpoint Face

Channel Bed — Large, Stabilizing Boulder — Boulder Knickpoint (Knickpoint Inclination) (b)

(1) an erosionally resistant layer that forms the knickpoint lip, (2) an underlying unit with lower resistance to erosion, and (3) the ability of stream flow to remove sediment from the base of the knickpoint. The removal of sediment from the base of the knickpoint can create a plunge pool by undercutting the resistant cap layer. The knickpoint then migrates upstream (retreats) as the material that forms the knickpoint face fails. Knickpoint retreat is commonly observed where streams are developed in alluvial materials characterized by varying resistances to erosion (Holland and Pickup 1976; Patton and Schumm 1981; Gardner 1983; Miller and others 1990), as is the case for most meadow complexes in the study area.

Most meadow systems are characterized by deposition of fine-grained silts and clays over the valley floor and the periodic deposition of sand and gravel both within the channel and as localized, lobate overbank deposits. The latter deposits tend to be associated with rare episodes of sediment influx to the drainage network during storm events. These diverse depositional sequences result in a layered stratigraphy that is prone to incision by knickpoint retreat. Erosionally resistant materials required for knickpoint retreat also appear to be related to soil development in both fine- and coarse-grained alluvium during periods of relative stability. Of particular importance are soils developed in the surface of Neoglacial (Qa1, fig. 2.1) deposits that possess significant quantities of clay and are particularly resistant to erosion. Another important property of these soils (and other units with relatively large amounts of silt and clay) is that the fine sediment limits vertical groundwater flow. As a result, where these fine-grained units are present, horizontal flows are enhanced, creating zones of groundwater seepage along the channel banks immediately above the less permeable layer. Bank seepage in these areas can be so significant that it results in erosion of less resistant (cohesive) bank materials, bank undercutting, and subsequent bank collapse. Although less obvious, groundwater flow also may lead to erosion and undercutting of materials beneath the knickpoint lip, particularly in areas that are characterized by upward flow gradients and/or artesian conditions (fig. 3.6a). Thus, knickpoint retreat appears to be aided by groundwater sapping processes, which tend to be spatially limited to meadow environments.

The mechanisms of channel incision correlate closely with the size and composition of material in the channel bed. Knickpoints along streams that traverse side-valley fans are composed of boulders and evolve by knickpoint inclination (fig. 3.6b). Knickpoints within meadows are composed of cohesive, fine-grained sediments and migrate upstream by means of knickpoint retreat. Upstream of meadows, knickpoints are generally lacking, and channel incision occurs by entrainment of individual clasts. Given that the current distribution of the geologic materials that form the channel bed is related to depositional processes that occurred in the past, it follows that the system's geological history has played a significant role in dictating the nature of modern channel processes.

An important observation from a management perspective is that once a drop in base level at the fan has taken place, further degradation is likely to occur somewhat rapidly. For example, aerial photographs suggest that the axial channel in Kingston 3 meadow (fig. 3.4) had been stable since at least 1965. Once base level had been lowered by a flood in 1995, the entire meadow system exhibited channel incision within a relatively short period of time (five years).

In many cases, wet meadows are characterized by an axial channel fed by upstream runoff, and one or more smaller tributaries fed predominantly by spring flow. During knickpoint migration, not all parts of the drainage network within these meadows are affected equally. For example, as the knickpoint migrated through Kingston 3 meadow, the base level drop along the axial stream created additional knickpoints within the spring-feed tributary channels. These knickpoints have not migrated more than a few meters upstream of the tributary's confluence with the axial channel, presumably because stream power dropped significantly (see Cosby and Whipple 2007). However, these knickpoints represent points of instability that can lead to rapid channel and valley incision under certain conditions.

Gully Formation Along Steep Valleys

As previously discussed, well-defined channel networks are incised by either knickpoint processes or entrainment of individual particles. In contrast, unincised meadows or meadows that possess shallow, discontinuous channels are usually entrenched by a different set of processes involving gully formation and headcut migration, both of which are promoted by groundwater sapping (sometimes called seepage erosion). The nature and rate at which these processes occur differ between basins, but basins can generally be grouped into two types: (1) those characterized by relatively steep valley floors that are underlain by highly permeable sediments; and (2) those that exhibit low-gradient valleys, relatively large meadows, and a mixture of sediment sizes within the valley fill. In this section, we discuss the formation of gullies and the resulting transport and deposition of sediment within basins that possess relatively steep and narrow valley floors.

Of particular concern is the potential for extremely rapid development of relative large gullies. This is prevalent within basins that are underlain by quartz monzonites and granodiorites of middle Jurassic age that weather into coarse sand and granule-sized sediment (called grus). Grus is particularly susceptible to erosion by groundwater because it is non-cohesive and highly permeable, allowing for rapid rates of groundwater flow. As a result, valley incision often involves a positive feedback mechanism in which the onset of incision and the formation of a distinct channel produce groundwater flow convergence, higher effective pore pressures, and enhanced seepage erosion and undercutting. As the channel grows, these processes are enhanced to the point that upstream headcut migration can occur with little or no overland flow, provided that the failed bank material is carried away from the base of the slope by groundwater discharge into the channel.

Perhaps the best example of this process (or sequence of processes) is provided by Marshall Canyon, a 4.9-km² basin located approximately 2 km south of Austin on the western flank of the Toiyabe Range. In May 1998, the valley floor in the upper section of the basin was rapidly incised over a period of a few days in response to heavy rainfall and melting of a relatively large winter snowpack (fig. 3.7a, b, and d). Germanoski and others (2001) found that erosion, deposition, and transport of sediment during and following the event occurred in distinct zones, called "process zones," along the valley bottom. These process zones were mapped on aerial photographs in June 1998 immediately following valley incision (fig. 3.8). The most significant zone of valley entrenchment (Erosion Zone 1; fig. 3.8) was located at the head of the drainage system in an area characterized by several side-valley springs and the convergence of low-order tributaries draining headwater reaches (fig. 3.8). The zone was

characterized by an unincised valley floor prior to the event. However, erosion created a flat-floored trench with nearly vertical walls. The trench was about 7 to 10 m wide, up to 6 m deep, and terminated upstream in three amphitheater-shaped, vertical headcuts that were separated by narrow "islands" of valley fill (fig. 3.7a). There was no evidence immediately after the event to suggest that the three headcuts were eroded by overland flow. Rather, it appeared that headcut development and migration primarily resulted from a combination of seepage erosion (sapping) and slope failure by mass wasting processes. Although headcut development and migration were not observed, the following factors were likely to have occurred in the process:

- Localized incision of the valley fill along a low-relief depression, creating a shallow, discontinuous gully system;

Figure 3.7. Major types of process zones recognized along the valley of Marshall Canyon: (a) Erosional Zone 1; (b) Transport Zone 1; (c) Depositional Zone 1; and (d) Incised channel within Erosion Zone 2. See fig. 3.8a for process zone locations.

- Convergence of both surface and, more importantly, groundwater flow as the depth of incision increased; and

- A shift in process mechanics away from incision by means of individual particle entrainment to incision by means of seepage erosion (sapping) and subsequent slope failure. The sapping process probably involved erosion of particles from the base of the trench, thereby undermining the headcut face and destabilizing the slope.

Downstream of Erosion Zone 1, sediment removed from the trench was transported through a V-shaped channel that was produced by incision during the high runoff years of 1983 and 1984 following partial burning of the basin by a wildfire in 1981. This V-shaped transport zone (Transport Zone 1) extended down-valley for approximately 100 m before terminating in a lobate-shaped deposit labeled "Depositional Zone 1" (figs. 3.7c and 3.8). The lobate deposit began as an inset channel fill that spilled onto the valley floor, covering a down-valley distance of approximately 60 m. Not all of the sediment that was cut from the trench in Erosion Zone 1 was deposited on the lobe within Depositional Zone 1. In fact, the majority of sediment produced by the event passed through the reach where it was routed into and out of Transport Zone 2 before coming to rest as a very large depositional lobe similar to that found upstream. The primary difference was that the second deposit was much larger than that found upvalley; it was almost 400 m long and had a maximum width of 75 m. Stratigraphic data show that a channel was present throughout this reach (Depositional Zone 2) prior to the 1998 event. The channel was completely filled to a depth of as much as 1.5 m during the event before deposition spilled onto the valley floor, creating overbank deposits with a maximum thickness of 0.4 m. Both the overbank lobate deposits and the channel fill were re-incised to depths ranging from 0.5 to 1.5 m immediately after sedimentation ceased.

Downstream of Depositional Zone 2, the valley floor is incised by two narrow (0.25 m wide) and deep (1.9 m) channels that terminate upstream in vertical headcuts (fig. 3.7d). Incision along this reach of the valley floor (Erosion Zone 2) appears to have started well before 1998 and is ongoing, although rather slowly. Farther downstream of the convergence, the two channels coalesce and the channel widens to a "bankfull" width of 4 m. Ultimately, the channel grades downstream onto the valley floor within Depositional Zone 3.

Field surveys and cartographic data show that the patterns of erosion, transport, and deposition are largely controlled by valley morphology. Erosion during the 1998 event occurred in areas where valley gradients and, therefore, shear stress were greatest (fig. 3.8). The transport zones created by flows in 1983 and 1984 also represent reaches of relatively high gradients in comparison to the depositional zones. These reaches did not incise in 1998, presumably because they had already been entrenched, and the V-shaped channels that were created were efficient at routing sediment downstream. In contrast to zones of erosion and transport, deposition occurred where channel gradients decreased and

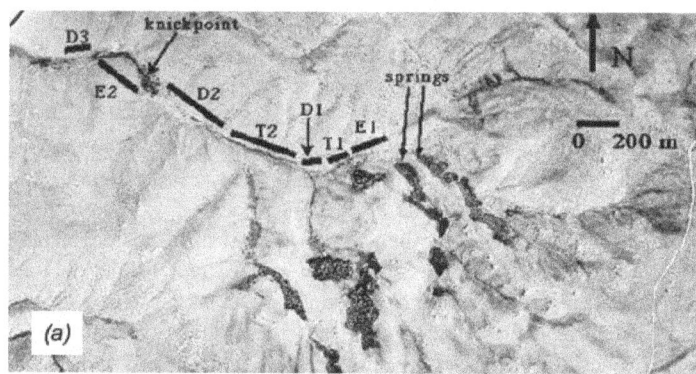

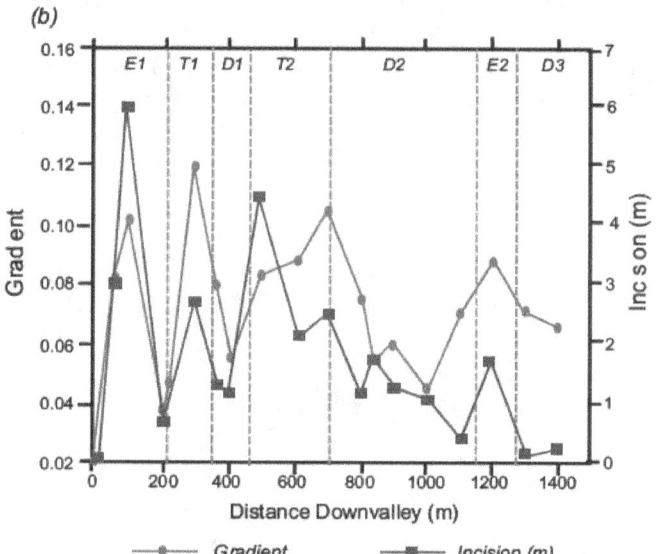

Figure 3.8. (a) Distribution of recognized process zones along the valley of Marshall Canyon in 1998; (b) changes in gradient and depth of incision along Marshall Canyon in 1998 as a function of process zone type. Gradient and depth of incision are relatively low in depositional zones compared to erosional zones.

valley floor widths increased (fig. 3.8). Thus, the observed pattern of erosion and incision following the 1998 event reflected a combination of channel gradients, valley width, the availability and nature of groundwater flow, and the system's geomorphic history.

The pattern of gully erosion and deposition that was observed in Marshall Canyon is common in other basins in the area, although the rate of gully development is much slower. In Corcoran Canyon (fig. 1.7), for example, incised channels are repeatedly associated with narrow, generally steeper reaches of the valley floor (fig. 3.9). In contrast, unincised reaches of the valley floor are associated with wider, lower-gradient valley segments. Importantly, most meadows are found within these wider, lower-gradient environments (figs. 3.9 and 3.10). While the meadows are associated with valley reaches that promote deposition, they may be affected by upstream migration of headcuts, which initially develop downstream along narrower, steeper transport zones where surface flows are concentrated and tractive forces are higher. In addition, incision appears to be enhanced by emergence

USDA Forest Service Gen. Tech. Rep. RMRS-GTR-258. 2011.

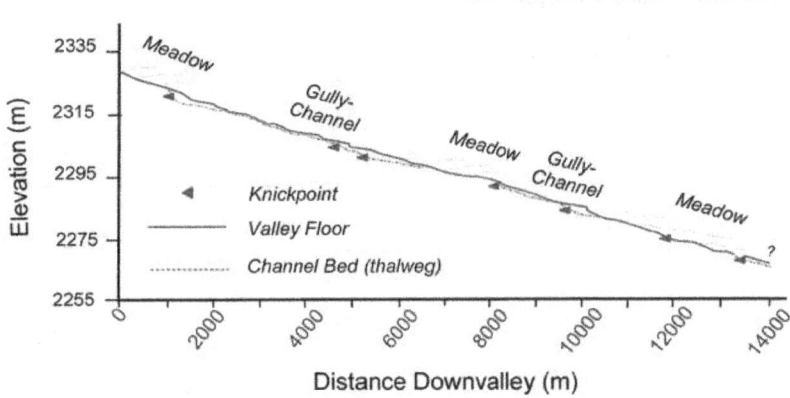

Figure 3.9. Spatial variations in valley width and gradients along Corcoran Canyon. Channel incision commonly begins along narrow, steep reaches with high erosive flows and migrates upstream where it may negatively impact the meadow complex.

of groundwaters under artesian conditions via springs that increase surface runoff at the downstream portion of the meadows. For instance, in Corcoran Canyon, multiple headcuts are found along the downstream segments of the meadows where groundwater springs provide additional water to the surface. In summary, entrenchment is promoted by a combination of factors, including narrow valleys that concentrate surface flows, steeper valleys that increase the flow's ability to entrain particles, and groundwater discharge that increases the magnitude and frequency of surface runoff. Reaches of a valley floor that are characterized by one or more of these properties are particularly sensitive to incision by gully formation and advancement.

Gully Formation, Headcut Migration, and Depositional Processes Along Low-Gradient Meadows

A few basins in central Nevada (such as Indian Valley and Lebeau) possess a number of very large, low-gradient meadow complexes (fig. 1.7). Although their valley floors may exhibit zones of sediment transport and deposition not all that different from those found in Marshall and Corcoran Canyons (fig. 3.10), the spatial scale over which the meadows exist leads to differences in the processes that govern valley entrenchment. The differences are significant enough

that they must be considered separately from those previously discussed when developing management strategies for meadow complexes.

To date, the most extensively studied valley of this kind is within the Indian Valley basin (fig. 3.11), a headwater drainage to the Reese River (fig. 1.7). While the remainder of this discussion primarily focuses on Indian Valley, the results can be applied cautiously to similar meadow/valley systems, including those found farther downstream along the Reese River (fig. 2.1).

The most distinctive features along the valley floor of Indian Valley are a series of discontinuous gullies. The term "discontinuous" refers to the fact that the entrenched valley segments are not interconnected. Rather, the gullies terminate downstream in fan-shaped deposits that grade smoothly onto the valley floor. In contrast, the upstream terminus is characterized by a prominent headcut that often exceeds several meters in height (fig. 3.12a). Between the up- and downstream termini, the character of the trench changes in a semi-systematic manner. For example, one intensively studied gully (fig. 3.13) is approximately 2.5 km in length. Within upstream areas, several subparallel trenches are tributaries to the main trench and each ends upstream in a headcut (fig. 3.13). The main trench is rectangular in shape and is up to 4 m deep and 30 m wide. Trench width and depth both decrease downstream until reaching the

USDA Forest Service Gen. Tech. Rep. RMRS-GTR-258. 2011.

31

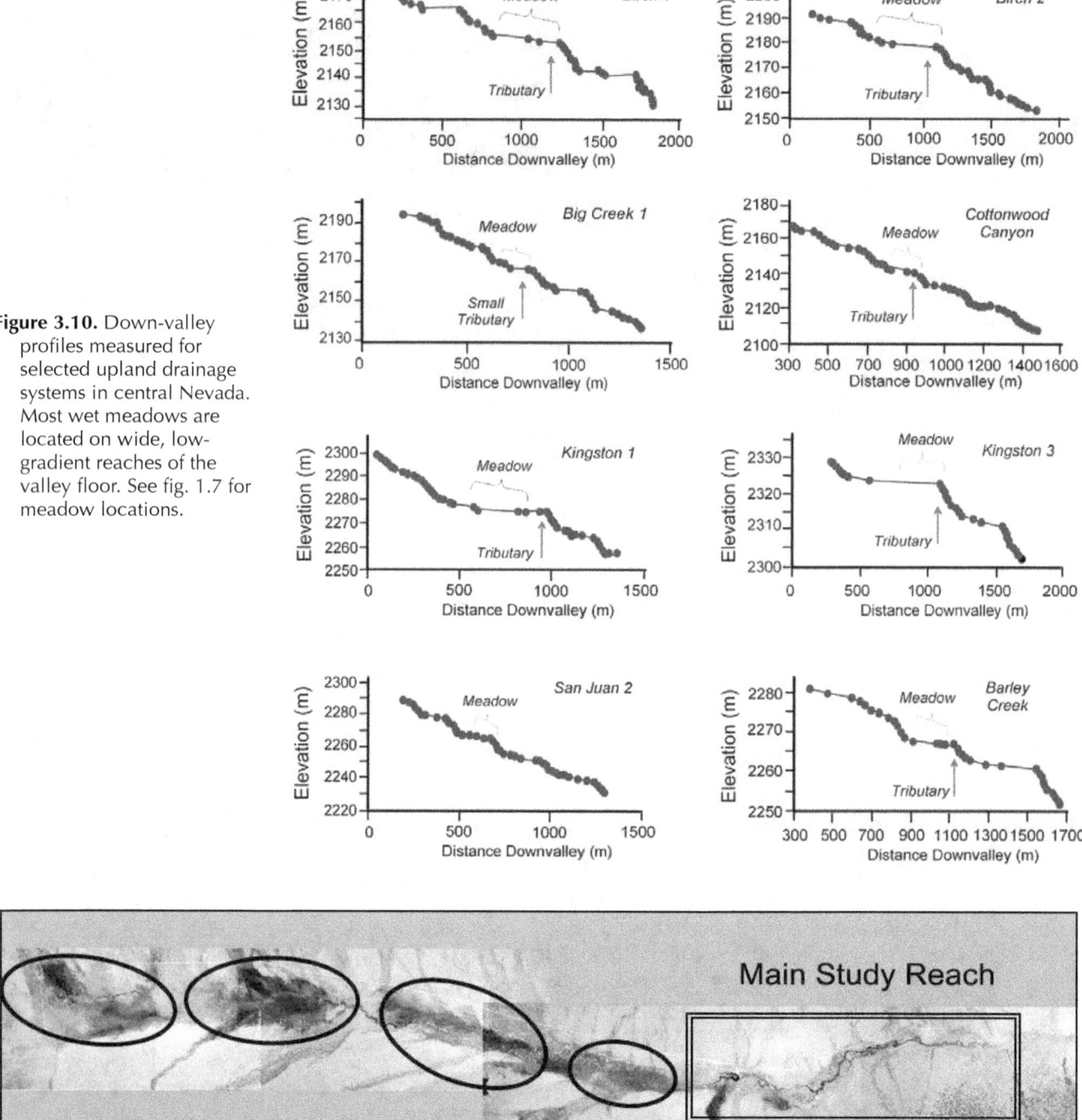

Figure 3.10. Down-valley profiles measured for selected upland drainage systems in central Nevada. Most wet meadows are located on wide, low-gradient reaches of the valley floor. See fig. 1.7 for meadow locations.

Figure 3.11. Aerial photograph of the Indian Creek valley showing the spatial distribution of wet meadows (circled). Entrenched reaches, generally located between meadows, are associated with zones of sediment transport.

unincised segment of the valley floor at the trench mouth. Throughout the incised reach, a stream channel is found on the trench floor. Along upstream segments of the trench, the channel is characterized by perennial flow, is bordered by well-defined floodplains and terraces, and is fine-grained (fig. 3.12c). Downstream, flow changes from intermittent to ephemeral and the size of the bed material increases until it is dominated by cobbles (figs. 3.12b and d). The shape of the stream channel also changes down-valley from a bed that exhibits deep, well-defined pools that are connected by narrow and much shallower runs to a relatively wide, featureless channel floor that encompasses most of the trench. Systematic variations in vegetation also occur in the downstream direction; upstream, the floodplain and terrace

32

USDA Forest Service Gen. Tech. Rep. RMRS-GTR-258. 2011.

Figure 3.12. Downstream changes in channel morphology along a discontinuous gully in Indian Creek valley. (a) Upstream headcut; (b) incised trench containing high water table and strip meadows; (c) incised trench located downstream of (b); (d) most downstream reach that is dry and characterized by renewed deposition.

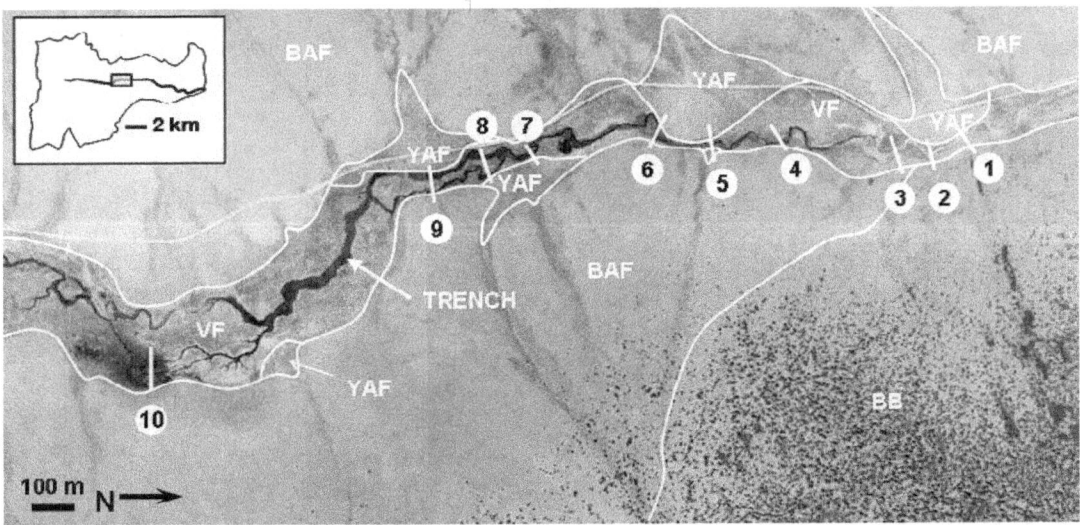

Figure 3.13. Aerial photograph of studied discontinuous gully system. Note that some gully headcuts are oriented at nearly right angles to the valley slope, suggesting erosion follows the direction of groundwater flow. Geomorphic units: VF = valley floor; TRENCH = incised trench long valley; YAF = young alluvial fans surface; BAF = older, bouldery alluvial fan surface; BB = basalt bedrock near surface associated with Black Mountain (northeast corner of photo). Groundwater measurements and vegetation surveys were made along transects (1 through 10). Index map shows study location and shape within the basin. See fig. 1.7 for basin location.

surfaces are covered by wet meadow species that creat strip meadows along the trench floor (fig. 3.12c). Downstream, dry meadow (or drier-end) species are dominant (figs. 3.12b and d).

The interactions and importance of surface- and groundwater flow to headcut migration in the Indian Valley meadows were analyzed by examining groundwater flow conditions in the vicinity of one headcut over a period of approximately five years, extending from 2002 to 2007 (fig. 3.14). The data

USDA Forest Service Gen. Tech. Rep. RMRS-GTR-258. 2011.

33

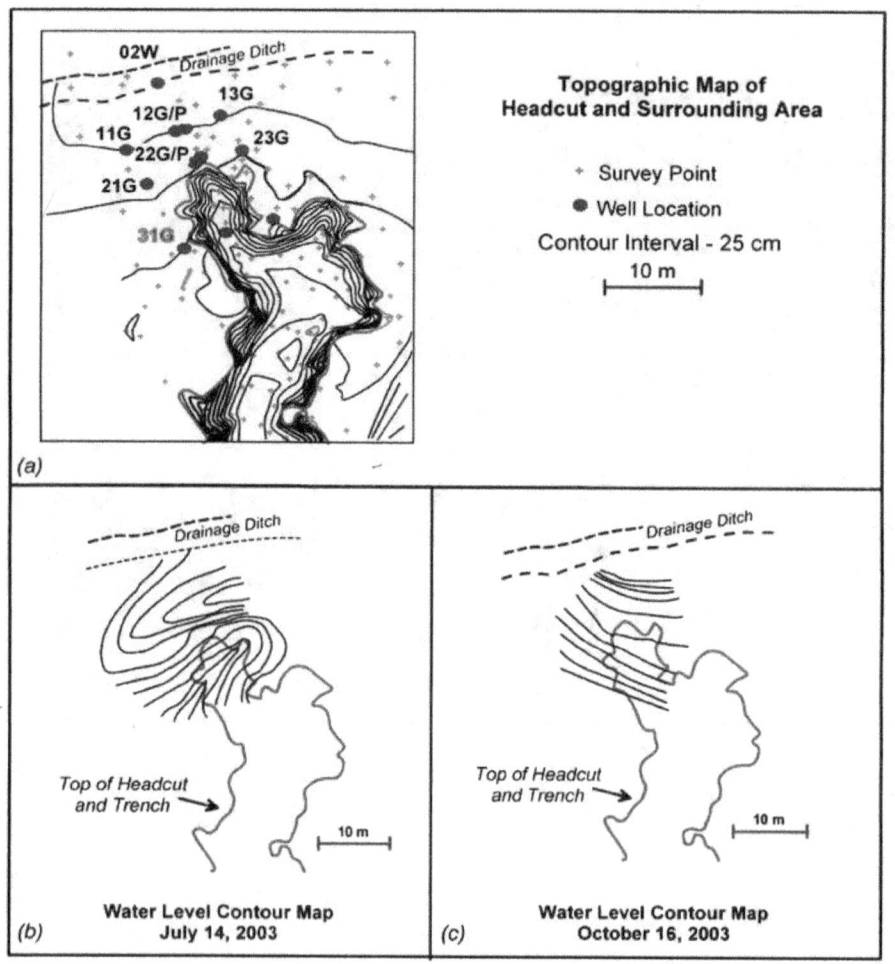

Figure 3.14. (a) Topography of an instrumented headcut in Indian Creek valley. Contour interval is 25 cm; (b) groundwater table on July 14, 2003; (c) groundwater table on October 16, 2003. The black arrow points to the top of the trench. Water table contours are based on measurements from 12 wells, shown in (a).

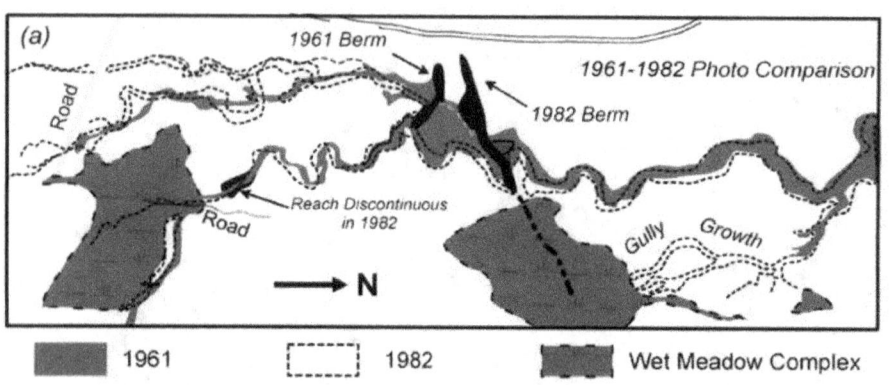

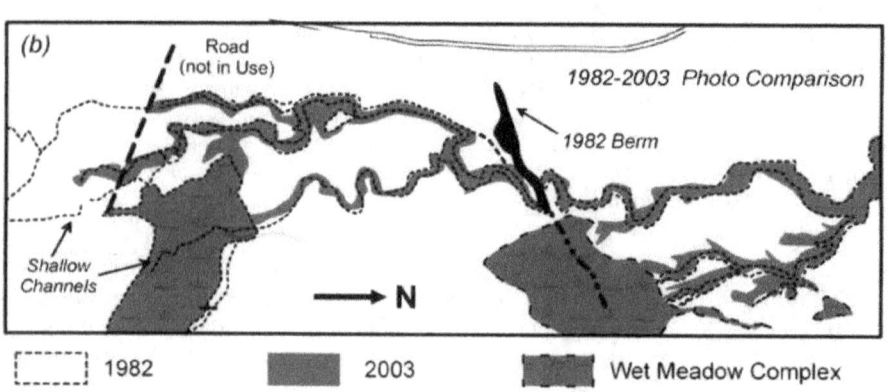

Figure 3.15. Extent of the discontinuous gully system in Indian Creek valley in 1961, 1982, and 2003. (a) Gully extension primary occurred between 1961 and 1982; (b) gully extension between 1982 and 2003 is thought to have primarily occurred during the 1982/1983 flood, the largest recorded during the past century.

Figure 3.16. Fracture exposed in the wall of a headcut in Indian Creek valley. These types of fractures presumably influence the dimensions of bank failure blocks and the rate at which headcut advancement can occur.

Fracture Plane

suggest that groundwater plays an extremely important role in controlling the nature and rate of headcut advancement. Indicators of the importance of groundwater on headcut migration are: (1) the amphitheater-shaped geometry of the headcuts, which is often used as an indicator of erosion by groundwater processes; (2) seepage from the headcut face and trench walls, particularly during the spring and early summer months; and (3) the cross-valley orientation of some tributary trenches that are aligned semi-parallel to the general direction of groundwater flow rather than with the predominant direction of surface runoff (fig. 3.15b).

Groundwater appears to influence headcut advancement by initiating mass wasting processes. It is well known that rising water tables and increased pore pressure tend to reduce the strength of alluvial materials, initiating episodes of bank failure (Thorne and Lewin 1979; Thorne 1982; Simon and others 1999). It can be hypothesized that observed slope failures along Indian Valley and other similar valleys correspond to wet periods of enhanced seepage and spatially, to zones of flow convergence as governed by the local groundwater flow system. The predominant mechanism of headcut advancement appears to be bank failure initiated by temporal and spatial variations in groundwater flow and subsequent weakening of the bank material strength. This suggestion is supported by modeling data generated by Johnson (2004). Using a program called Slope/W by Geo Slope International, he found that bank stability decreased with increasing head levels at the headcut instrumented in Indian Valley (fig. 3.14) and that seasonal slope failure was likely during the late spring when local groundwater levels were at their highest.

Figure 3.17. Wall of trench located downstream of the headcut shown in fig. 3.16. The eroded "alcove" positioned along the base of the bank was likely caused by groundwater as it emerged from the valley fill. This type of undercutting often leads to bank failure.

Seepage Erosion

USDA Forest Service Gen. Tech. Rep. RMRS-GTR-258. 2011.

35

Montgomery (1999) found that headcut advancement in California's Tennessee Valley also was tied closely to groundwater-related bank failure mechanics. He argued that advancement resulted from development of vertical fractures during periods of drying (desiccation) and subsequent failure of the blocks of bank materials that were defined by the fractures as water levels rose. The annual rate of headcut advancement was dependent on the distance of the fractures from the bank face because only one block would fail during an annual wetting and drying cycle. The importance of fracture formation to headcut advancement within Indian Valley appears to be variable. Some headcuts clearly developed pressure-release fractures during desiccation, and the size and rate of failure was controlled by fracture dimensions (fig. 3.16). In contrast, fractures were not observed at other headcuts, and failed blocks of bank material exhibited a rotational movement. Field observations suggest that differences in fracture development were associated with variations in the grain size distribution of the bank material, with fractures forming in finer-grained sediment composed of expandable clays.

The upstream migration of headcuts by the groundwater-enhanced failure mechanism just described can continue only if the failed bank material is removed from the base of the slope. Until the debris is removed, the slope is stabilized by the buttressing effects of the failed sediment (Carson and Kirkby 1972). Although seepage was observed to remove some of the basal bank material, most material was likely removed by small- to moderate-sized surface flows. Thus, headcut advancement involves both a groundwater component that initiates bank failure and a surface water component that removes failed bank material. During low to moderate runoff years, headcuts tend to precede up-gradient, parallel to groundwater flow because elevated groundwater levels are most likely to lead to headcut instability and failure, all other factors being constant. The development of the headcut, then, is a self-enhancing process because once it begins to form, the trench will create a convergence of surface- and groundwater flow, both of which will promote headcut advancement. That is, trench development creates the conditions that are conducive to further valley incision and upstream headcut migration.

Another means through which groundwater influences headcut migration is known as seepage erosion or "sapping." Sapping refers to the application of an upward force by groundwater on individual particles, which reduces their effective particle weight and facilitates particle entrainment (Howard and McLane 1988). Over time, entrainment and transport of particles produces a hollow or alcove in the trench wall that leads to bank failure by mass wasting processes (fig. 3.17). Sapping is exacerbated by high rates of groundwater discharge, which are associated with highly permeable materials, steep groundwater gradients, and layered geologic materials with contrasting hydraulic properties that encourage horizontal flow.

A closely related process to sapping is called "piping," a phenomenon that involves the enlargement of existing macropores and cavities by groundwater flow (Anderson and Burt 1990). The formation of pipes is generally associated with burrows, decaying roots, or other openings created by plants and animals. The process tends to be particularly prevalent in clay-rich soils characterized by shrink-swell processes, which amplify the rate of erosion (Heppell and others 2000). Like sapping, piping can locally undermine the trench wall and lead to slope failure. Piping is so prevalent in Corcoran Canyon that pipe collapse and the subsequent removal of the failed bank material by overland flow is the dominant mechanism of meadow degradation. Both piping and sapping processes were observed along the trench walls of Indian Valley. However, the distribution of pipes and undermined banks resulting from seepage erosion is not temporally and spatially extensive enough to account for all of the advancement of headcuts observed within Indian Valley. Nonetheless, sapping and piping are extremely important processes because they can erode fine-grained particles from beneath many types of headcut treatments that are constructed of rock, logs, and other materials, rendering the treatments ineffective in a short period of time.

Figure 3.18. Headcut associated with a shallow, discontinuous channel within a wet meadow of Indian Creek valley. Headcut migration occurs by plunge-pool erosion and undermining of the headcut face during surface runoff. Photograph taken in June 1996 during the falling limb of the annual snowmelt event.

USDA Forest Service Gen. Tech. Rep. RMRS-GTR-258. 2011.

The short-term rates of headcut advancement within the gullies monitored in Indian Valley were on the order of 1 m/year. The comparison of aerial photographs between 1961 and 2003 show that headcuts periodically have advanced much more rapidly than was measured in the field during the observation period (fig. 3.15). It is unlikely that such rapid rates of migration (particularly between 1961 and 1982) could occur by means of the groundwater-induced failure mechanism previously described. Thus, it is thought that rapid headcut advancement occurs by means of repeated plunge-pool erosion and undermining of the headcut, followed by the failure and rapid removal of the material during major runoff events such as those in 1973, 1975, 1978, or 1983/1984 (fig. 3.13). This argument is extremely important because it suggests that the mechanisms of headcut erosion differ between periods of "average" and "high" runoff and that while the rates of advancement are driven by slower-acting groundwater processes during periods of average runoff, they are controlled by surface flows in the latter. Management strategies aimed at reducing the rate of headcut advancement need to consider both sets of processes to be effective.

A question of significant concern from a management perspective is: how do the large, advancing headcut systems initially form? Montgomery (1999) argues that within California's Tennessee Valley, abrupt channel heads are created once incision by entrainment of individual particles exposes the soil B-horizon. In the B-horizons, the soil structure, including vertically oriented fractures, allows for the repeated failure of blocks of soil from a near-vertical face. The abrupt break in topography can then extend deeper during upstream headcut advancement. Both field and aerial photographic data show that, in addition to the large gully systems, the valley floor within the wet meadow complexes of Indian Valley exhibit two distinct types of shallow, discontinuous channels. One type of channel is fed by overland flow, which enters along a uniformly graded slope. Erosion and incision along these channels occurs by the removal of individual particles by runoff. Channels of the second type tend to be slightly deeper, and their beds are characterized by one or more small headcuts developed below the zone of rooting (fig. 3.18). Headcut migration tends to occur by bank failure along the headcut face. Assuming that these two types of discontinuous channels represent an evolutionary sequence that culminates in the large discontinuous gullies, the development of headcuts along the stream in Indian Valley would appear to be similar to that suggested by Montgomery (1999). In these cases, incision

Figure 3.19. Cattle trail leading to the edge of a headcut in Indian Creek valley. The spatial correlation between cattle trails and gullies suggest that, in some cases, overland flow is concentrated within the trail and is capable of eroding the valley fill.

Figure 3.20. Spring, or blowhole, on the valley floor of Indian Creek valley. These springs create shallow channels that may eventually be enlarged to create larger gully systems.

USDA Forest Service Gen. Tech. Rep. RMRS-GTR-258. 2011.

37

begins with erosion of the valley floor by the entrainment of individual particles and evolves into a gully once incision has reached a sufficient depth to allow for block failure from a near-vertical face. Once developed, the self-enhancing nature of the headcuts caused by the convergence of surface and groundwater flow allows headcuts to grow deeper as they advance upstream.

Incision of the valley floor by particle entrainment and headcut advancement are both promoted by saturated conditions. This is likely to explain the tendency for shallow channels to be concentrated within wet meadows as opposed to drier areas of the valley floor. In contrast, re-deposition of sediment downstream within the trench or on the valley floor is likely to be associated with a loss of stream power (less influent flow) and an increase in suspended sediment concentration.

The gully development and expansion that was previously described requires the initial erosion of the valley floor by overland flow. The ability of surface flows to entrain particles is strongly governed by the area's microtopography and vegetation characteristics. Any activity that promotes flow concentration or reduces vegetative cover (or stem density/roughness) tends to promote particle entrainment. In Indian Valley, a large number of shallow channels and headcuts are fed by minor (<20 cm deep) linear depressions that are devoid of significant vegetation. These depressions are associated with cattle trails, suggesting that the initial erosive process required for gully development could be promoted by livestock (fig. 3.19). Other activities such as roads and diversion structures that were intended to reduce channelized erosion also created zones of concentrated flow. Thus, these wet meadows appear to be particularly sensitive to anthropogenic activities, including the installation of rehabilitation structures, which divert flow to other locations of the valley floor in an attempt to reduce erosion in an existing gully. However, natural processes also can initiate shallow channel systems. One such process is the development of vertical springs or blowholes, in which water under extreme pressure rises to the surface of the meadow and flows down-valley, creating a channel system (fig. 3.20).

Groundwater measurements along the instrumented trench of Indian Valley show that gully heads are characterized by effluent flow associated with groundwater convergence on the headcut (fig. 3.14). Downstream, the in-flow of water from the subsurface becomes seasonally variable before eventually changing to a condition in which water is lost from the channel throughout the year. Thus, sediment deposition at the mouth of the gullies appears to be related to a change in the relations between the surface and groundwater flow systems in the vicinity of the trench. In the case of the large, deep gullies, these relations are strongly controlled by regional physical features such as the nature of the underlying bedrock and valley morphology (see discussion on Indian Valley hydrology in the following section and Jewett and others 2004), which produce zones of downward groundwater flow. However, the observed influent and effluent conditions also are related to the evolution of the gully. As headcuts advance upvalley, groundwater levels downstream of the headcuts drop, eventually leading to a loss of water through the trench floor and to sediment deposition (Jewett and others 2004).

Channel Avulsion

The majority of meadow complexes found in central Nevada are dominated by fine-grained, often organic sediments. Locally, these fine-grained sediments are buried by thin (<1 m thick) sand and gravel deposits (fig. 3.21). In some cases, the sands and gravels completely fill a paleochannel and spill onto the valley floor as lobate, convex-up accumulations. In other locations, the sands and gravels can only be found as convex-up bars. Laterally, the deposits are discontinuous, thinning toward the margins and in the downstream direction.

Field and aerial photographic data suggest that these coarse-grained deposits were produced by avulsion. Avulsion is a process by which the channel is abruptly relocated from one position on the valley floor or floodplain to another. In a review of avulsion processes, Jones and Schumm (1999) subdivided avulsions into four groups based on the factors that lead to channel relocation. However, while one avulsion process may dominant the system, others may contribute to channel relocation and, within a given region, avulsion may be caused by more than one set of factors. Therefore, care must be taken when attributing causes of avulsion for a particular stream. Nonetheless, avulsion within meadow complexes of central Nevada appears to be related to clogging of the channel and loss of flow capacity as a result of stream bed aggradation. The loss of channel capacity leads to overbank flooding and the scouring of a new channel system that bypasses the aggraded reach. This process is well illustrated by a 1983 event that occurred along Cottonwood Creek on west side of the Toiyabe Range (fig. 1.7).

In Cottonwood, gravel-sized sediment filled a short-reach of the axial channel at the upstream end of a wet meadow complex (fig. 3.22). The coarse sediment was then ramped onto the meadow surface by overbank flood waters, creating several gravel bars that were oriented at about a 35° angle from the axial channel alignment (fig. 3.22). The bars were approximately 15 m long, 5 m wide, and buried finer-grained meadow sediments. Flow that emanated from around the bars coalesced downstream in a shallow depression in the meadow surface and rapidly eroded a narrow, approximately1.5 to 3 m deep channel into the valley fill (fig. 3.22). The newly cut channel allowed flows from upstream to bypass the aggraded reach, and a piece of the pre-existing channel down-valley of the sediment-clogged stream section remained as an abandoned channel (fig. 3.22). Over the next several years, the newly cut channel continued to incise and widen to accommodate the incoming flows from upstream. Comparison of channel photos with cross sectional profile data indicated that much of the channel enlargement occurred between 1997 and 1999 (when the first cross-section was surveyed), presumably during the relatively high runoff year of 1998 (fig. 3.22).

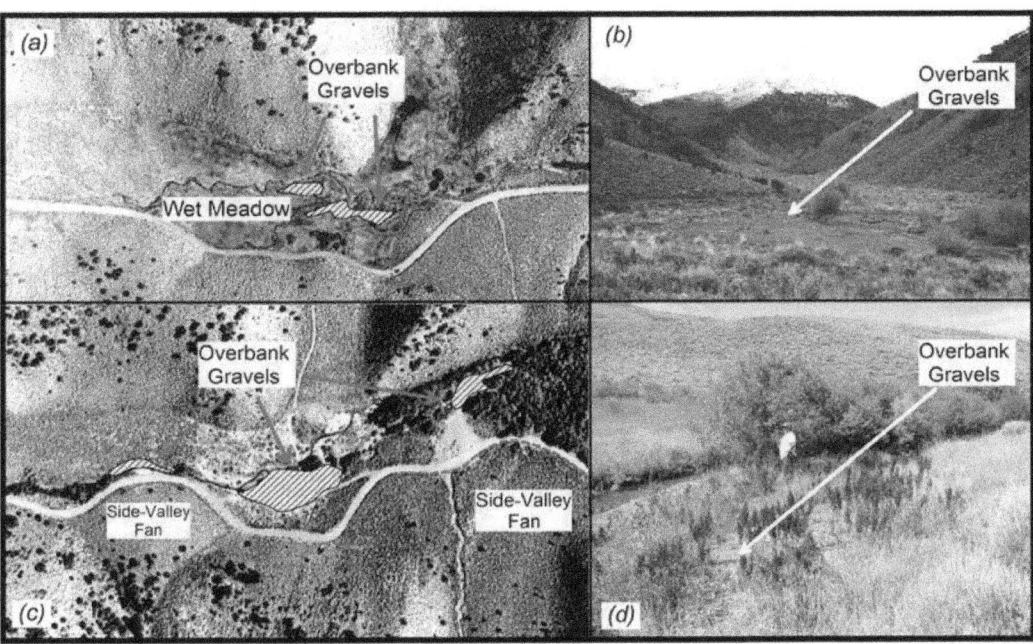

Figure 3.21. Course gravel deposits located on the valley floor of Kingston (a, b, c) and Birch (d) Canyons. These deposits are thought to have formed during channel filling and avulsion that resulted from the localized influx of coarse-grained sediment. Flow in (a) and (b) is from left to right.

A similar process likely occurred within Birch 2 meadow (fig. 1.7). However, it differed from the avulsion described for Cottonwood in that overbank flood waters flowed down-valley into an existing spring channel that was dominated by fine-grained sediment. The spring channel was subsequently converted into the axial drainage system through erosive processes that deepened and widened the original channel.

The frequency at which avulsion occurs varies from one meadow to another. However, it is clear that channel avulsion is a fundamental process associated with meadow development. For example, older bars partially covered by fine-grained sediment are visible as topographic highs within the Cottonwood meadow. In addition, the valley fill within Kingston 3 meadow (fig. 1.7) exhibits thin, laterally discontinuous sand and gravel lenses that are interspersed with finer-grained sediments (fig. 3.23). These lenses presumably represent the deposition of sand and gravel during channel avulsions, followed by burial with silts and clays during overbank flooding. Radiocarbon (C-14) dates obtained from organic materials in the cores show that these gravel deposits date back at least 8000 years BP, indicating that avulsion has been an integral part of meadow aggradation and development throughout the Holocene.

The idea that channel bed aggradation leads to avulsion may seem to contradict suggestions that channels within the upland basins of central Nevada are sediment starved and tend to incise. Both hypotheses can be correct because aggradation that is associated with avulsion is produced by the rapid, temporary influx of coarse sediment to the drainage network. This aggradation represents a short-term condition that is superimposed on a longer-term tendency for channel incision. In Cottonwood, the near instantaneous influx of gravel-sized sediment to the meadow was created by rapid remobilization of material stored behind a series of upstream beaver dams that were breached during the high flows of

1983. Other potential sources of sediment that may rapidly deliver coarse sediment to the drainage network are mass wasting events (such as landslides), localized trenching of side-valley fans during episodes of extreme runoff, and/or the dissection of roads by runoff (fig. 3.24).

Stratigraphic and cartographic data show that avulsions are primarily limited to meadows; reaches of the stream channel without meadows show little evidence of past avulsion episodes (Miller and others 2001). This observation results from the tendency of sediment that is rapidly flushed into the drainage network to be redeposited within the meadow complex. Aggradation within the meadow is probably induced in large part by changes in channel gradient that often occur as a result of long-term aggradation of the valley floor upstream of side-valley alluvial fans and other valley constrictions. Jones and Schumm (1999) argue that aggradation and subsequent avulsion also may be related to encroachment of riparian vegetation, which leads to a loss of channel capacity, an increase in channel roughness, and a reduction in flow velocities. The association of localized aggradation and avulsion in meadow areas that are heavily overgrown by willows, such as in Kingston Canyon and Birch Creek (fig. 3.25), suggests that riparian vegetation may contribute to aggradation in some upland watersheds.

Summary

Channel incision, gully formation, and avulsion have significantly affected meadow complexes in central Nevada. The most widespread impacts are associated with incision, which has been observed in most upland meadow complexes in the region. The mechanisms of incision vary as a function of the underlying bedrock and grain size of erodible material. Incision by the entrainment and transport of individual grains occurs along reaches that are characterized by loose,

USDA Forest Service Gen. Tech. Rep. RMRS-GTR-258. 2011.

39

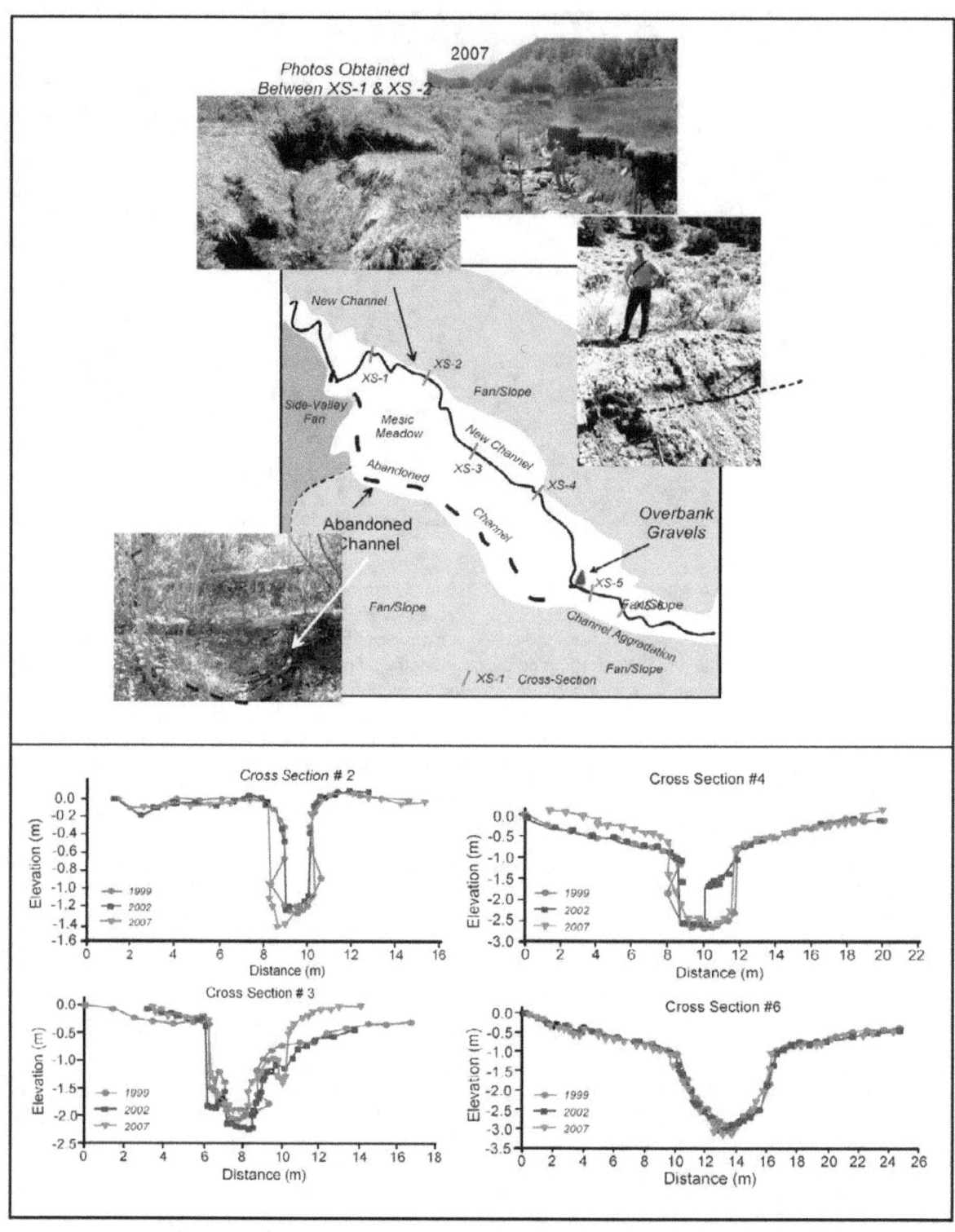

Figure 3.22. Channel changes associated with an avulsion that occurred in 1983 along Cottonwood Creek. Upstream reaches of the abandoned channel were filled with sediment that was derived from behind failed beaver dams. Aggradation within the channel led to overbank flows, deposition on the valley floor, and downstream incision of a new channel. Cross sections illustrate changes in the resulting incised channel from 1999 to 2007.

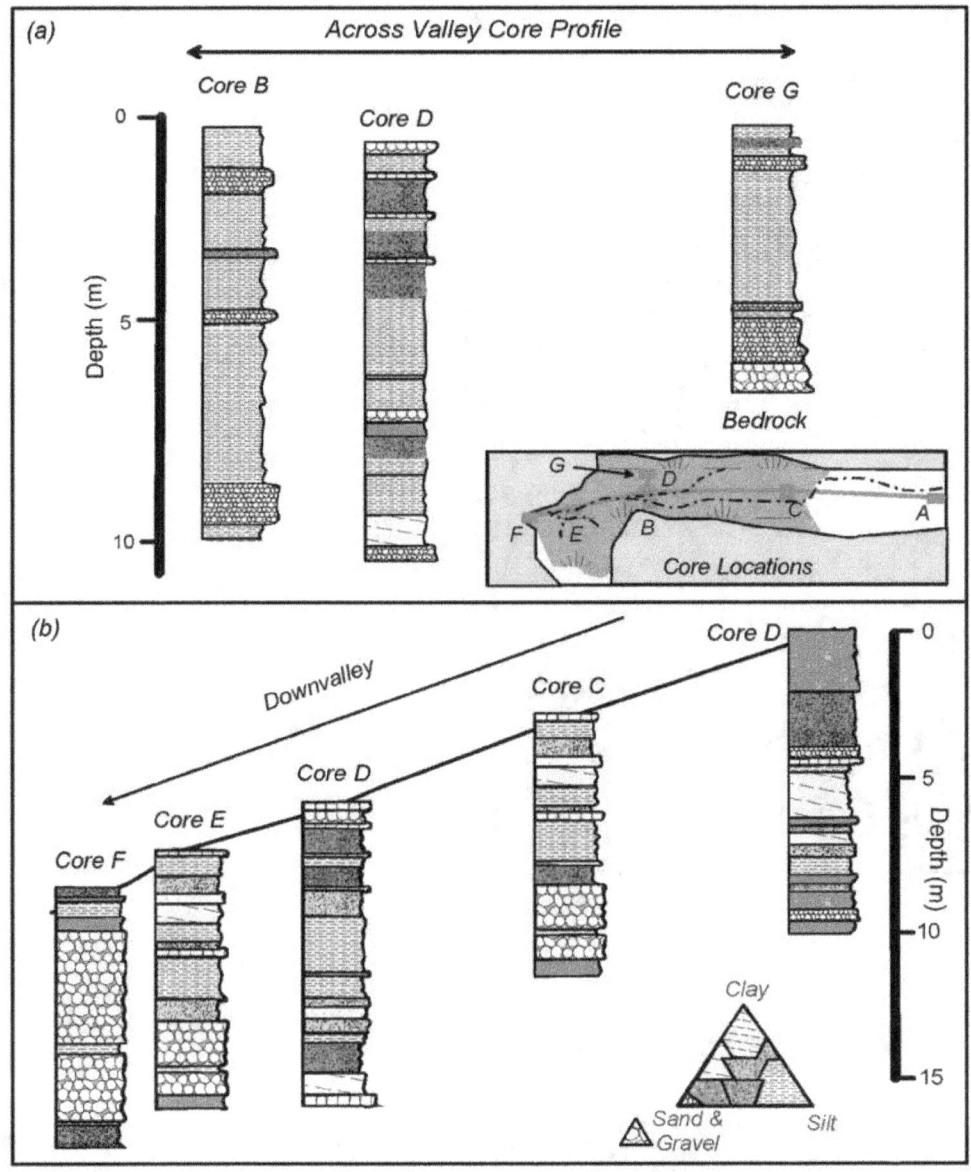

Figure 3.23. Stratigraphic units observed in cores extracted from Meadow #3 in Kingston Canyon. The spatially discontinuous nature of the sand and gravel units suggests that they were formed by avulsion processes similar to those observed along Cottonwood Creek.

coarse-grained sediment; whereas incision by knickpoint formation and migration occurs along stream segments that are characterized by fine-grained, more cohesive sediments. In many instances, incision is initiated by a drop in base level along a convexity in the longitudinal profile that is created by a side-valley alluvial fan, or by deposition upstream of a bedrock valley constriction. Once initiated, incision progresses upstream as the channel adjusts to the lowered base level.

Gully formation is predominantly limited to valley systems without an integrated drainage system. Once gullies have formed, the rate of headcut advancement varies as a function of the overland flow intensity. During extreme events, gully formation occurs by means of repeated plunge-pool erosion and undermining of the headcut, followed by failure and rapid removal of the failed bed and bank material. During years characterized by low to moderate runoff events, headcut advancement is controlled primarily by groundwater sapping processes. Therefore, to be effective,

management strategies that are aimed at reducing the rate of headcut advancement need to consider processes that occur during both low flow and high flow years. In addition, observations from Indian Valley indicate that meadow complexes are sensitive to activities that may concentrate flow on the surface, including trails created by livestock.

Channel avulsion is primarily restricted to low-gradient, meadow environments and is induced by the temporary influx of coarse sediment, which causes localized channel aggradation and filling. The resulting reduction in channel capacity (cross-sectional area) forces water over the channel banks and results in valley entrenchment at a new location within the meadow complex. In some cases, the overbank waters are diverted into smaller spring channels, which are subsequently converted into the axial drainage system. Data from recent avulsions suggest that it may take a few decades for an incised channel produced by avulsion processes to acquire the morphology that is typical of channels up- or downstream of the site.

USDA Forest Service Gen. Tech. Rep. RMRS-GTR-258. 2011.

41

Figure 3.24. Potential sources of temporary sediment influx to axial drainage systems in the upland watersheds of central Nevada. (a) Trenching of previously unincised hillslope hollows during extreme runoff events; (b) the trenching of roads, in this case, Slaughterhouse Canyon in 1997; (c, d) the breaching of beaver dams and the subsequent erosion of stored sediment.

Figure 3.25. Gravel deposition and channel accretion along segments dominated by streamside willows.

References

Anderson, M.G.; Burt, T.P. 1990. Subsurface runoff. In: Anderson, M.G.; Burt, T.P., eds. Process Studies in Hillslope Hydrology. Chichester: John Wiley: 365-400.

Carson, M.A.; Kirkby, M. 1972. Hillslope Form and Process. London: Cambridge University Press. 475 p.

Chambers, J.C.; Farleigh, K.; Tausch, R.J.; Miller, J.R.; Germanoski, D.; Martin, D.; Nowak, C. 1998. Understanding long- and short-term changes in vegetation and geomorphic processes: The key to riparian restoration. In: Potts, D.F., ed. Proceedings: Rangeland management and water resources. American Water Resources Association and Society for Range Management. 27-29 May 1998; Reno, NV. Herndon, VA: American Water Resources Association and Society for Range Management: 101-110.

Cosby, B.T.; Whipple, K.X. 2007. Knickpoint initiation and distribution within fluvial networks: 236 waterfalls in the Waipaoa River, North Island, New Zealand. Geomorphology, Special Paper, The Bedrock Geology of Channels: 1462-1476.

Gardner, Thomas W. 1983. Experimental study of knickpoint and longitudinal profile evolution in cohesive, homogenous material. Geological Society of America Bulletin. 94: 664-672.

Germanoski, D.; Ryder C.H.; Miller, J.R. 2001. Spatial variation of incision and deposition within a rapidly incised upland watershed, central Nevada. Proceedings of the 7th Federal Interagency Sedimentation Conference; 25-29 March 2001, Reno, NV. Subcomittee on Sedimentation. v. 2: 141-148.

Germanoski, D.; Miller, J.R. 2004. Basin sensitivity to channel incision in reponse to natural and anthropogenic disturbance. In: Chambers, J.C.; Miller, J.R., eds. Great Basin Riparian Ecosystems—Ecology, Management, and Restoration. Covello, CA: Island Press: 88-123.

Gilbert, Grover K. 1896. Niagra Falls and their history. National Geographical Monograph 1: 203-236.

Heppell, C.M.; Burt, T.P.; Williams, R.J. 2000. The use of tracers to aid the understanding of the herbicide leaching in clay soils. In: Foster, I.D.L., ed. Tracers in Geomorphology. Chichester: John Wiley: 309-332.

Holland, W.N.; Pickup, G. 1976. Flume study of knickpoint development in stratified sediment. Geological Society of America Bulletin. 87: 76-82.

Howard, A.D.; McLane, C.F., III. 1988. Erosion of cohesionless sediment by groundwater seepage. Water Resources Research. 24: 1659-1674.

Jewett, D.G.; Lord, M.L.; Miller, J.R.; Chambers, J.C. 2004. Geomorphic and hydrologic controls on surface and subsurface flow regimes in riparian meadow ecosystems. In: Chambers, J.C.; Miller, J.R., eds. Great Basin Riparian Ecosystems—Ecology, Management, and Restoration. Covello, CA: Island Press: 124-161.

Johnson, R. 2004. Groundwater conditions that influence sapping induced slope failure in an actively eroding trench system in Indian Creek Valley, central Nevada. Cullowhee, NC: Western Carolina University. Thesis. 48 p.

Jones, L.S.; Schumm, S.A. 1999. Causes of avulsion: an overview. Special Publications in Association of Sedimentology. 28: 171-178.

Miller, J.R.; Ritter, D.F.; Kochel, C.R. 1990. Morphometric assessment of lithologic controls on drainage basin evolution in the Crawford Upland, south-central Indiana. American Journal of Science. 290: 569-599.

Miller, J.R.; Germanoski, D.; Waltman, K.; Tausch, R.; Chambers, J. 2001. Influence of late Holocene hillslope processes and landforms on modern channel dynamics in upland watersheds of central Nevada. Geomorphology. 38: 373-391.

Montgomery, D. 1999. Erosional processes at an abrupt channel head: implications for channel entrenchment and discontinuous gully formation. In: Darby, S.E.; Simon, A., eds. Incised River Channels: Processes, Forms, Engineering and Management. New York: John Wiley and Sons: 247-276.

Patton, P.C.; Schumm, S.A. 1981. Ephemeral-stream processes: implications for studies of quaternary valley fills. Quaternary Research. 15: 24-43.

Phipps, R.L. 1985. Collecting, preparing, cross dating, and measuring tree increment cores. U.S. Geological Survey, Water Resources Investigative Reports. 85-4148.

Pickup, G. 1975. Downstream variations in morphology, flow conditions and sediment transport in an eroding channel. Zeit. Geomorphologie. 19: 433-459.

Sigafoos, R.S. 1964. Botanical evidence of floods and flood-plain deposition. U.S. Geological Survey Professional Paper 485-A. Washington, DC: U.S. Government Printing Office. 35 p.

Simon, A.; Curini, A.; Darby, S.; Langendon, E.J. 1999. Streambank mechanics and the role of bank and near-bank processes in incised channels. In: Darby, S.E.; Simon, A., eds. Incised River Channels: Processes, Forms, Engineering and Management. Chichester: John Wiley and Sons: 123-151.

Thorne, C.R. 1982. Processes and mechanisms of river bank erosion. In: Hey, R.; Bathurst, J.; Thorne, C., eds. Gravel-Bed Rivers. Chichester: John Wiley and Sons: 1-37.

Thorne, C.R.; Lewin, J. 1979. Bank processes, bed material movement, and planform development in a meandering river. In: Rhodes D.D.; Williams G.P., eds. Adjustments of the fluvial system. Dubuque: Kendal Hunt: 117-137.

Schumm, S.A. 1999. Causes and controls of channel incision. In: Darby, S.E.; Simon, A., eds. Incised River Channels: Processes, Forms, Engineering and Management. Chichester: J. Wiley & Sons: 19-33.

USDA Forest Service Gen. Tech. Rep. RMRS-GTR-258. 2011.

43

Chapter 4:   Hydrologic Processes Influencing Meadow Ecosystems

Mark L. Lord, David G. Jewett, Jerry R. Miller, Dru Germanoski, and Jeanne C. Chambers

Introduction

The hydrologic regime exerts primary control on riparian meadow complexes and is strongly influenced by past and present geomorphic processes; biotic processes; and, in some cases, anthropogenic activities. Thus, it is essential-to understand not only the hydrologic processes that operate within meadow complexes but also the interactions of meadow hydrology with other processes that affect these ecosystems. Regional- and watershed-scale analyses have contributed to the understanding and management of meadows. However, investigation of meadow-scale characteristics and processes have shown that local factors can override larger-scale influences and that some processes, especially those related to groundwater hydrology, cannot be fully explained by topographically defined watershed-scale characteristics (Montgomery 1999; Winter 2001; Devito and others 2005). In this chapter, we provide an overview of the hydrologic setting within the Great Basin and describe and explain key aspects of meadow hydrology for specific sites within selected watersheds in central Nevada. Next, we discuss generalities in the hydrologic characteristics of 56 meadows that were assessed in these upland watersheds. We conclude by providing an approach for characterizing hydrologic conditions based on hydrologic setting, groundwater conditions, vegetation patterns, and stream connections.

Hydrologic Characteristics and Processes

General Hydrologic Setting

The geomorphic and hydrologic characteristics of the Great Basin provide a framework to understand general hydrologic processes and patterns at both watershed and meadow scales. The geology, topography, and climate of the Great Basin are highly variable across the region and, consequently, the hydrology of the area is complex. Regional groundwater flow patterns are strongly controlled by southwest-northeast trending fault-block mountain ranges and, in some locations, include deep, interbasin flow through permeable bedrock units that connect basins (Mifflin 1988; Plume 1996; Maurer and others 2004). In general, mountain ranges and flanking alluvial fans are groundwater recharge areas, whereas the centers of many basins are groundwater discharge zones (Maurer and others 2004). The types of geologic units that underlie the basins and that form the adjacent mountain ranges exert strong controls on groundwater flow

rates and paths. Most bedrock units have low permeability. Intrusive igneous rocks and metamorphic rocks generally exhibit low permeability and act as barriers to groundwater flow (Plume 1996; Maurer and others 2004). However, highly fractured basalt, a volcanic rock, may have hydraulic conductivity values up to about 400 m/day. Sedimentary rocks have a wide range of permeabilities; at the high end, some carbonate rocks with fractures widened by solution have hydraulic conductivity values up to 1000 m/day (Maurer and others 2004). Unconsolidated deposits are commonly of fluvial origin, and although their hydraulic conductivity is highly variable, it may be as high as 670 m/day. Faults can differ in permeability from surrounding earth materials by up to several orders of magnitude. In general, faults in unconsolidated materials restrict groundwater flow, and faults in bedrock enhance flow (Maurer and others 2004).

The locations, volumes, and timing of groundwater recharge and discharge are critical to sustaining montane riparian meadow complexes. The interactions of groundwater and stream water are important to understanding these systems (Winter 1999; Jewett and others 2004; Newman and others 2006; Stonestrom and others 2007). Groundwater recharge in the arid- to semi-arid southwestern United States tends to be focused in stream beds and limited areas of headwater regions of mountains rather than over broad, diffuse areas as is common in more humid regions (Wilson and Guan 2004; Constantz and others 2007; Prudic and others 2007). Perennial streams, springs, and wetlands are generally groundwater discharge sites that are supported by deeper, regional groundwater flow systems (Jewett and others 2004; Anderson and others 2006; Newman and others 2006; Patten and others 2008). Conceptual models of groundwater and stream water interaction in the Great Basin show that streams gain in the mountains and lose in the basins (Mifflin 1988). At smaller scales, however, the patterns are more complicated. A given stream channel may change between gaining and losing over short distances or seasonally (Jewett and others 2004; Newman and others 2006; Prudic and others 2007).

General Relationship of Meadow Vegetation to Hydrology

Montane riparian meadow complexes of the central Great Basin are characterized by herbaceous wet and mesic plant communities dominated by sedges, rushes, and grasses (Weixelman and others 1996; Chambers and others 2004). Meadow vegetation patterns are partly controlled by geomorphic setting, soil type, and human uses, but the depth to

A.

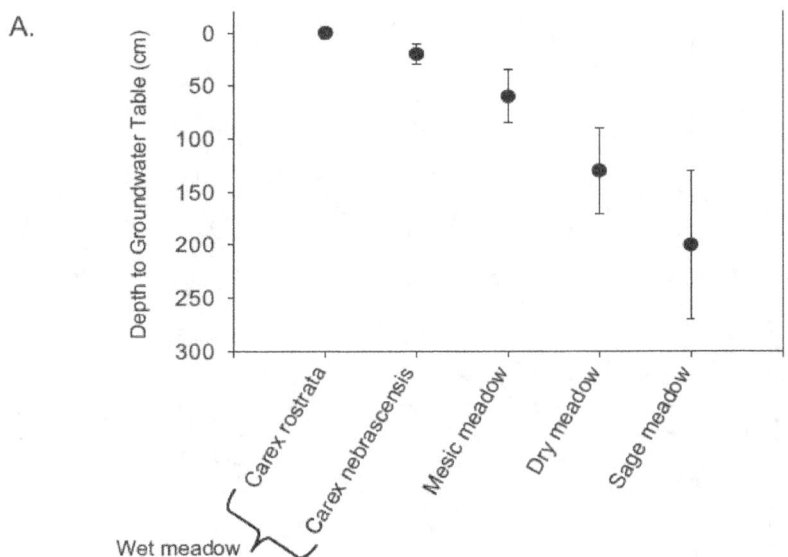

Figure 4.1. (a) General relationship between depth to groundwater table and vegetation type; both *Carex* species are part of the wet plant community (Chambers and others 2004). (b) Seasonal relationship between water table depth and vegetation type at Kingston 3 meadow, 2003 to 2006.

B.

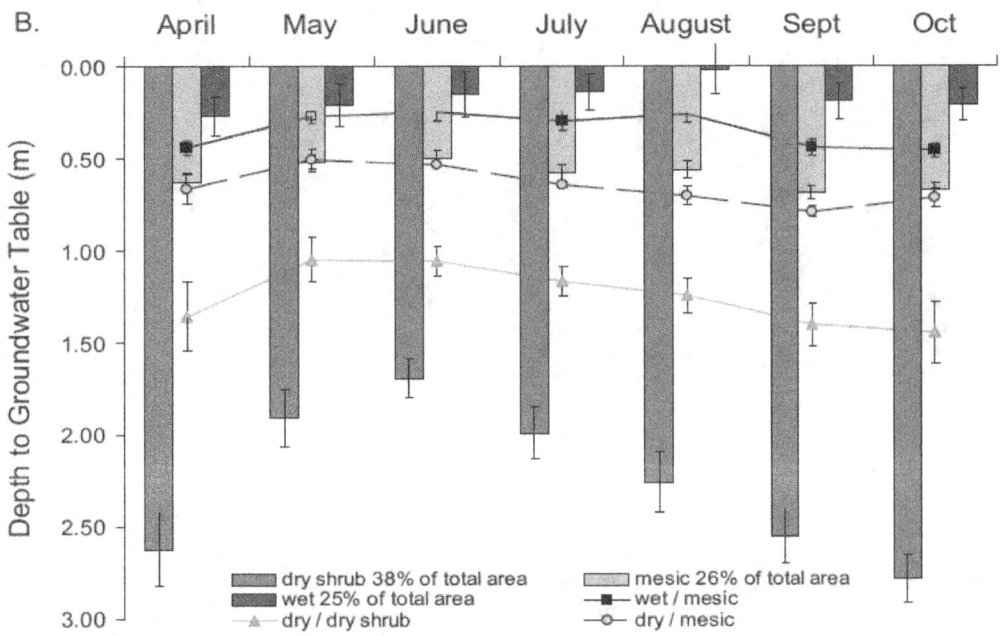

the water table is the dominant controlling factor at most sites (Allen-Diaz 1991; Chambers and Miller 2004). Different meadow plant communities tend to occur along gradients that are controlled by water table elevation (or depth) (Castelli and others 2000; Jewett and others 2004; Dwire and others 2006). The relationships between depth to groundwater and meadow vegetation types are well-defined for upland meadows in the central Great Basin (fig. 4.1a; Castelli and others 2000; Martin and others 2001; Chambers and others 2004). In general, wet meadow communities require water table depths during the growing season of less than 30 cm, mesic meadow communities require about 55 cm, and dry meadow communities require about 120 cm (Castelli and others 2000; Jewett and others 2004). Widespread stream incision of meadow ecosystems is considered the most important threat to this scarce, ecologically important resource

that supports a high percentage of the Great Basin's biodiversity. The magnitude, location, and frequency of stream incision are influenced by climate, bedrock geology, alluvial stratigraphy, vegetation, groundwater-stream water interactions, and anthropogenic activities (e.g., Germanoski and Miller 2004; Weissmann and others 2004). Stream incision often results in declines in meadow water tables and can cause shifts in plant community types from wetter to drier (Chambers and others 2004). The response of plant communities to stream incision is largely controlled by the meadow groundwater hydrology, especially the traits of interaction between groundwater and stream channels. Understanding the linkages among stream, hydrologic, and vegetation processes in meadow complexes is fundamental to effective management, stabilization, and restoration of these riparian ecosystems.

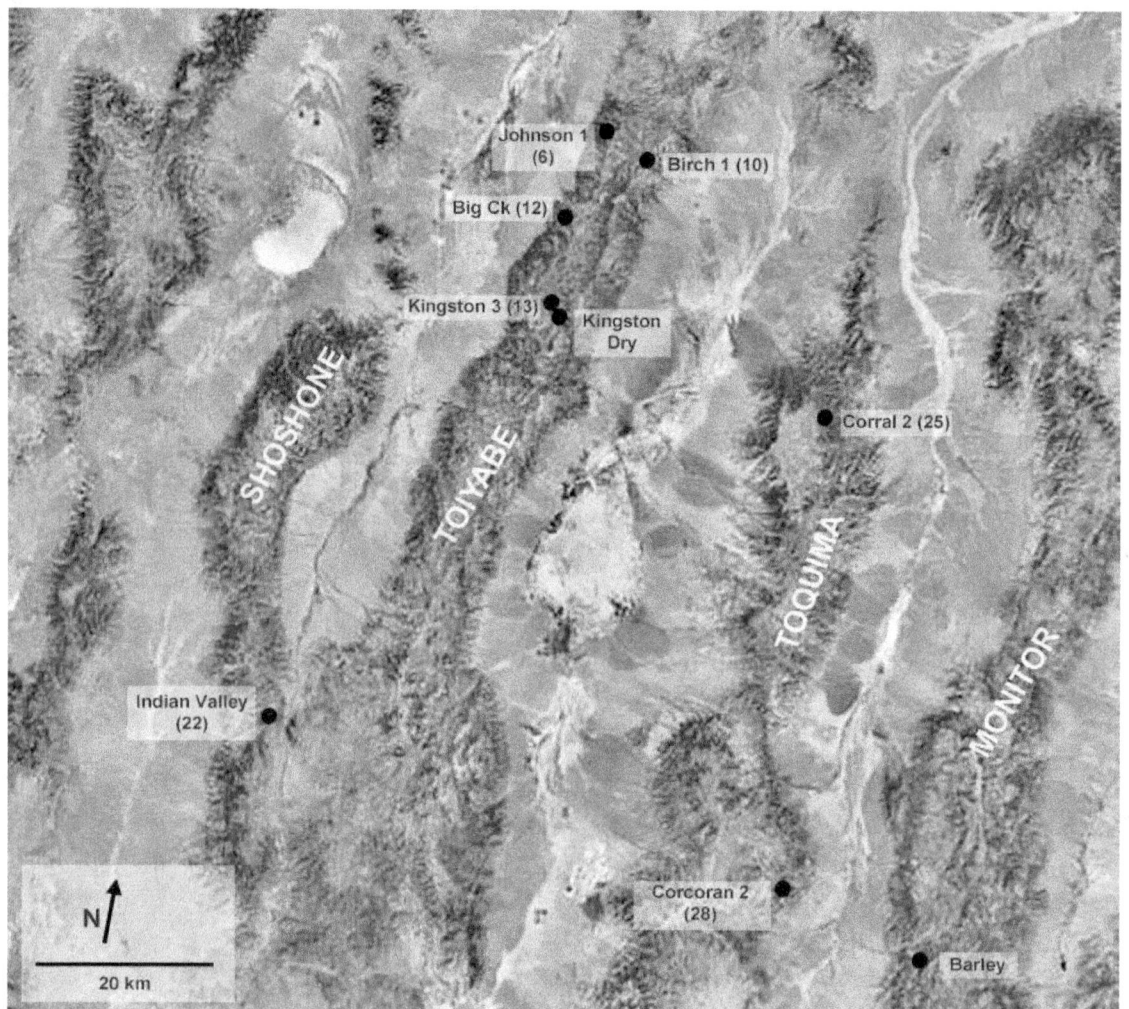

Figure 4.2.
Satellite image of central Nevada mountain ranges showing locations of three heavily instrumented meadow sites (yellow circles) and other meadows referenced in this chapter. Meadow names and number in parentheses match the study site map in fig. 1.7.

Hydrologic Study Approach

The characterization of meadow hydrology was conducted using (1) data collected at meadows that are dispersed across the Great Basin of central Nevada, and (2) intensively monitored and studied meadows that were chosen to represent the larger meadow population. The study population included 56 meadows located in 33 watersheds over 6 mountain ranges in the central Great Basin (fig. 1.7). All of the meadows that were studied are located in the mountains; range in elevation from 2023 m to 2631 m; and, with few exceptions, are located within the Humboldt-Toiyabe National Forest. Detailed hydrologic, stratigraphic, and geomorphic data were collected at six meadows to document processes, test hypotheses, establish causal relationships, and provide a basis for interpreting the hydrology of the entire meadow population (fig. 4.2; table 4.1). Three of the six meadows (Kingston 3, Big Creek, and Indian Valley) were studied intensely; data were collected on water table depth, stream discharge, stream and channel bed temperature, geophysical properties, stratigraphic layers from sediment cores, and plant species and communities. These three sites were chosen because they are representative of other meadow complexes and because multiple years of physical and vegetation data were available. The Kingston 3 meadow, which was established as an experimental site in 2003, was the most studied site. Water table depths were collected monthly during the growing season from 1997 to 2008. Well depths ranged from about 0.5 m to 8 m. Groundwater levels and water temperature were measured hourly in 24 wells using automated water level loggers (pressure transducers). These data were used to document diurnal and seasonal variations in groundwater levels and longer-term patterns in groundwater flow.

This chapter summarizes data from the three intensively studied sites and integrates results with information that was collected at other meadows. Collectively, an improved understanding has emerged of meadow processes; hydrologic, geomorphic, and vegetation interactions; and management implications.

Table 4.1. Types of data collected at eight sites in the central Great Basin (figs. 4.2 and 1.7). Two sites, Barley and Kingston Dry, were studied to examine the formation or destruction of meadows; Barley did support a meadow prior to stream incision.

Topic	Data type	Big Creek (12)	Indian Valley (22)	Kingston 3 (13)	Barley	Birch 1 (10)	Corcorcan 2 (28)	Johnson 1 (6)	Kingston Dry
Geology	Sediment cores (stratigraphy, texture, % organic)	3	3	14	4	2	0	4	2
	Down-hole geophysics (resistivity)			•					o
Ground-water	Water chemistry	o	o	•		o			o
	Groundwater well level data (monthly)	54	60	99	4	4	3		4
	Continuous water level and temperature	•	o	•					
	Hydraulic conductivity data (slug/bail tests)	o	o	•					
Stream water	Longitudinal and cross section repeat surveys	o	o	•					
	Stream water and stream bed temperature surveys	o	o	•			o		
	Water chemistry	o	o	•			o		o
	Continuous water level and temperature data	•	o	•					
	Stream gaging	•	o	•			o		
Meadow	Plant community maps	X	X	X		X	X	X	
	Spring location, size, and type maps	X	X	X		X	X	X	
	Ground-penetrating radar survey data	•	•	•	•	•	•	•	•
	Seismic survey data	•	•	•			•		•
	Geomorphic map	X	X	X					

\# Number of wells and sediment cores at meadow
• Extensive at meadow (>6 locations in meadow)
o Minimal at meadow (<6 locations in meadow)
X Data were collected and mapped at meadow for listed topic

Hydrogeologic Settings of Kingston 3, Big Creek, and Indian Valley Meadows

The general hydrogeologic settings where meadows have formed were discussed in Chapter 2. Briefly, the major factors required for meadow formation are a sufficient supply of water and a hydrogeologic setting that detains groundwater, thereby creating a shallow water table. There are a number of geologic and geomorphic settings that have created these conditions, but a pervasive trait is the occurrence of fine-grained (low hydraulic conductivity) sediments in the down-valley portion of the meadow, which are commonly present where there is a local reduction in the cross section of axial valley fill. Whereas low-permeability sedimentary materials detain groundwater flow to support wet meadow vegetation, most meadows terminate down-valley where unconfined, high-permeability sedimentary layers permit rapid draining and lowering of the groundwater table.

A common geomorphic setting for meadow complexes is immediately upstream of where side-valley alluvial fans project across axial valleys (Chapter 2; Miller and others 2001).

Because the three intensively studied meadow complexes are discussed extensively in this chapter, their geomorphic settings are described here. The valley of Kingston Canyon has numerous side-valley alluvial fans (fig. 4.3a). However, some have created the hydrogeologic conditions necessary to support meadow complexes (such as Kingston 3) while others have not. One such area (Dry Kingston, fig. 4.3a) was studied to understand how the hydrology of this "dry" site differs from those that support wetlands (table 4.1). Within Kingston 3, the channel is locally incised by as much as 2 m below the valley floor. Stream incision is deepest immediately upstream of the side-valley alluvial fan and decreases upvalley.

The Big Creek basin is located in the Toiyabe Range of central Nevada, to the west and across the divide from the Kingston Canyon basin (fig. 4.2). Like Kingston 3, the meadow at the Big Creek field site is located upstream of a valley constriction that was created by coalescing alluvial fans that nearly extend across the entire width of the valley floor to the north (fig. 4.4). Another side-valley alluvial fan enters the axial valley near the southern end of the site. The Big Creek site is approximately 250 m long and ranges from 20 to 60 m wide. The site has a perennial stream,

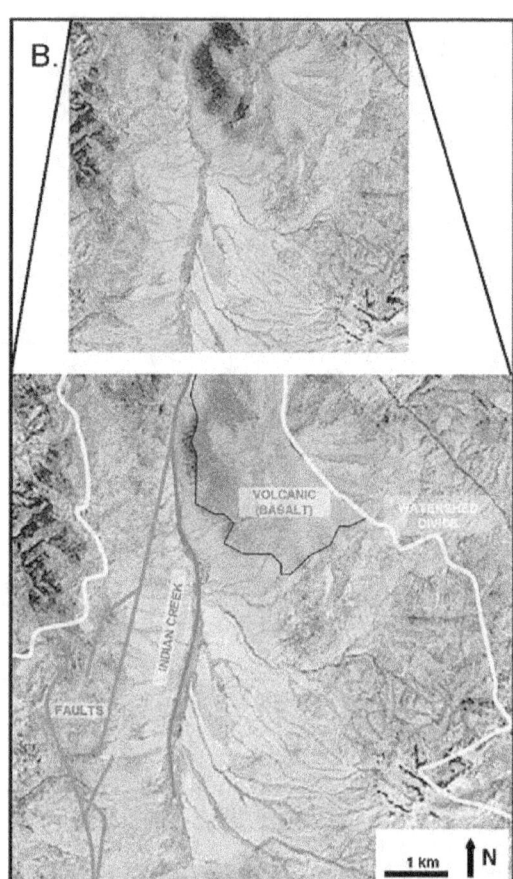

Figure 4.3. (a) Southerly view of Kingston Canyon showing setting common to many meadow complexes, with meadows immediately upstream of a side-valley alluvial fan (AF). The Kingston 3 meadow has 99 groundwater wells and a stream gage; it was the site of many detailed geologic, hydrologic, and vegetation studies (table 4.1). (b) Satellite image of Indian Valley showing meadow upstream of valley constriction caused by a volcanic mountain. Geology modified from Kleinhampl and Ziony (1985).

flowing south to north, in a channel incised up to approximately 1 m below the valley floor. The channel traverses the entire meadow system and links upstream and downstream reaches of the basin. Six small, spring-fed gullies flow across the wet meadow to the incised axial channel. The site is bounded laterally by steep hillslopes that rise sharply above the valley floor (fig. 4.4).

The Indian Valley meadow complex (fig. 4.3b) occurs in a different type of setting than Kingston 3 and Big Creek (fig. 4.4). Its origin is due to a remnant of a basaltic volcanic mountain located upslope of Black Mountain. Upvalley (south) of Black Mountain, a series of broad meadow complexes are present that developed on a relatively thin (about 8 m) sequence of primarily fine-grained alluvial sediments underlain by low-permeability volcanic rocks: rhyolite and tuffs (Kleinhampl and Ziony 1985; Jewett and others 2004). The meadow complex diminishes completely downvalley due to well-developed, incised channels underlain by coarser-grained alluvium and higher-permeability basaltic bedrock (Jewett and others 2004). In some locations in the meadow, incision exceeds 4 m. Source areas of water for this meadow complex are broad, old alluvial fans and faults (fig. 4.3b).

Groundwater Hydrology of the Study Meadows

Groundwater Spatial Patterns. Groundwater flow rates, seasonal patterns, and flow directions vary within a meadow and among meadows and reflect the geologic complexities discussed previously. The primary controls on groundwater conditions at a given location are: (1) stratigraphy (i.e., the type, geometry, continuity, and sequence of underlying geologic units); (2) hydraulic conductivity of subsurface materials; (3) the water source, particularly whether it is part of a local or regional aquifer groundwater flow system; (4) whether the source waters that directly support the meadow complex are diffuse or discrete (that is, derived from a thick, sedimentary unit or through faults and fractures in bedrock); and (5) the relationship of groundwater to stream channels. The Kingston 3 meadow was used to demonstrate groundwater flow patterns because of the extensive stratigraphic and hydrologic data available for this site. Information also was used from the Indian Valley site (fig. 4.2).

Like many Great Basin meadows, the hydrologic sources of Kingston 3 are springs and artesian conditions, and these

48

USDA Forest Service Gen. Tech. Rep. RMRS-GTR-258. 2011.

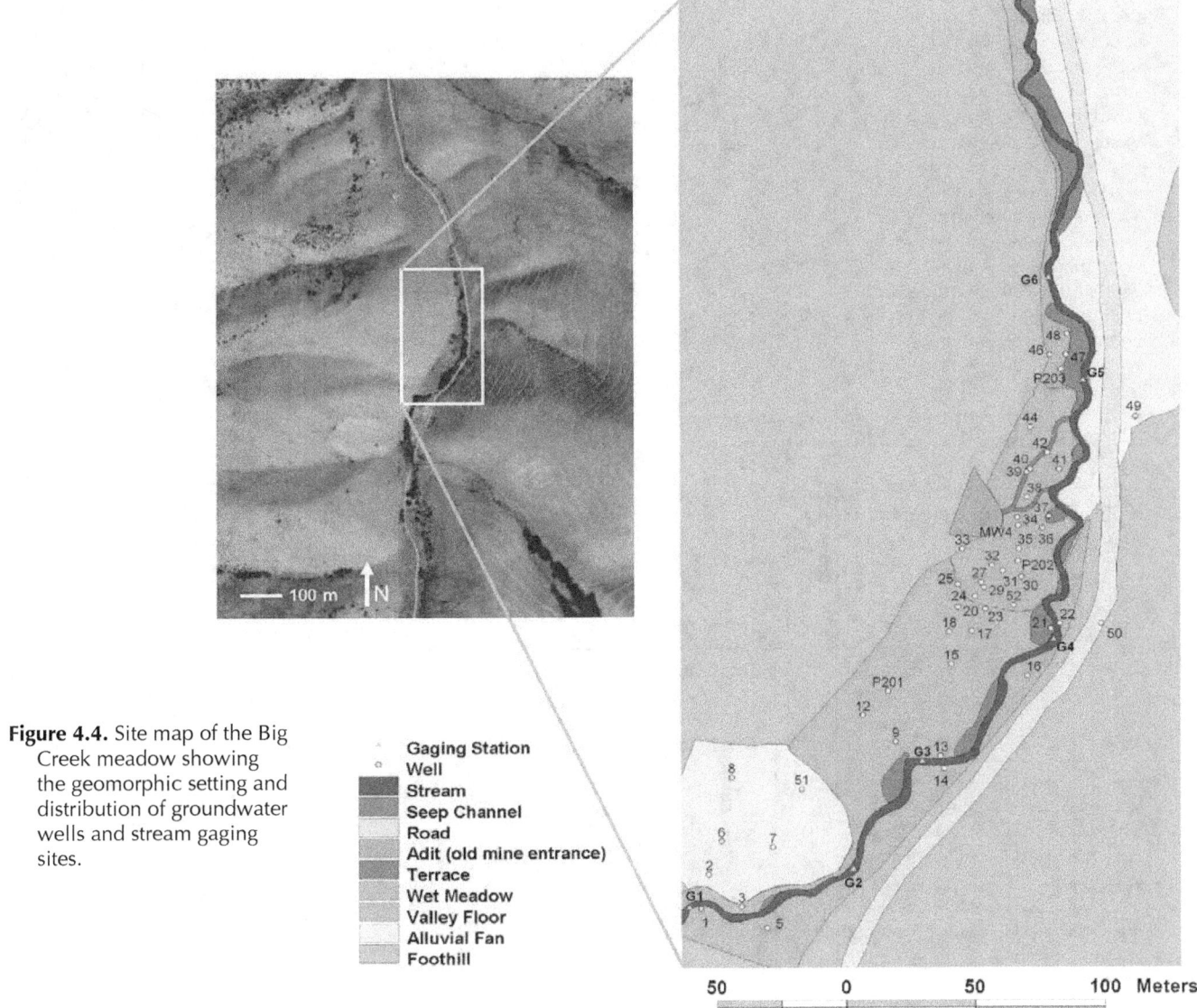

Figure 4.4. Site map of the Big Creek meadow showing the geomorphic setting and distribution of groundwater wells and stream gaging sites.

Legend:
- Gaging Station
- Well
- Stream
- Seep Channel
- Road
- Adit (old mine entrance)
- Terrace
- Wet Meadow
- Valley Floor
- Alluvial Fan
- Foothill

directly reflect the complexity of the subsurface geology. The water table depth at the Kingston 3 meadow is shallowest at valley floor edges and slopes toward the stream; the water table drops about 12 m in elevation over the length of the meadow (about 350 m) (fig. 4.5). An examination of the longitudinal, hydrogeologic cross-section demonstrates the influence of geology on groundwater flow patterns (fig. 4.6). In the upstream portion of the meadow, sediments are mostly fine-grained alluvial deposits created by axial valley streams. Down-valley, the coarse-grained sediments deposited by side-valley fans become more dominant. The interfingering of axial valley deposits with side-valley fan deposits resulted in many discontinuous sedimentary units with strongly contrasting hydraulic conductivities, which contributed to confining layers, artesian conditions, and points of emergence (or discharge) for springs. Discontinuous units also were produced by channel avulsion processes. Slug tests, an in-well method, were used to determine hydraulic conductivity of subsurface materials. The tests showed values that ranged over three orders of magnitude (10^{-2} to 10^{-5} cm/s) but

that probably under-represented the variability because in establishing the well field, groundwater wells were preferentially screened in coarser-grained sediments. The meadow's down-valley terminus coincides with the occurrence of continuous sand and gravel deposits (well 10.1; fig. 4.6), which permit more rapid groundwater flow and a lowering of the water table depth. The influence of stratigraphy of the valley fill and groundwater is indicated by the relationship of the shallow groundwater table and groundwater head levels from deeper wells (about 8 m). For example, as seen in fig. 4.6, the water table slopes down-valley and becomes more shallow downstream. The deep wells, however, are bound by fine-grained stratigraphic units, causing the head levels to become increasingly artesian down-valley, reaching levels up to 2 m above the ground surface, before continuous gravel layers are encountered and water pressure is released.

A three-dimensional understanding of the stratigraphy was obtained by detailed ground penetrating radar (GPR) surveys (Sturtevant 2007). As suggested by the core data, a facies map produced from the GPR surveys showed that

USDA Forest Service Gen. Tech. Rep. RMRS-GTR-258. 2011.

49

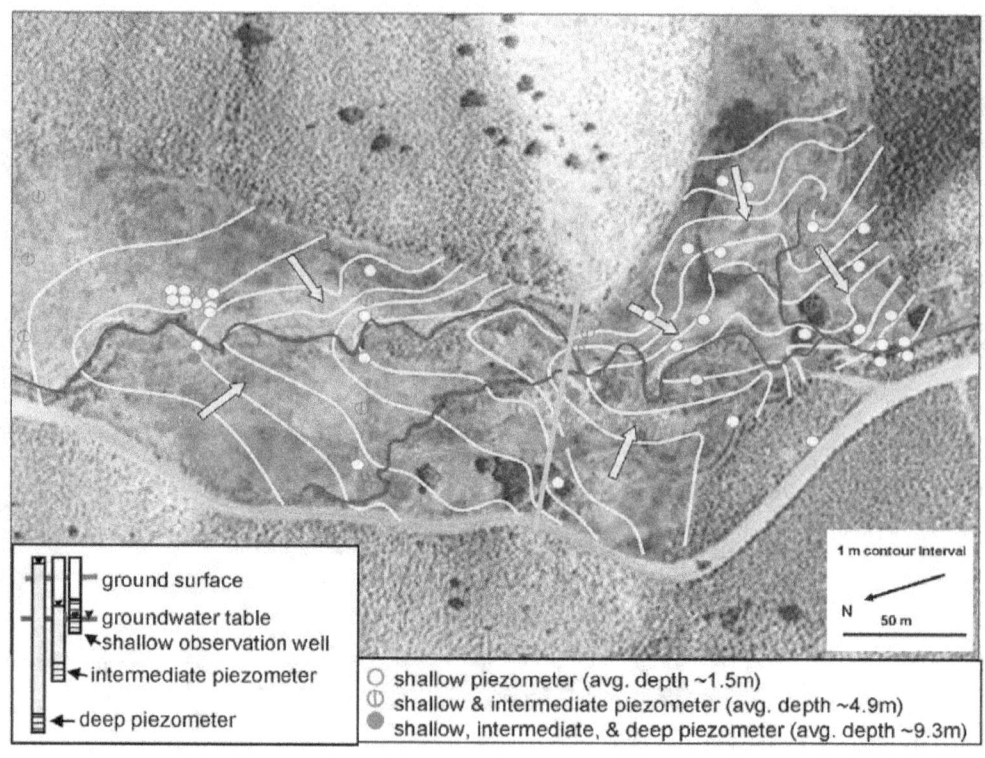

Figure 4.5. Kingston 3 meadow groundwater table and well sites. The stream is mostly gaining through the meadow, except at the downstream end where it is losing; the water table drops about 12 m over the length of the meadow. Groundwater table map is for August 2003, but overall patterns change little with time. The meadow is instrumented with groundwater wells (circles); most well sites have nests of piezometers (n = 99; schematic lower left). Green line (center) is location of water table profile in fig. 4.10. Stream flow is south (right).

ground surface
groundwater table
shallow observation well
intermediate piezometer
deep piezometer

○ shallow piezometer (avg. depth ~1.5m)
◐ shallow & intermediate piezometer (avg. depth ~4.9m)
● shallow, intermediate, & deep piezometer (avg. depth ~9.3m)

1 m contour interval

N 50 m

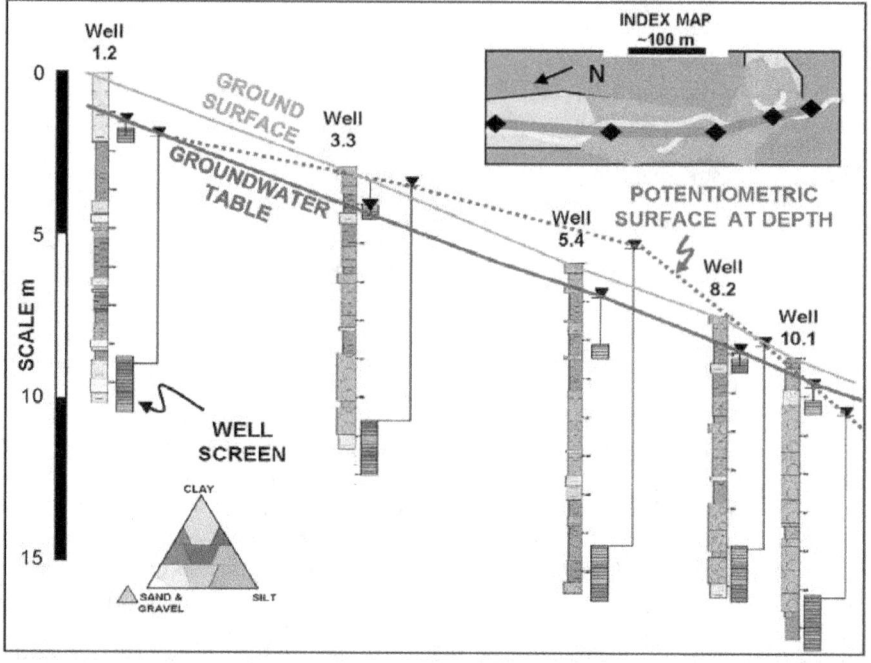

Figure 4.6. Longitudinal hydrogeologic section of down-valley axis of Kingston 3 meadow. Lithologic columns show a coarsening down-valley; about three-quarters of the most downstream core in the meadow (well 10.1) is composed of gravel. The water table, determined from the shallow wells, becomes closer to the surface down the meadow. The deep groundwater shows an increase in artesian conditions (see potentiometric surface) down the valley, up to the point where the meadow terminates around well 10.1.

the valley fill is characterized by many discontinuous layers that generally coarsen down-valley (fig. 4.7). The map also showed the occurrence of gravel deposits along the eastern valley floor margin, where numerous springs discharge to the surface.

Groundwater table and flow patterns in the meadows also vary along the valley floor before reaching the side-valley fan deposits. In the Kingston 3 meadow, the variability of groundwater levels decreases down-valley in both shallow and deeper groundwater systems (fig. 4.8). Over a five-year period, groundwater levels at the upstream end of the meadow varied about an order of magnitude more than at

down-valley sites. The opposite pattern is present at the Indian Valley meadow complex (fig. 4.9), where down-valley wells show much more variability than upstream sites. This contrast reflects differences in the hydrogeologic settings of the two sites. At Indian Valley, the stratigraphy is less complex than at Kingston 3 meadow and the conditions contributing to shallow water tables are gradually lost over about 1 km (Jewett and others 2004). At the Kingston 3 meadow, marked changes in hydrogeology occur over just a few meters in some places.

The characteristics of the connection between groundwater and surface water are strong determinants in how the

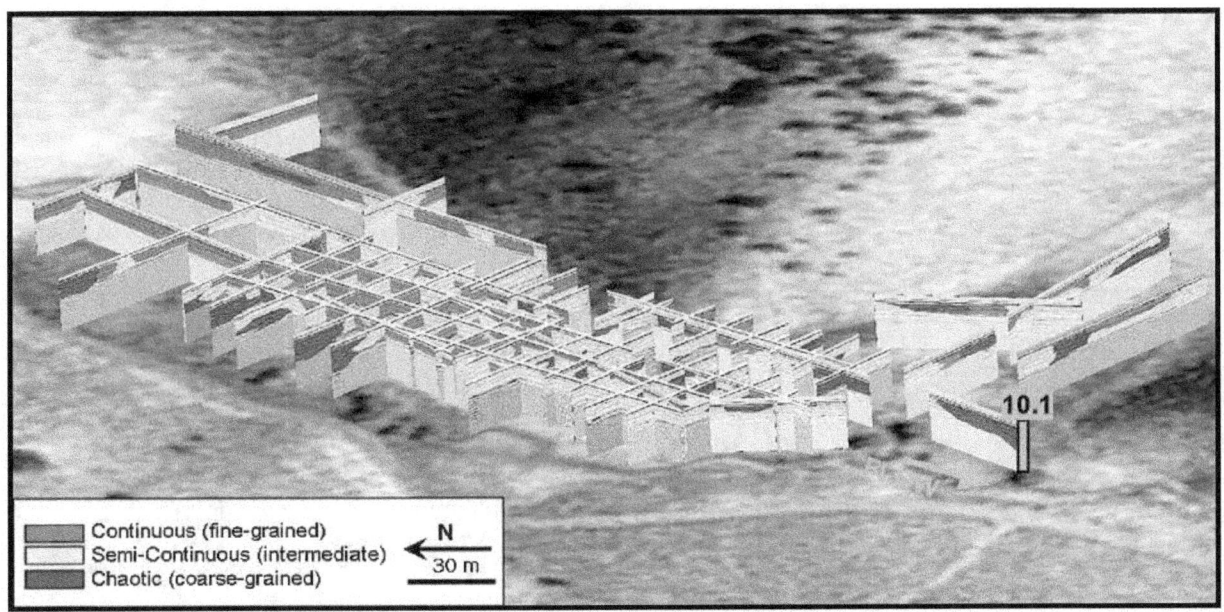

Figure 4.7. Ground-penetrating radar facies map of Kingston 3 meadow (from Sturtevant 2007). Upstream units are generally fine-grained and continuous, whereas downstream units are coarser-grained and discontinuous. The coarse-grained area at well site 10.1 (see longitudinal section of fig. 4.6) coincides with the down-valley meadow terminus, a loss of artesian conditions, and groundwater with a downward flow direction. These changes in conditions are attributed to the continuity of the coarse-grained sediments that permit rapid drainage of groundwater that supports the meadow upvalley.

Figure 4.8. Water levels in nested piezometer sites along the down-valley axis (fig. 4.5) at Kingston 3 meadow; elevation is relative. Groundwater levels at all depths are most variable upvalley. Water levels in the deep wells are above the groundwater table throughout most of the meadow and have heads up to 3 m higher than the water table in the lower part of the meadow (e.g., P84D). The increased artesian conditions down the meadow are caused by fine-grained, confining stratigraphic units, which lead to high fluid pressure.

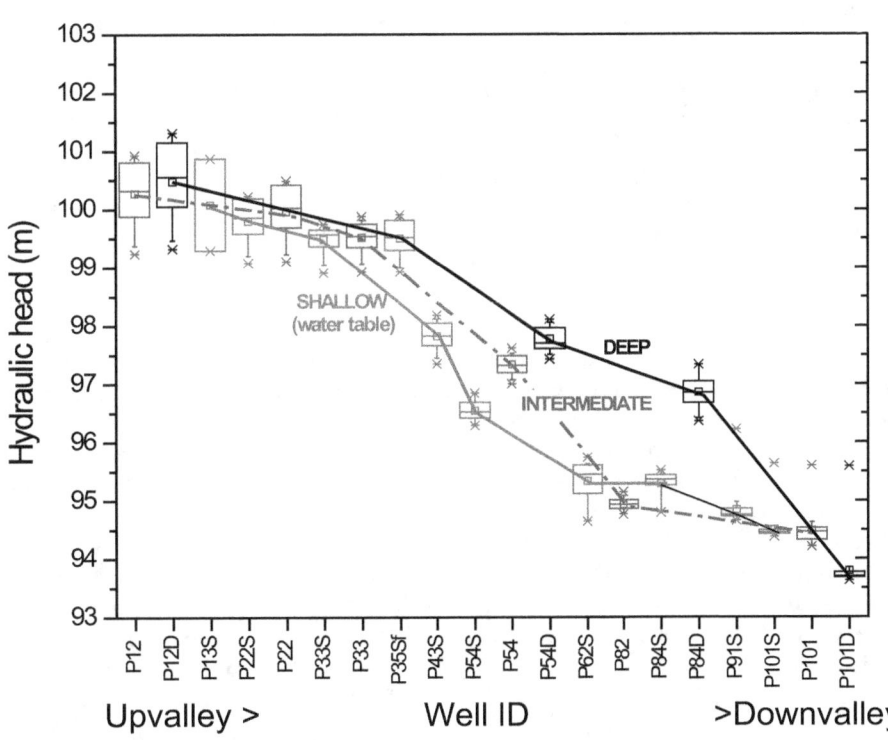

water table and, therefore, vegetation types respond to stream incision or migration (Chapter 5). Streams can be viewed as gaining or losing depending on whether the groundwater flows toward the stream or drains away from the stream. At Kingston 3 meadow, much of the stream is fed directly by shallow groundwater, thus the groundwater table adjacent to the stream slopes to the level of the stream (fig. 4.10a). In

a losing reach, stream water drains into the groundwater so that the water table slopes away from the channel. This is the case for some reaches of the stream in Indian Valley (fig. 4.10b), where the hydrogeologic conditions no longer support shallow water tables.

The source area of the groundwater supporting meadows also controls the spatial characteristics of the groundwater

USDA Forest Service Gen. Tech. Rep. RMRS-GTR-258. 2011.

51

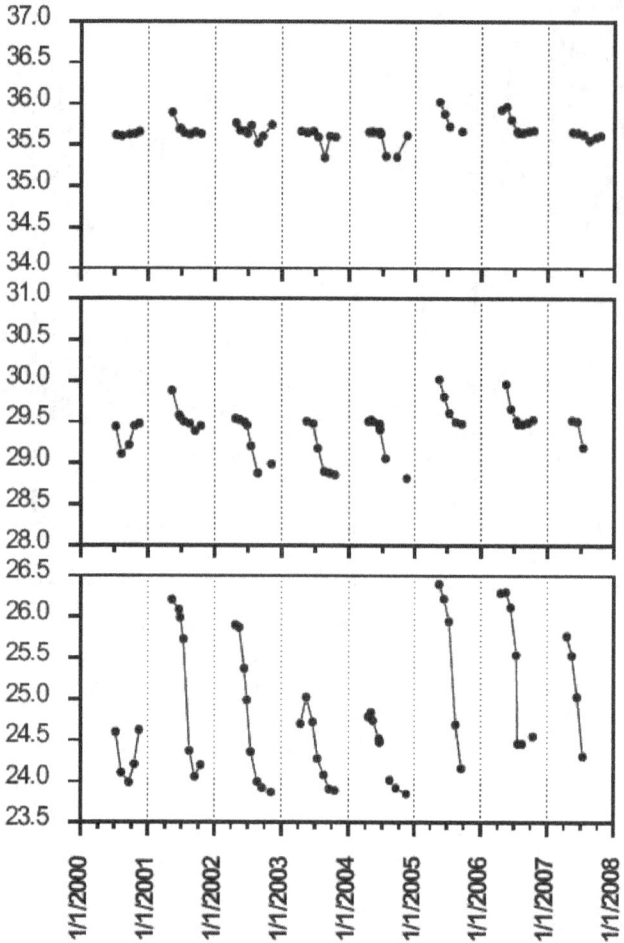

Figure 4.9. Groundwater table elevations in floor of incised trench, from upstream (well 8B), midstream (well 5B), and downstream (well 3B) reaches at Indian Valley; elevation is relative. Note that seasonal water table variations increase downstream from less than 0.5 m to over 2 m.

table and flow patterns in meadows. Overall, meadow complexes are groundwater discharge sites, though patterns vary depending on the size of the groundwater catchment area and when the recharge occurs for that groundwater body. For example, discharge areas of regional (large-scale) groundwater flow systems tend to have less variation in head levels at daily and seasonal scales and are important to sustaining many springs and wetlands (Mifflin 1988; Wilson and Guan 2004; Anderson and others 2006; Winter 2007; Patten and others 2008). The influence of different groundwater sources is evident at Kingston 3 meadow. The upstream portion of the meadow is fed by groundwater moving downstream through the valley fill. These areas show strong seasonal and diurnal variations in water levels (well 33; fig. 4.11). In the mid- and downstream portion of the meadow, water table depths show little seasonal variation and, in some cases, have trends opposite to those in the upstream portion of the meadow (fig. 4.11). These traits are indicative of regional groundwater discharge sites (Winter 2004; Jewett and others 2004; Newman and others 2006; Prudic and others 2007). Based on the groundwater level and water chemistry data at

Kingston 3 meadow (Tennant and others 2006), the meadow complex has three primary groundwater sources: axial valley water; alluvial tributary water that joins the meadow from the east; and, as indicated by seismic data, water from a subsurface fault that outcrops under a portion of the west margin of the valley side. The influence of these sources also is reflected in fig. 4.5, which shows contours of relative water table depths throughout the meadow.

Groundwater Interaction with Stream Water. Evidence for multiple groundwater sources supporting meadow complexes can be found by examining the interaction between groundwater and stream water. In fig. 4.11, the discharge pattern of the stream in Kingston 3 meadow (Stm, bottom graph) reflects a complicated composite of different groundwater sources. The stream is perennial within the meadow but it is intermittent immediately upstream of the meadow and typically flows from late spring to mid-summer during snowmelt runoff. Interactions between surface water and groundwater were evaluated by repeated, detailed stream discharge measurements of the stream and its tributaries (fig. 4.12a). Hydrologic budget analysis of stream discharge showed that axial valley groundwater feeds the upstream end of stream (above gage station K4) but that the spring-fed tributaries are the primary source of flow downstream. When tributary inputs to flow are subtracted, the stream is losing in some reaches of the meadow, especially downstream of gage station K2. For example, for the 2004 data shown in fig. 4.12a, the stream loses over 30 percent of its flow between stations K2 and K1.

Spatial changes along the stream within the meadow also were evaluated by installing temporary piezometers directly in the stream bed to a depth of 0.5 m. This simple method can be used to determine if the stream is gaining or losing by comparing the water level in the piezometer to the stream water level (Wanty and Winter 2000). The collected data are consistent with stream discharge measurements. The vertical hydraulic gradient was 0.3 m/m upward at the upstream end of the meadow and 0.06 m/m downward in the downstream portion of the meadow.

Repeated surveys of stream water and stream bed (15 cm deep) temperatures were conducted along the length of the stream and its tributaries (fig. 4.12b) to identify gaining and losing stream segments and changes in groundwater sources (Constantz 1998; Kalbus and others 2006). The temperature profile data showed three distinct patterns in stream water temperature: warming in the upstream segment of the meadow, cooling to the middle segment of the meadow, and subsequent warming downstream (fig. 4.12b). The locations of the pattern changes are consistent with the flow data on gaining and losing reaches.

Many studies have documented the importance of understanding the exchange between groundwater and surface water on stream biotic productivity, the hyporheic zone, and biogeochemical cycling (e.g., Hunt and others 2006; Newman and others 2006). However, as seen in Kingston 3 meadow, changes in this interaction can occur over short distances and time intervals, so generalizations about a stream reach being gaining or losing may oversimplify

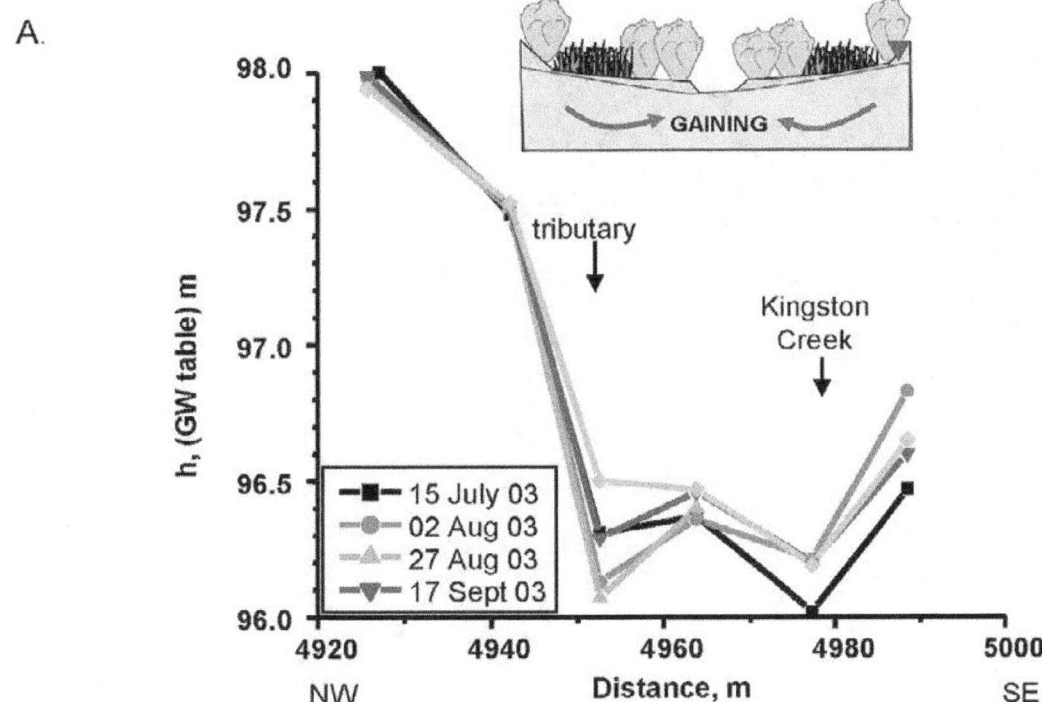

A.

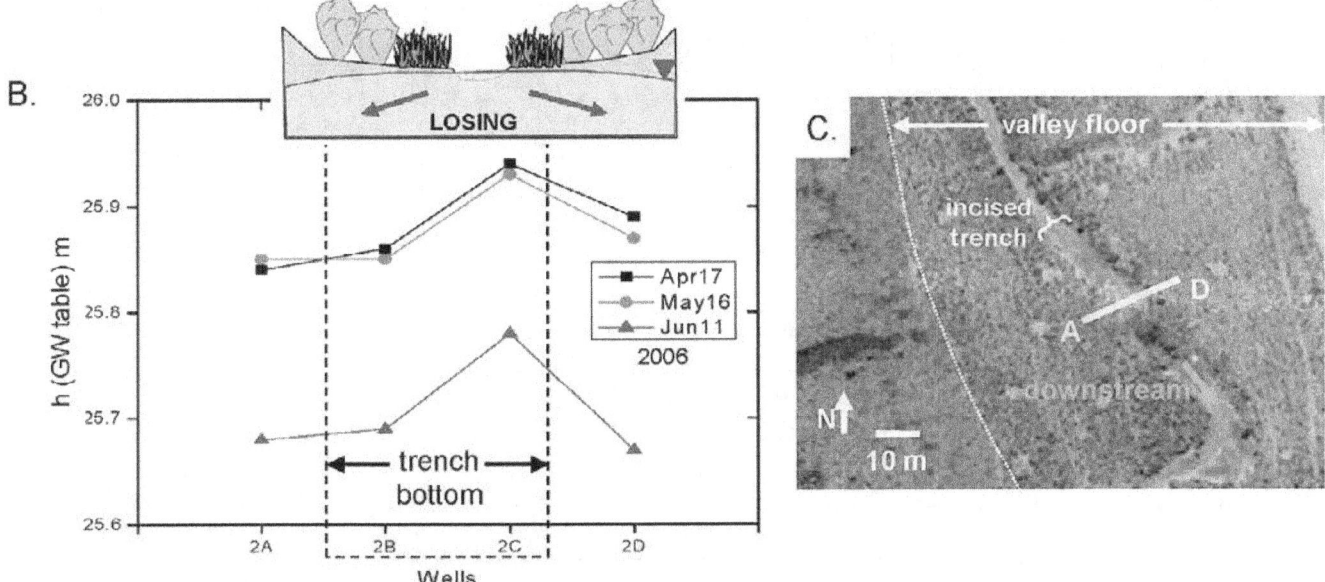

B.

C.

Figure 4.10. Groundwater table profiles across a gaining and losing channel reach. Schematic diagrams show relationship of water table and flow directions to stream. (a) Gaining reach at Kingston 3 meadow; water table slopes toward channel (profile location shown by green line on fig 4.5). (b) Losing reach at Indian Valley meadow; water table slopes away from channel of incised trench. (c) Aerial photograph shows geomorphic setting. Upstream portions of Indian Valley are mostly gaining but become losing down-valley with distance from the water sources and as the permeability of the subsurface materials increases.

reality. Newman and others (2006) indicated that small-scale changes in the type of exchange between groundwater and surface water are relatively common in semi-arid systems and can result from changes in geology and variations in runoff inputs.

Meadow Hydrology Temporal Patterns. While some temporal patterns relate to spatial controls were discussed previously, natural events (precipitation, snowmelt, occurrence and length of growing season, climatic change, etc.) also have significant effects on hydrologic processes. We

USDA Forest Service Gen. Tech. Rep. RMRS-GTR-258. 2011.

53

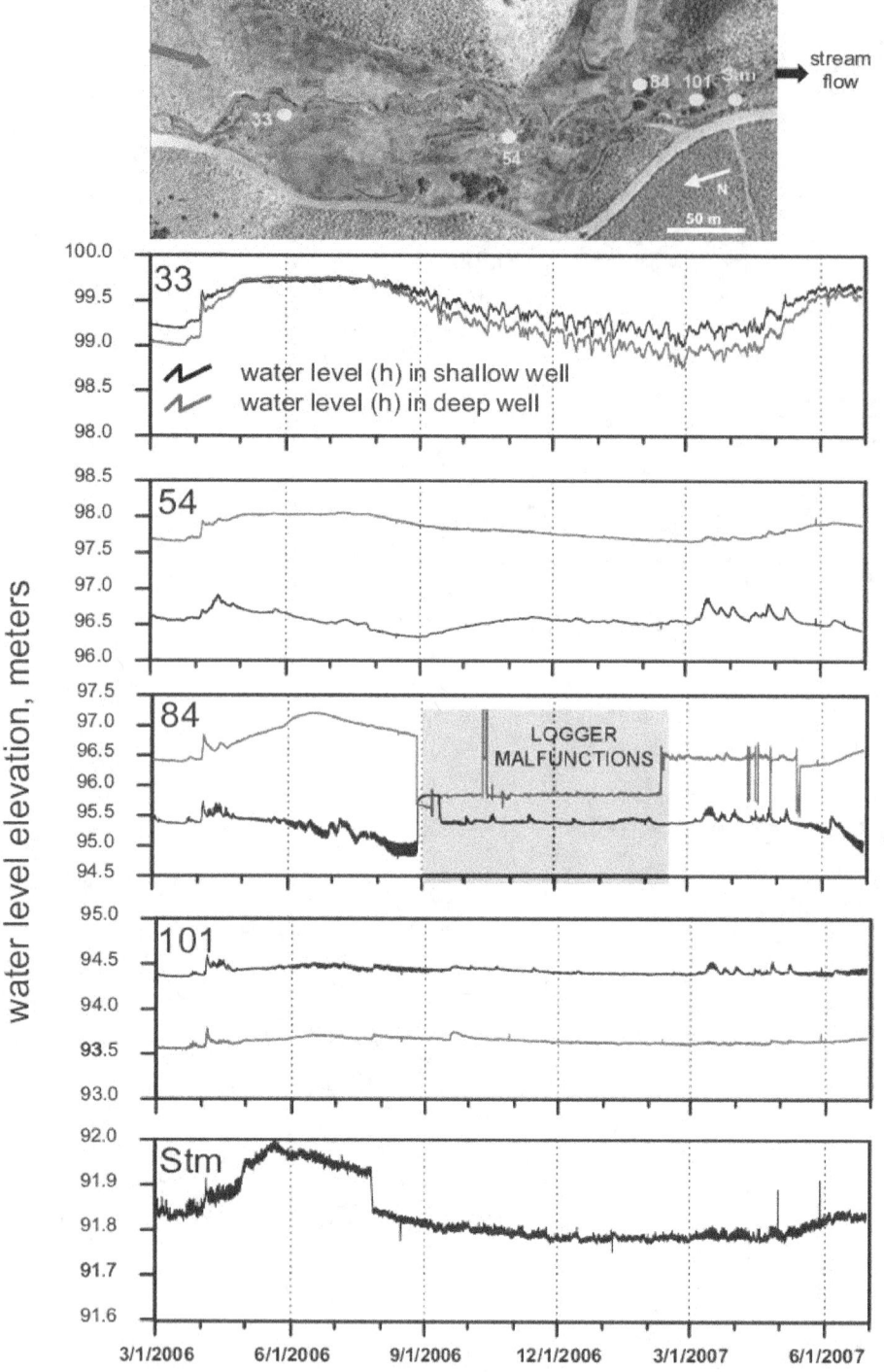

Figure 4.11. Groundwater and stream water levels (Stm) of Kingston 3 meadow sites. Groundwater plots show water levels of deep and shallow wells in successively down-valley wells, from top to bottom. Well site 33 shows a smooth seasonal signal, fed by axial valley groundwater (index map, blue arrow), while well sites 54 and 85 are more flashy and are influenced strongly by groundwater from the high-gradient tributary valley (orange arrow). Vertical hydraulic gradient is small at well site 33, strongly upward at sites 54 and 84, and downward at site 101.

use the hydrologic and hydrogeologic data from the Big Creek study site to illustrate short-term and long-term temporal patterns in meadow hydrology. The Big Creek site has been continuously monitored since it was instrumented with 54 piezometers in 1997 (Jewett and others 2004).

The Big Creek meadow is located upstream of a valley constriction that is created by coalescing alluvial fans that extend nearly across the entire width of the valley floor to the north (fig. 4.4). Another side-valley alluvial fan enters the axial valley near the southern end of the site. Sources of

water to the groundwater system at the Big Creek site are subsurface flow moving down-valley in the valley-fill sediments, the side-valley alluvial fan located near the southern boundary of the site, and discharge from the stream. Contour lines of water table surface (fig. 4.13) indicate that the main direction of subsurface groundwater flow is down-valley in a southwest to northeast direction. The largest component of groundwater flow is water moving through the thick valley-fill sediment sequence. The lateral constriction caused by narrowing of the valley on the north end of the site combined

54

USDA Forest Service Gen. Tech. Rep. RMRS-GTR-258. 2011.

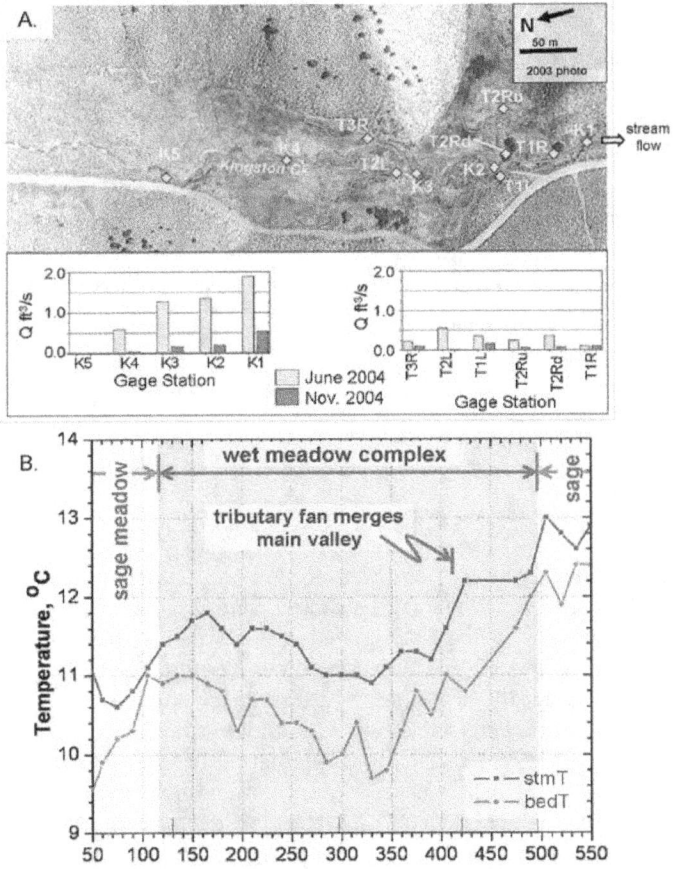

Figure 4.12. (a) Stream discharge data in Kingston meadow for summer and fall 2004. Data show strong seasonality, with flow in the main channel that is over three times greater in June than in November. In the upstream, flow in the main channel is primarily from groundwater; downstream from mid meadow, most flow is from tributaries. (b) Stream water and stream bed (depth ~15 cm) temperature plot shows increased temperature at about 350 m, reflecting warmer groundwater contribution from the east tributary valley.

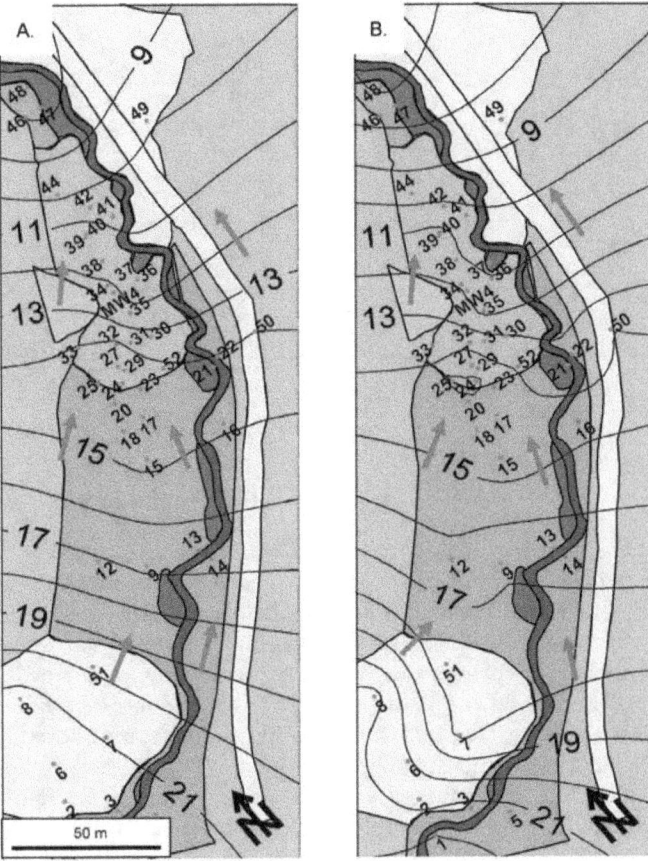

Figure 4.13. Big Creek water table maps illustrating (a) high water table conditions (25 June 1997) and (b) low water table conditions (09 August 2000). Water table elevation values are relative; 1 m contour interval. Arrows show groundwater flow directions; stream flow is northerly (top). Base maps are fig. 4.4.

with a vertical thinning of the valley-fill sediments creates a bottleneck for subsurface flow. This flow constriction produces saturated soils and groundwater discharge zones that are characteristic of the meadow complexes. The configuration of the water table (fig. 4.13) also suggests that the side-valley alluvial fan in the southern area of the site as well as the stream influence groundwater flow patterns. The pattern of the water table near the side-valley alluvial fan indicates it is a source of subsurface flow. The water table contours slope toward the stream (gaining) in some places and away from the stream (losing) in others (fig. 4.13, arrows).

The impact that different water sources have on the groundwater system varies over time due to seasonal changes and fluctuations in timing and amounts of annual precipitation. Figure 4.13 presents water table maps for both a wet season monitoring event (that is, high water table conditions; 25 June 1998; fig. 4.13a) and a dry season monitoring event (low water table conditions; 09 August 2000; fig. 4.13b). During wetter conditions, the water table is higher across the site, with the greatest increases in the sage meadow zone located in the upper region of the site (for example, water levels near piezometer No. 7 increased by approximately 3 m). Water table elevations in the wet meadow zone also increased but not by nearly as much. The water table in the wet meadow zone is at or near the ground surface, and higher water levels (greater hydraulic heads) result in increased groundwater discharge, which flows across the ground surface in small channels and eventually enters the stream. Field observations revealed that the area of saturated soils, indicating groundwater discharge, was greatest when the water table was high.

Both maps of the water table (fig. 4.13) show that the side-valley alluvial fan in the southern area of the site and the stream traversing the entire site have an influence on groundwater flow patterns, but that influence is less pronounced when the water table is higher. During wet conditions (fig. 4.13a), water level contours only deflect slightly down-valley near the side-valley alluvial fan, suggesting that the fan supplies flow to the subsurface. However, the magnitude of subsurface flow that was contributed by the

USDA Forest Service Gen. Tech. Rep. RMRS-GTR-258. 2011.

55

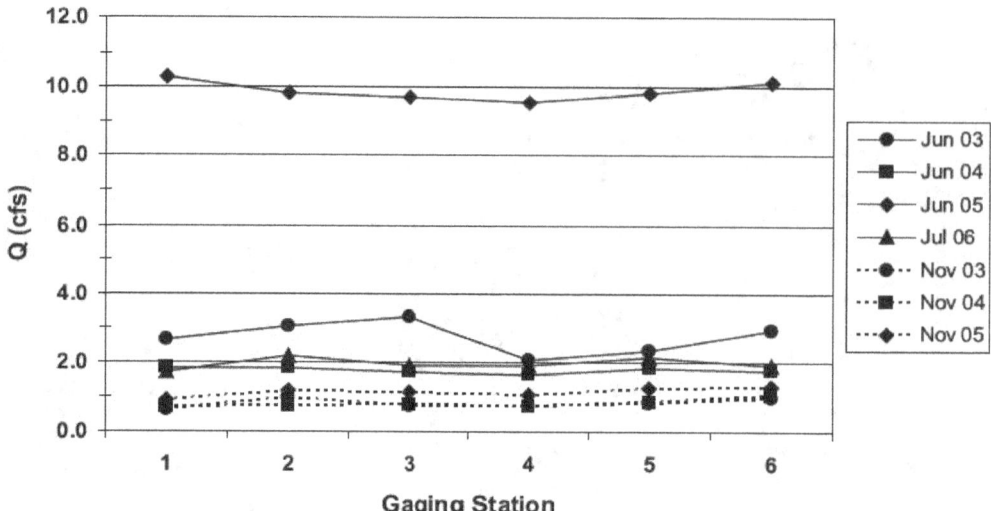

Figure 4.14. Stream discharge (2003 to 2006), Q (in cfs), measured at six gaging stations located along the stream at the Big Creek study site. See fig. 4.4 for gaging station location G1 to G6.

fan relative to the contribution provided by subsurface flow in the valley-fill sediments is greater during drier conditions (fig. 4.13b). The impact of groundwater flow to and from the stream channel also is more evident during drier conditions. The downstream reach of the stream adjacent to the wet meadow (fig. 4.13; light blue) is gaining during both wet and dry conditions. However, upstream the influence of the stream on groundwater flow patterns increases as site conditions become drier and the water table elevation decreases (fig. 4.13b).

To examine the temporal and spatial interaction between surface and subsurface flow, stream discharge was measured at six gaging stations during the spring/summer and fall seasons from 2003 to 2006. The locations of the gaging stations are shown in fig. 4.4. Figure 4.14 shows the discharge measured at each gaging station (in cubic feet per second, cfs) for seven dates over three years. Stream flow ranged from 0.6 to 3.3 cfs, except during a high flow event recorded in June 2005 when discharge measured 10.3 cfs. During this event, a gradual decline in streamflow was observed from stations G1 to G4 indicating losing conditions upstream. Stream discharge gradually increased from stations G4 to G6, suggesting gaining conditions downstream. Stream flow recorded during the other spring/summer measurement events ranged from 1.7 to 3.3 cfs. In June 2003, gaining conditions occurred upstream (between G1 and G3) followed by losing conditions mid-stream (between G3 and G4) and gaining conditions downstream. The length of the upstream segment that exhibited gaining conditions decreased as stream discharge decreased. Stream flow was lowest during the fall (November 2003 to 2005; 0.6 to 1.3 cfs) following the dry summer season. Fall gaging records showed that flow in the stream increased only slightly from location to location in the downstream direction.

Water table depth data that were collected over time provide a glimpse of the hydroperiod, or the frequency and amplitude of water-level fluctuations (Winter and others 1998), for different portions of the Big Creek meadow. Figure 4.15a illustrates the water table depth (mean depth ± 1 standard deviation) from 1997 to 2006 for piezometers

located in the sage, dry, and wet meadow zones. Water table depth is greatest in the sage meadow zone. Average water table depths in the sage-dominated meadow range from 2.5 to 3.5 m below the ground surface, but depth to the water table varies greatly across this zone (as depicted by the error bars). Average water table depths in the dry meadow zone range from 0.5 to 1 m and are less variable. The water table is closest to the surface in the wet meadow, with the average depth generally less than 0.5 m. Water table depths in the wet meadow are the least variable. As the hydraulic head in this zone increases, the water level can only rise to the ground surface, after which further increases in the hydraulic head are marked by increases in groundwater discharge.

Average depth to water table also reflects the amount of precipitation received in the Big Creek watershed (fig. 4.15b). The water table was highest (that is, the depth to water was at a minimum) during the wet years of the late 1990s, and it was lowest from 1999 to 2004 in response to lower than average precipitation. Groundwater levels increased in 2004 and 2005 as annual precipitation increased. Water table depths generally reflected the influence of evapotranspiration during the growing season for both the dry and wet meadow zones. During most years for which data are available, water table depths declined during the growing season in the dry and wet meadow zones. This trend was likely due to increased plant transpiration and evaporation from the wet meadow surface. Water levels showed a rebound in the fall when evaporation was less, plants became dormant, and transpiration was minimal.

Hydrographs (time series data of water table depths from piezometers and the stream), also exhibited these seasonal and annual trends and fluctuations (fig. 4.16). Three piezometers (P-201, P-202, and P-203) were instrumented with water-level loggers to obtain continuous water level records. P-201 was located in the sage meadow zone, P-202 was in the wet meadow zone, and P-203 was just down-gradient of the wet meadow at the northern end of the site (fig. 4.4). The stream also was instrumented with a datalogger that was located at gaging station G5 (fig. 4.4). The hydrographs for P-201, P-202, and P-203 exhibited the same annual pattern.

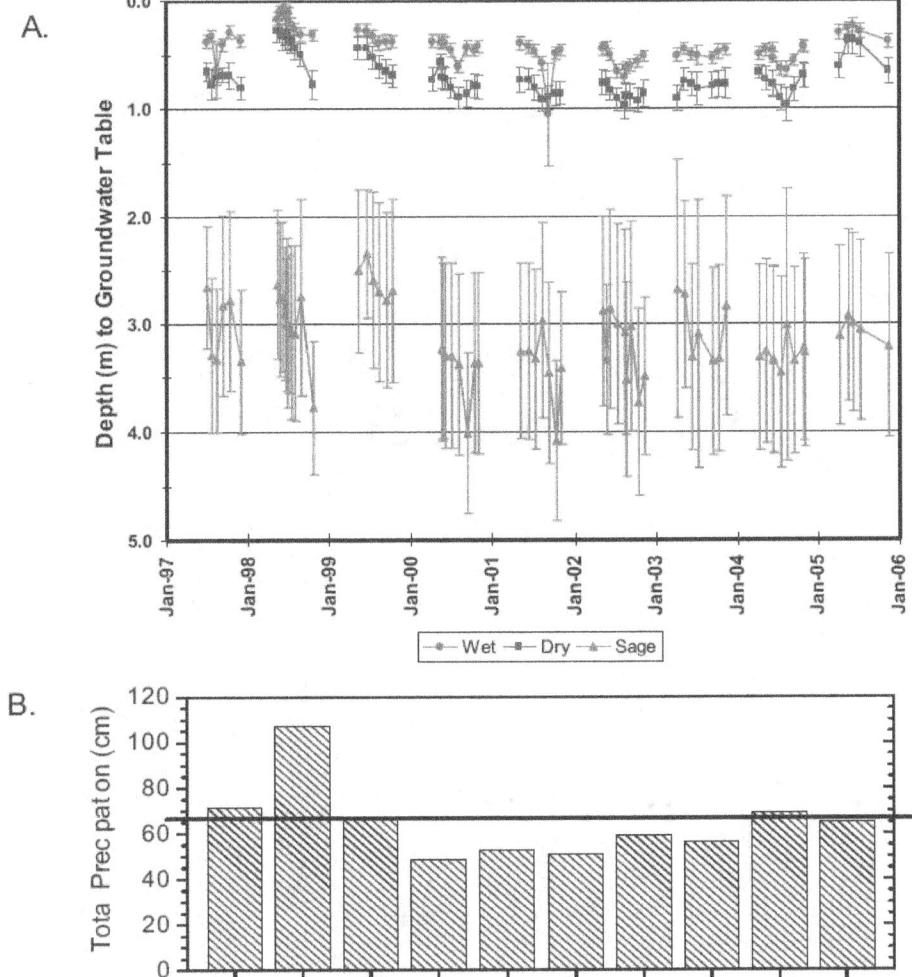

A.

B.

Figure 4.15. (a) Average depth to groundwater (± 1 SD) in piezometers located in wet, dry, and sage plant communities of the Big Creek meadow, January 1997 to January 2006. Water level measurements were taken monthly during growing season, five to six times per year. (b) Total water year precipitation at Big Creek SNOTEL site; line is 27-year average (66.8 cm).

still affected the water table in the sage meadow, but the change in the water level was not as rapid as where the water table was closer to the surface.

Although not measured, plant transpiration and surface evaporation appeared to affect the water table depth in and around the meadow complex. Water level fluctuations were greatest during the growing season and least during the non-growing season (fig. 4.16). These fluctuations were more pronounced in piezometers located in or near the wet meadow (P-202 and P-203). The daily periodicity of the water level fluctuations was evident when portions of the hydrographs were enlarged in order to better observe the diurnal fluctuations during portions of the growing season (June to July 2004) and the non-growing season (November to December 2004) (fig. 4.17). During the growing season, water levels began to drop about the time sunlight hit the meadow. The water table declined throughout the day and reached the lowest levels in the evening when the meadow became shaded from the sun by the surrounding steep terrain. The level of the water table then recovered (rose) overnight. The hydrograph for P-202, which was located in the wet meadow, showed the greatest fluctuation in water levels, up to 17 cm daily from October 2003 to 2006. The same periodicity in water level fluctuations was present in the hydrograph for P-203, but the magnitude of the diurnal change was less. This piezometer was located just outside of the wet meadow zone and was probably affected by different soil:plant water relations. The P-201 (sage meadow) hydrograph showed minimal change, but the daily periodicity was still evident. Diurnal fluctuations also were evident in the stage records for the stream and were probably due to a daily decrease in baseflow to the stream from subsurface sources because of evapotranspiration demands.

Water-level elevations were at their highest during the spring snowmelt, which usually occurs in May (fig. 4.16). Water levels decreased throughout the growing season probably due to reduced rainfall in the summer months and the loss of water through increased evapotranspiration. As the growing season ended, water levels increased. Water table elevations also showed a slow increasing trend throughout the period of record (2003 to 2006). This corresponds to the general increase in annual precipitation since the 2000 water year (fig. 4.15b). In addition, the hydrographs showed the influence of storm events on the water table. P-202 and P-203 were responsive to precipitation events because they were located in or near the wet meadow, where the water table is near the ground surface. P-201 was not as responsive to precipitation events because it was located in the sage meadow where the water table depth was greatest. Large precipitation events

Daily water level fluctuations in the hydrographs were minimal or nonexistent during the non-growing season (fig. 4.17). Diurnal fluctuations occurred in piezometer P-202, but the magnitude of change was less than that observed during the growing season. These fluctuations may have been due to evaporation of water from groundwater discharge

USDA Forest Service Gen. Tech. Rep. RMRS-GTR-258. 2011.

57

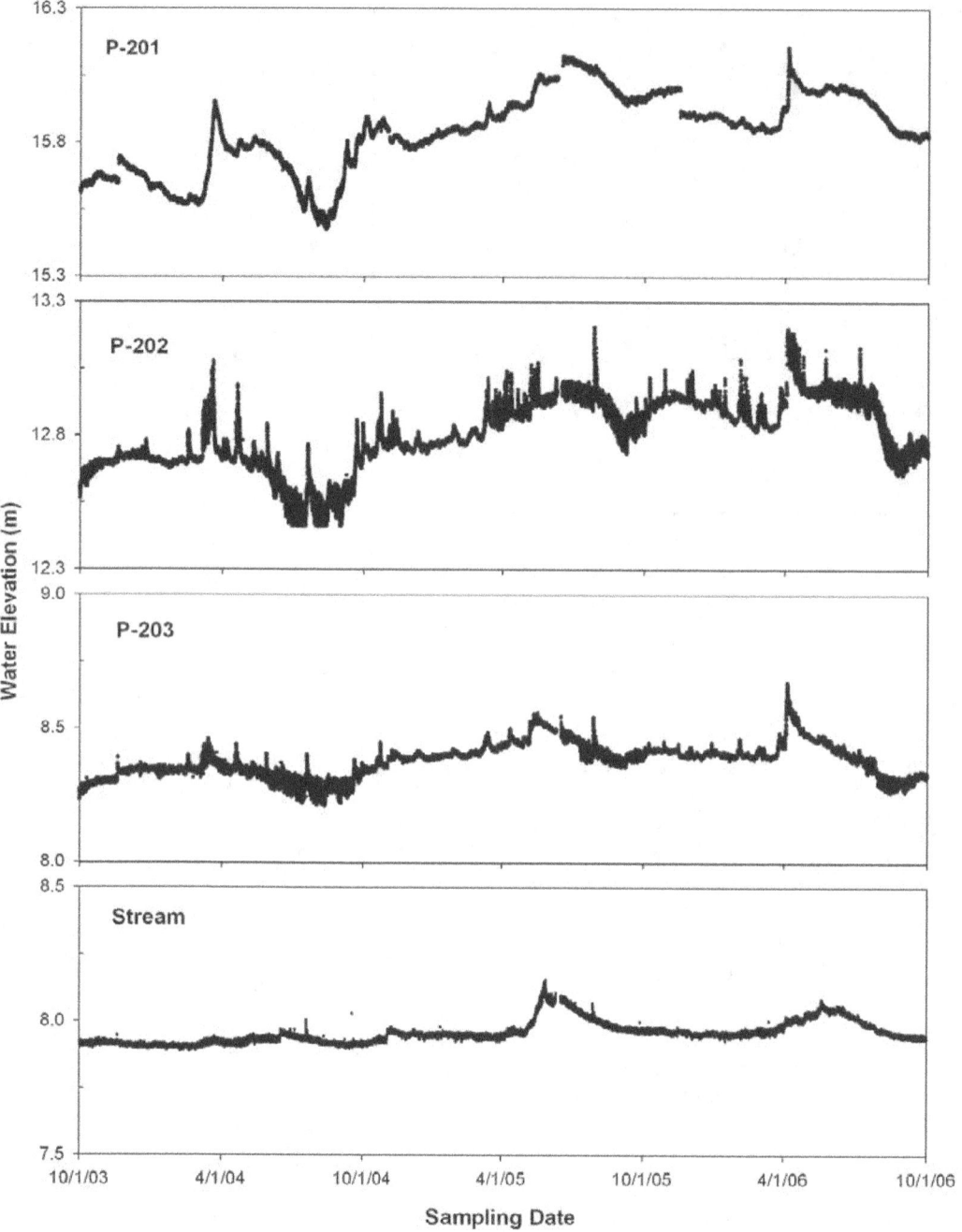

Figure 4.16. Three-year hydrographs for piezometers instrumented with dataloggers in Big Creek meadow.

zones when sunlight was on the wet meadow. Diurnal fluctuations were not observed in the other hydrographs.

The temporal changes in hydrologic processes and patterns at the Big Creek site illustrate the role of multiple variables on meadow conditions. There are predictable seasonal cycles of fluctuations in water table depths that correspond with timing of plant growth cycles, snowmelt runoff, and precipitation. Water level data from four groundwater wells and the creek at Kingston 3 meadow (figs. 4.2 and 4.3) illustrate this pattern. Figure 4.18 shows water level data for the 2005 calendar year that were normalized to percent of maximum water level. That is, all water level data

were recalculated for each well to percent of maximum water level for 2005. For three well locations (101S, 87D, and 33D) and the stream, water levels patterns showed two distinct patterns: rising water levels that were most pronounced from May through June, and falling water levels. While the recession began immediately after maximum water levels for most sites, the water table at the site of well 33D remained high from mid-May to August before declining. The rising stage occurred over a shorter time period than the falling stage. This pattern was especially pronounced at well 33D, where more than 50 percent of the annual rise occurred over a two-week period—a similar pattern to Kingston 3 meadow,

USDA Forest Service Gen. Tech. Rep. RMRS-GTR-258. 2011.

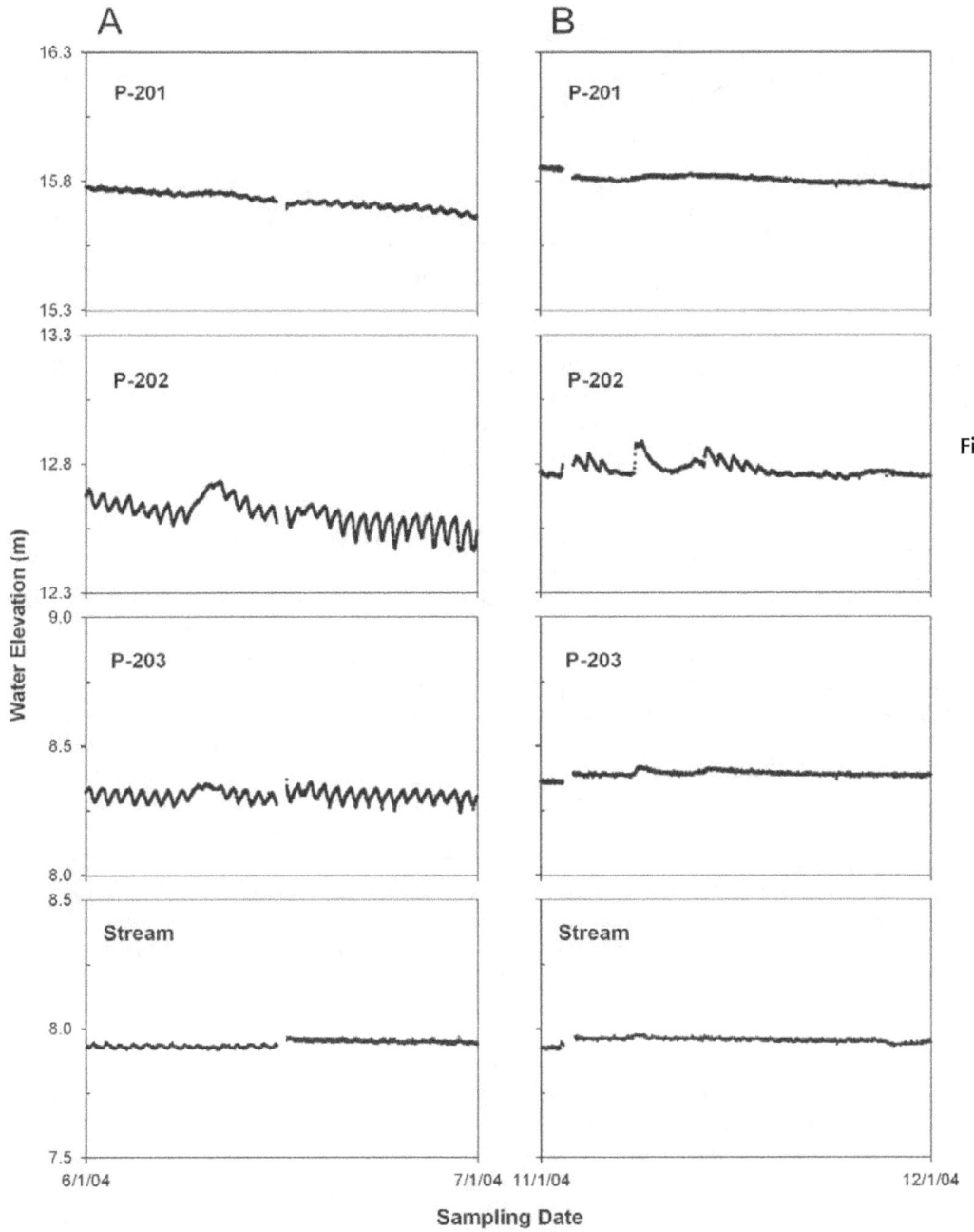

Figure 4.17. Sections of hydrographs in fig. 4.16, illustrating water level fluctuations recorded during (a) a growing season (June 2004) and (b) a non-growing season (November 2004) in Big Creek meadow.

adjacent to the stream. Differences in responses between sites were most likely due to differences in the timing and location of groundwater recharge for different groundwater sources. The short timeframe for the rising portion of the hydrographs suggests that the meadow may be very sensitive to changes that occur in the amount or timing of recharge in the source regions. These general patterns are consistent with studies of groundwater recharge in arid and semi-arid regions, where groundwater recharge through losing streams (that is, stream-focused recharge) is an important process (Constantz and others 2007; Prudic and others 2007). From a management perspective, this suggests that source areas for groundwater recharge need to be considered when evaluating meadows for management activities (Chapter 5).

General Hydrologic Traits of the Study Meadows

In general, the riparian meadow complexes in the mountains of the central Great Basin are groundwater discharge zones with shallow water table depths that commonly have springs, artesian conditions, and perched water tables. However, the specific traits of each meadow may vary widely. These variations result in large part from the stratigraphic and geomorphic conditions that have developed over hundreds to thousands of years along the hillslopes and valley bottoms, but particularly within and immediately adjacent to meadow boundaries. Individual meadow characteristics

USDA Forest Service Gen. Tech. Rep. RMRS-GTR-258. 2011.

59

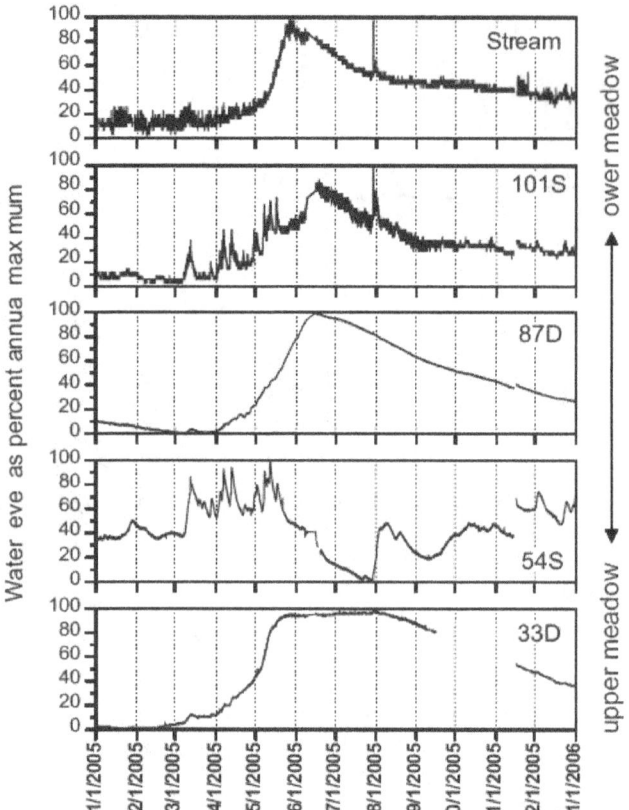

Figure 4.18. Groundwater and stream water level plots showing annual water level patterns as a percent of annual maximum water level in the Kingston 3 meadow. Annual hydrographs for all sites, except well 54S, show a relatively short period of rising levels and a much longer period of declining levels. At the stream and well sites 33 and 87, about three-quarters of the annual rise occurs within one month.

result from the cumulative interplay of vegetation, watershed and stream physical processes, climate, and anthropogenic activities. Despite the variation in meadow conditions and processes, general hydrologic traits are apparent based on observations at the 56 meadows studied.

In about half of the meadows studied, the shallowest water table is located in the center of the valley rather than adjacent to or nearby a stream. This observation is supported by the mapped spring locations and groundwater-dependent wet meadow vegetation. In other meadows, the shallowest water table occurs at the edge of the valley floor against the valley hillslopes and is typically fed by springs or occurs next to shallow streams. Stream channels are present in all meadow complexes, but they vary greatly in size, flow characteristics, bank materials, and the degree to which they affect meadow hydrology.

In many meadow complexes, springs create perennial channels and support shallow groundwater tables. Springs emerge at sharp breaks in slope or where there are heterogeneities in the underlying geology, such as faults (Chapter 2). Springs are present in 75 percent of the meadows, and

20 percent of the meadows have more than 10 mapped springs. They vary in shape, size, and flow rate and range from discrete, bubbling springs at the head of channels (fig. 4.19a), to diffuse seep zones on the valley floor or along channel banks (fig. 4.19b), to piped flow out of exposed banks (fig. 4.19e). Springs often are associated with shallow water tables and wet meadow vegetation unless they have well-developed or incised drainage channels. Springs are important to many wetlands in the Great Basin and in other arid and semi-arid regions (Tooth and McCarthy 2007; Patten and others 2008). Perennial springs in these regions are commonly sustained in part by deep outflow from regional groundwater systems (Anderson and others 2006).

Artesian conditions, where groundwater is under enough pressure to rise above the land surface, have been observed in piezometers of most instrumented meadows (fig. 4.19c). A natural expression of artesian conditions is a bubbling spring on a horizontal ground surface. At the Kingston 3 meadow, three artesian "pipes" have been identified (fig. 4.19f). These pipes are naturally formed vertical shafts that range in diameter from about 15 to 50 cm and that connect the land surface to a confined aquifer (up to 1.5 m deep). The pipes probably formed by erosion of unconsolidated sediments by high-pressure groundwater from an underlying confined aquifer as it worked its way to the surface. Another expression of artesian conditions is a blister or spring mound (Ashley and others 2002; Tooth and McCarthy 2007). Artesian blisters represent areas where very low-permeability soil has blocked and been elevated by an accumulation of upward moving groundwater. Walking on one of these blisters is very much like walking on a waterbed. In the central Great Basin, blisters reach up to 0.5 m in height, are several square meters in area, and have been observed in six meadows.

Perched groundwater conditions are very common in the meadows. Perched conditions occur where shallow groundwater is underlain by a low-permeability layer that is separated by unsaturated materials from the deeper, regional groundwater table. Some meadow complexes (e.g., Johnson and Corcoran; fig. 4.2) are largely supported by perched water tables. Groundwater wells can be used to determine if conditions are perched (fig. 4.20b); however, the presence of a small, shallow stream immediately adjacent to sagebrush often indicates perched conditions in the field (fig. 4.19d). Another indicator of low-permeability layers is how wet and mesic plant communities are distributed in relation to small-scale topography. The Corcoran meadows are blanketed by a fine-grained, low-permeability unit (a paleosol) that maintains the high water table conditions to support wet and mesic communities even on gentle slopes (fig. 4.20a). Low-permeability, buried soils also were shown to play an important role in supporting near-surface water and associated wetland ecosystems in California's central valley (Rains and others 2006).

Stream channels are present in all meadow systems but vary in the degree to which they directly influence meadow water tables and vegetation. In some cases, the effects are negligible, but in others, they are highly significant. Reasons for this variation are differences in the path of the

Figure 4.19. Hydrologic features common to meadows. (a) springs; (b) groundwater seeps along channel sides; (c) artesian conditions (picture of flowing well); (d) perched water table, commonly characterized (as in this photo) by a wet meadow stream immediately adjacent to sage brush; (e) groundwater piping in fine sediments (see flow at arrow); and (f) artesian pipes: photo shows arm down muddy water flowing to surface from confined aquifer.

channel with respect to the meadow, the size of the channel, the nature of the subsurface materials, the interaction with groundwater, and the water source (groundwater, runoff, or both) (Chapter 5). Stream channels produced the deposits in the geologic past that created the hydrologic conditions necessary to support these meadows but do not necessarily control the current hydrologic state of the meadows. The location of meadows is explained by groundwater conditions, but that does not mean that streams are unimportant to the present or, especially, future status of meadows.

An important trait of the relationship of stream channels to meadow hydrology is whether the stream reach is being fed by groundwater (gaining) or is recharging groundwater (losing). In a gaining stream reach, the depth of the water table increases with distance from the stream, whereas the water table depth decreases with distance from a losing stream (figs. 4.10a and b). Riparian vegetation patterns can be used to infer if a stream reach is gaining or losing because groundwater-dependent plant communities can serve as a proxy for average depth to the groundwater table. At the Kingston 3 meadow, the plant communities became drier closer to the stream (fig. 4.21), indicating a gaining stream (an inference supported by groundwater well data). At the Corcoran meadow (fig. 4.20c), the plant communities became drier toward the margins of the valley indicating a losing system.

The significance of stream connection, or control, on the groundwater table can be assessed by comparing vegetation on either side of a stream. In Cottonwood Canyon, the creek has dry vegetation (sage brush) on one side and mesic vegetation (baltic rush) on the other side; this suggests that the groundwater flow direction is from the wetter to the drier side and, importantly, that stream incision has intercepted and lowered the groundwater table (fig. 4.20d). In this case, the stream may have contributed to some loss in the area of wet meadow complexes. Alternatively, some streams do not alter the groundwater flow patterns or table in the meadow, as reflected in the similar plant communities on both sides of the stream (Birch 1; fig. 4.20e). Although these streams have not yet lowered the groundwater table enough to cause shifts in plant community types, future stream incision may affect the groundwater table and plant communities.

Some channels are completely disconnected from the groundwater under most conditions as they do not support perennial streams. These channels, such as in lower Indian Valley, are typically larger than perennial spring channels (fig. 4.20e) and have developed to convey seasonal discharge typically associated with snowmelt runoff (fig. 4.20f). Most of the time, these channels have little affect on groundwater because the channel bed is well above the water table. When they do transmit runoff, they are sites of stream-focused groundwater recharge (Constantz and others 2007).

USDA Forest Service Gen. Tech. Rep. RMRS-GTR-258. 2011.

61

Figure 4.20. Photographs display meadow traits that reflect hydrologic characteristics and interrelationships between vegetation, hydrogeologic setting, and stream channel. (a) Wet meadow vegetation occurrence over slopes reflects a continuous blanket of near-surface, fine-grained sediments. This is comon in meadows with perched water tables. (b) Perched water table supporting wet meadow complex; yellow line marks a dry, groundwater well that is set in saturated meadow soils. (c) A losing stream is indicated by wet meadow species centered in the meadow with successively drier vegetation types away from the meadow axis. (d) Channel incision has caused a drop in the water table on left bank, as indicated by sage; because groundwater flow is from right to left, the water table on the right bank has been less affected. (e) Minor channel incision has had no significant effect on groundwater, as indicated by wet meadow vegetation on both banks. (f) Dry, bouldery channel is a seasonal runoff channel, mostly from snow melt, that has little relationship to the groundwater hydrology that supports the adjacent meadow.

Creation of new channels or enlargement of existing channels can partly or completely degrade the hydrologic framework necessary to support a meadow. Stream incision and subsequent channel adjustments can occur over a few years to decades, with subsequent effects on both water table depths and vegetation. Thus, an important consideration in evaluating the effects of streams on meadows is to determine whether the present-day stream is connected to the meadow and, if the stream is actively incising, how groundwater hydrology may change.

Springs, artesian conditions, and perched water tables in meadows of the central Great Basin indicate the presence of heterogeneous geologic materials that cause complex groundwater conditions. The typical meadow has a geologic setting with complex stratigraphy characterized by strongly contrasting hydraulic conductivities and high hydraulic gradients. Consequently, any changes in the meadow systems, whether by streams, people, or climate, are likely to result in a complex response that may vary from meadow to meadow or even within one meadow.

Approach for Assessing the Hydrologic Status of Meadows

A general assessment of the current status of meadows can be made based on the hydrogeologic setting, groundwater sources, the occurrence and effects of stream incision, and stream-subsurface water interactions. Table 3.2 illustrates the use of field indicators to characterize six meadow complexes that were evaluated in this study. Part of this assessment was based on using meadow vegetation patterns to interpret hydrologic characteristics. This approach was justified by the strong relationship between plant community type and depth to groundwater table (figs. 4.1a and b and 4.21; Allen-Diaz 1991; Chambers and others 2004; Jewett and others 2004). In

62

USDA Forest Service Gen. Tech. Rep. RMRS-GTR-258. 2011.

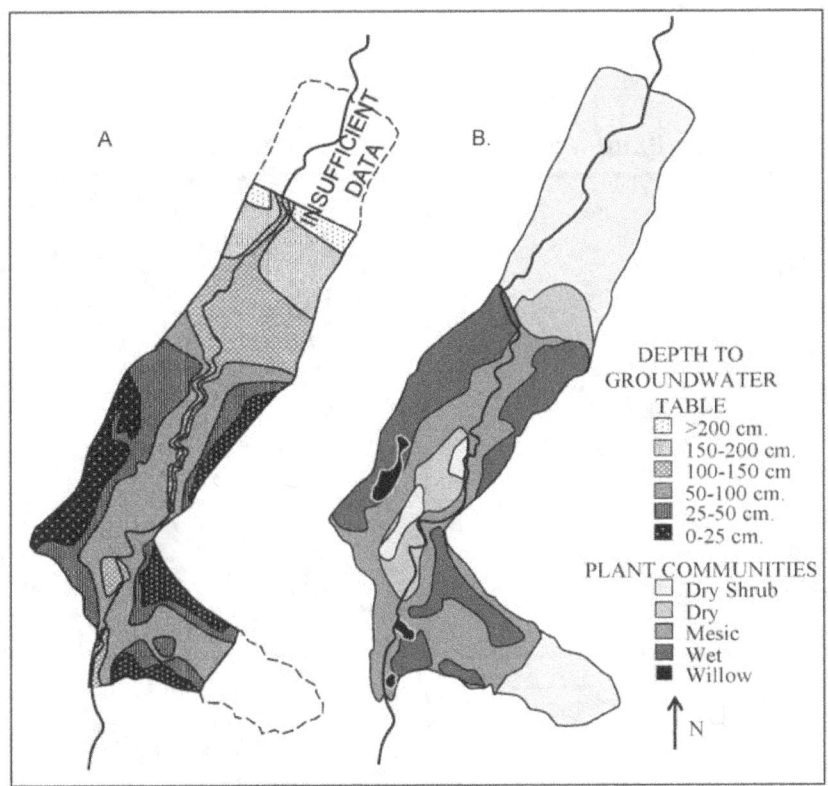

Figure 4.21. Maps of the Kingston 3 meadow; downstream is south. (a) Depth of groundwater table below ground. (b) Plant communities. The depth to groundwater is shallowest at the valley sides and is deepest upvalley and adjacent to the stream. In general, the vegetation and depth to water table patterns are very similar, especially where the water table is most shallow.

DEPTH TO
GROUNDWATER
TABLE
- >200 cm.
- 150-200 cm.
- 100-150 cm
- 50-100 cm.
- 25-50 cm.
- 0-25 cm.

PLANT COMMUNITIES
- Dry Shrub
- Dry
- Mesic
- Wet
- Willow

N

some cases, interpretation of the relationship can be complicated by the lag in time for certain vegetation types to adjust to new hydrologic conditions. For this and other reasons, these assessment examples are not intended to substitute for field work with detailed observations. However, the examples demonstrate that important inferences regarding meadow processes can be made based on relatively simple field observations of vegetation patterns, stream characteristics, and the locations and types of springs.

Kingston 3 (table 4.2, trait E) is an example of a meadow system with complex stratigraphy and an incised stream, which have caused some meadow degradation. This meadow complex is located upstream of an alluvial fan and has a complex geologic setting and discontinuous stratigraphy with highly variable permeability. Stream incision has resulted in a drop in the water table adjacent to the stream and, as previously noted, the stream is gaining through much of the meadow. An increase in the depth to the water table adjacent to the stream has resulted in conversion from wet to mesic or dry meadow vegetation and, in some locations, encroachment of sagebrush (fig. 4.21). Wet meadow communities are associated with springs at the edges of the valley floor or side-valley alluvial fans, and artesian conditions are common. Although meadow vegetation in Kingston 3 appears largely adjusted to the current hydrologic regime, a lag in the response of long-lived riparian species like *Juncus balticus* and *Iris missouriensis* often occurs after stream incision (Chambers and others 2004). Also, because stream incision and subsequent channel adjustments can continue over years to decades (or longer), interpreting the relationships between

water table depths and meadow vegetation requires accounting for the degree and activity of incision and determining the traits of the stream connection to the meadow hydrology.

In contrast to Kingston 3, Birch 1 (table 4.2, trait B) is a meadow system with simple stratigraphy that has been minimally degraded by stream incision. This meadow complex is located upvalley of a bedrock constriction and has largely continuous geologic units. The groundwater sources are from the upstream axial valley fill and side-valley areas that include numerous springs in the northeast portion of the meadow. The water table is largely perched in the down-valley portion of the meadow, which is capped by a low-permeability sediment/soil layer. The side-valley tributary is incised through much of the upper portion of the meadow and has caused a shift to drier meadow vegetation in that area. In contrast, despite over 1 m of incision in the main channel, there has been little affect on water table and vegetation, probably because of the perched water table.

Summary of Meadow Hydrologic Processes and Properties

The meadow complexes of the central Great Basin are groundwater-dependent ecosystems that, in some cases, are threatened by stream incision. In general, the headwater zones of watersheds that support meadow ecosystems are groundwater recharge areas, and groundwater recharge often occurs along the bed of losing streams primarily during seasonal snow melt. The meadows down-valley are

USDA Forest Service Gen. Tech. Rep. RMRS-GTR-258. 2011.

63

Table 4.2. Types of meadow complexes in the central Great Basin. The left column describes key hydrologic characteristics and the current relationship of the stream to meadow hydrology and vegetation patterns. The middle and right columns show a map of the plant communities in the meadow and an aerial photograph of the meadow, respectively.

Meadow Traits	Meadow Plant Map	Meadow Aerial Photograph
A. Simple, Not Degraded by Stream Hydrogeologic Setting • bedrock constriction • continuous geologic units Hydrology • GW source is down valley • springs common in low permeability sediment layer Stream Connections • gaining • incision has little effect on GW & vegetation patterns	 N 50 m	 BARLEY TRIB
B. Simple, Minimally Degraded by Stream Hydrogeologic Setting • bedrock constriction • continuous geologic units Hydrology • GW source is down & side valley • springs common in low permeability sediment layer • perched GW table downmeadow Stream Connections • gaining some; perched some • >1 m of incision has little effect on GW & vegetation patterns	 100 m N	 BIRCH 1
C. Simple, Stream Degraded Hydrogeologic Setting • downstream valley constriction & alluvial fan Hydrology • GW source is center and down valley • artesian conditions and springs common Stream Connections • gaining • incision has likely breached confined aquifer and has effected riparian GW & vegetation patterns	 50 m N	 BARLEY 1

Table 4.2 continued.

D. Complex; Minimally Degraded by Stream

<u>Hydrogeologic Setting</u>
- Draped, old alluvial fans
- dominantly fine-grained geologic units

<u>Hydrology</u>
- GW source is down valley & center valley upwelling
- perched water tables

<u>Stream Connections</u>
- losing, perched
- incision has had little effect on GW & vegetation patterns

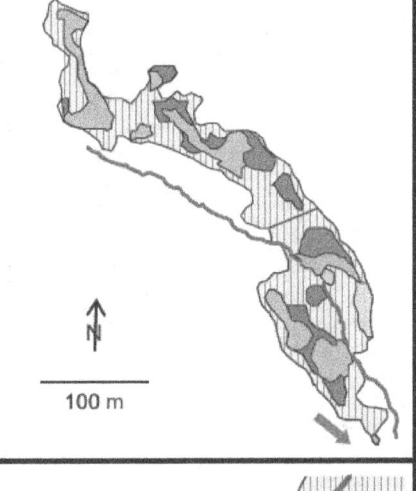

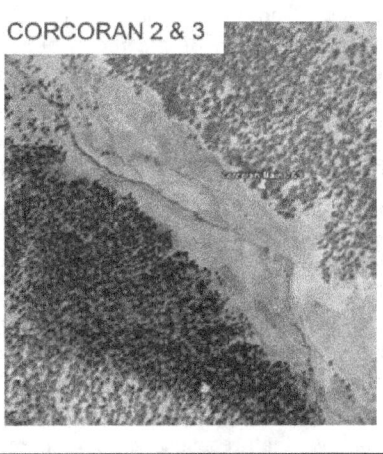

CORCORAN 2 & 3

100 m

E. Complex, Stream Degraded

<u>Hydrogeologic Setting</u>
- upstream of alluvial fan
- complex geologic setting
- discontinuous hydrogeologic units with high variability in permeability

<u>Hydrology</u>
- GW source is valley sides and springs
- artesian conditions common

<u>Stream Connections</u>
- gaining overall
- incision has effected riparian GW & vegetation patterns

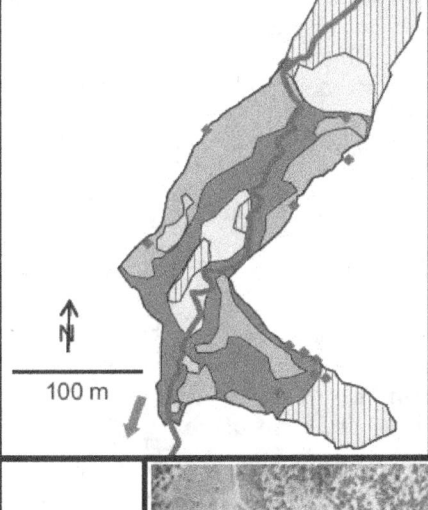

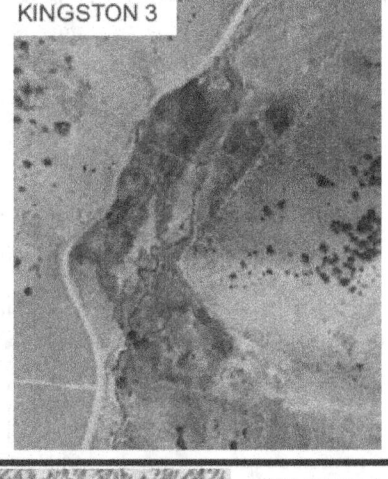

KINGSTON 3

100 m

F. Complex, Degraded by Stream

<u>Hydrogeologic Setting</u>
- upstream of alluvial fan
- heterogeneous geologic units

<u>Hydrology</u>
- GW source mostly side valley
- few springs

<u>Stream Connections</u>
- gaining
- incision has altered GW & vegetation patterns
- GW support for most meadows on valley floor is lost

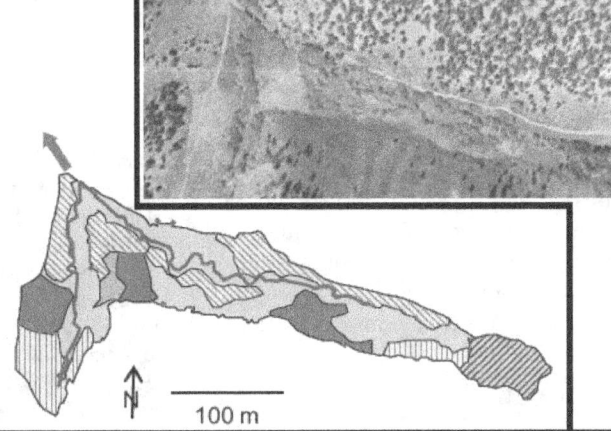

SAN JUAN 1

100 m

Legend: Plant Communities and Water Features

	Wet		Mesic Shrub		Dry Shrub		Willow
	Mesic		Dry		Rose Shrub		Aspen
	Upland Plants	◆	Spring		Stream		Stream Flow

USDA Forest Service Gen. Tech. Rep. RMRS-GTR-258. 2011.

65

discharge areas, although some stream channel reaches vary between gaining and losing over short distances or among seasons. The hydrologic regime exerts primary control on riparian meadow complexes and is strongly influenced by past and present geomorphic processes; biotic processes; and, in some cases, anthropogenic activities. There is a variety of specific geologic and geomorphic settings that create the shallow water tables necessary to support wet meadow vegetation, but a pervasive trait is the occurrence of low-permeability, fine-grained sediments in the down-valley portion of the meadow.

In most meadows, the shallowest part of the water table is at the valley margins or in the central part of the valley floor and is not adjacent to a stream channel. Springs, artesian conditions, and perched water tables are common meadow features, especially in meadows underlain by complex stratigraphy. Stream- and groundwater levels vary during the growing season at daily scales, among seasons with the highest water tables during summer, and over years with weather patterns and climatic change. Meadow plant communities occur along gradients that are controlled by the depth of the water table and, thus, are key indicators of the hydrogeologic setting of meadows.

Stream channels are present in all meadows but vary in the degree that they influence meadow water tables and vegetation. Stream incision lowers groundwater tables; causes shifts in vegetation from wetter to drier species; changes groundwater flow paths; and, in extreme cases, causes permanent loss of meadow complexes. The specific response of the water table and vegetation to stream incision varies greatly with groundwater budgets, hydraulic conductivity of sediments, stream processes, and stratigraphy. The geomorphic and hydrologic characteristics of individual meadows vary considerably, and effective management and restoration requires a basic understanding of their hydrogeomorphic settings, especially the connectedness of groundwater systems with stream channels. Research on the meadows in the central Great Basin provides the necessary information for managers to assess the key hydrologic traits of meadow ecosystems and the relationships among the hydrogeomorphic setting, the stream channel, and the vegetation communities. For example, complex vegetation patterns along a stream channel likely indicate stratigraphic complexity where stream incision has significantly lowered the water table.

References

Allen-Diaz, Barbara H. 1991. Water table and plant species relationships in Sierra Nevada meadows. American Midland Naturalist. 126: 30-43.

Anderson, K.; Nelson, S.; Mayo, A.; Tingey, D. 2006. Interbasin flow revisited: the contribution of local recharge to high-discharge springs, Death Valley, CA. Journal of Hydrology. 323: 276-302.

Ashley, G.M.; Goman, M.; Hover, V.; Owen, B.R.; Renaut, R.W.; Muasya, A.M. 2002. Artesian blister wetlands, a perennial water resource in the semi-arid rift valley of east Africa. Wetlands 22: 686-695.

Castelli, R.M.; Chambers, J.C.; Tausch, R.J. 2000. Soil-plant relations along a soil-water gradient in Great Basin riparian meadows. Wetlands. 20: 251-266.

Chambers, J.C.; Miller, J.R., eds. 2004. Great Basin Riparian Ecosystems—Ecology, Management, and Restoration. Covello, CA: Island Press. 304 p.

Chambers, J.C.; Tausch, R.J.; Korfmacher, J.L.; Miller, J.R.; Jewett, D.G. 2004. Effects of geomorphic processes and hydrologic regimes on riparian vegetation. In: Chambers, J.C.; Miller, J.R., eds. Great Basin Riparian Ecosystems—Ecology, Management, and Restoration. Covelo, CA: Island Press: 196-231.

Constantz, J. 1998. Interaction between stream temperature, streamflow, and groundwater exchanges in alpine streams. Water Resources Research. 34: 1609-1615.

Constantz, J.; Adams, K.S.; Stonestrom, D.A. 2007. Overview of ground-water recharge study sites—Chapter C. In: Stonestrom, D.A.; Constantz, J.; Ferré, T.P.A.; Leake, S.A. Ground-water recharge in the arid and semiarid southwestern United States. U.S. Geological Survey Professional Paper. 1703: 61-82.

Devito, K.; Creed, I.; Gan, T.; Mendoza, C.; Petrone, R.; Silins, U.; Smerdon, B. 2005. A framework for broad-scale classification of hydrologic response units on the Boreal Plain: is topography the last thing to consider? Hydrological Processes. 19(8): 1705-1714.

Dwire, K.A.; Kauffman, J.B.; Baham, J.E. 2006. Plant species distribution in relation to water-table depth and soil redox potential in montane riparian meadows. Wetlands. 26: 1.

Germanoski, D.; Miller, J.R. 2004. Basin sensitivity to channel incision in response to natural and anthropogenic disturbance. In: Chambers, J.C.; Miller, J.R., eds. Great Basin Riparian Ecosystems—Ecology, Management, and Restoration. Covello, CA: Island Press: 88-123.

Hunt, R.J.; Strand, M.; Walker, J.F. 2006. Measuring groundwater–surface water interaction and its effect on wetland stream benthic productivity, Trout Lake watershed, northern Wisconsin, USA. Journal of Hydrology. 320: 370-384.

Jewett, D.G.; Lord, M.L.; Miller, J.R.; Chambers, J.C. 2004. Geomorphic and hydrologic controls on surface and subsurface flow regimes in riparian meadow ecosystems. In: Chambers, J.C.; Miller, J.R., eds. Great Basin Riparian Ecosystems—Ecology, Management, and Restoration. Covello, CA: Island Press: 124-161.

Kalbus, E.; Reinstorf, E.; Schirmer, M. 2006. Measuring methods for groundwater-surface water interactions. Hydrology and Earth System Sciences Discussions. 10: 873-887.

Kleinhampl, F.J.; Ziony, J.I. 1985. Geology of northern Nye County, Nevada. Nevada Bureau of Mines and Geology Bulletin 99A. 172 p.

Martin, D.W.; Chambers, J.C. 2001. Effects of water table, clipping, and species interactions on *Carex nebrascensis* and *Poa pratensis* in riparian meadows. Wetlands. 21: 422-430.

Maurer, D.K.; Lopes, T.J.; Medina, R.L.; Smith, J.L. 2004. Hydrogeology and hydrologic landscape regions of Nevada. U.S. Geological Survey Scientific Investigations Report 2004-5131. 41 p.

Mifflin, M.D. 1988. Region 5, Great Basin. In: Back, W.; Rosenshein, J.S.; Seaber, P.R., eds. Hydrogeology, the geology of North America, Vol. O-2. Boulder, CO: Geological Society of America: 69-78.

Miller, J.R.; Germanoski, D.; Waltman, K.; Tausch, R.; Chambers, J. 2001. Influence of late Holocene hillslope processes and landforms on modern channel dynamics in upland watersheds of central Nevada. Geomorphology. 38: 373-391.

66

USDA Forest Service Gen. Tech. Rep. RMRS-GTR-258. 2011.

Montgomery, D. 1999. Erosional processes at an abrupt channel head: implications for channel entrenchment and discontinuous gully formation. In: Darby, S.E.; Simon, A., eds. Incised River Channels. New York: John Wiley and Sons: 247-276.

Newman, B.D.; Vivoni, E.R.; Groffman, A.R. 2006. Surface water-groundwater interactions in semiarid drainages of the American southwest. Hydrological Processes. 20: 3371-3394.

Patten, D.T.; Rouse, L.; Stromberg, J.C. 2008. Isolated spring wetlands in the Great Basin and Mojave Deserts, USA: potential response of vegetation to groundwater withdrawal. Environmental Management. 41: 398-413.

Plume, R.W. 1996. Hydrogeologic framework of the Great Basin region of Nevada, Utah, and adjacent states. U.S. Geological Survey Professional Paper 1409-B. 64 p.

Prudic, D.E.; Niswonger, R.G.; Harrill, J.R.; Woods, J.L. 2007. Streambed infiltration and ground-water flow from the Trout Creek Drainage, an intermittent tributary to the Humboldt River, north-central Nevada—Chapter K. In: Stonestrom, D.A.; Constantz, J.; Ferré, T.P.A.; Leake, S.A., eds. Ground-water recharge in the arid and semiarid southwestern United States. U.S. Geological Survey Professional Paper. 1703: 313-351.

Rains, M.C.; Fogg, G.E.; Harter, T.; Dahlgren, R.A.; Williamson, R.J. 2006. The role of perched aquifers in hydrological connectivity and biogeochemical processes in vernal pool landscapes, Central Valley, California. Hydrological Processes. 20: 1157-1175.

Stonestrom, D.A.; Constantz, J.; Ferré, T.P.A.; Leake, S.A. eds. 2007. Ground-water recharge in the arid and semiarid southwestern United States. U.S. Geological Survey Professional Paper 1703.

Sturtevant, K.A. 2007. Integrating multiple geophysical methods to analyze geologic controls of riparian meadow complexes, Central Great Basin, NV. Department of Geology, State University of New York at Buffalo. Thesis. 378 p.

Tennant, C.; Morgan, V.; Means, C.; Lord, M.L.; Jewett, D.G. 2006. Hydrogeologic setting and characteristics of riparian meadow complexes in the mountains of central Nevada: a case study. Geological Society of America Abstracts with Programs Vol. 38. Paper 9-5.

Tooth, S.; McCarthy, T.S. 2007. Wetlands in drylands: geomorphological and sedimentological characteristics, with emphasis on examples from southern Africa. Progress in Physical Geography. 31(3): 3-41.

Wanty, R.B.; Winter, T.C. 2000. A simple device for measuring differences in hydraulic head between surface water and shallow ground water. U.S. Geological Survey Fact Sheet FS-077-00. 2 p.

Weissmann, G.S.; Zhang, Y.; Fogg, G.E.; Mount, J.F. 2004. Influence of incised-valley-fill deposits on hydrogeology of a stream-dominated alluvial fan. Society of Sedimentary Geology Special Publication No. 80: 15-28.

Weixelman, D.A.; Zamudio, D.C.; Zamudio, K.A. 1996. Central Nevada riparian field guide. R4-ECOL-TP. Ogden, UT: U.S. Department of Agriculture, Forest Service, Intermountain Region.

Wilson, J.L.; Guan, H. 2004. Mountain-block hydrology and mountain-front recharge. In. Phillips, F.M.; Hogan, J.; Scanlon, B., eds. Groundwater recharge in a desert environment: the southwestern United States. Washington, DC: American Geophysical Union. 23 p.

Winter, T.C. 1999. Relation of streams, lakes, and wetlands to groundwater flow systems. Hydrogeology Journal. 7: 28-45.

Winter, T.C. 2001. The concept of hydrologic landscapes. Journal of American Water Resources Association. 37(2): 335-349.

Winter, T.C. ed. 2004. Hydrological, chemical, and biological characteristics of a prairie pothole wetland complex under highly variable climate conditions—the Cottonwood Lake area, east-central North Dakota. U.S. Geological Survey Professional Paper 1675. 109 p.

Winter, T.C. 2007. The role of ground water in generating streamflow in headwater areas and in maintaining base flow. Journal of the American Water Resources Association. 43(1): 15-25.

Winter, T.C.; Harvey, J.W.; Franke, O.L.; Alley, W.M. 1998. Ground water and surface water: a single resource. U.S. Geological Survey Circular 1139.

USDA Forest Service Gen. Tech. Rep. RMRS-GTR-258. 2011.

67

Chapter 5:   Meadow Sensitivity to Natural and Anthropogenic Disturbance

Jerry R. Miller, Mark L. Lord, and Dru Germanoski

Introduction

Investigations of geomorphic responses to natural and anthropogenic disturbances have revealed marked differences in the rate, magnitude, and nature by which different watersheds, or components of a given watershed, adjust to perturbations. These differences in response are often characterized using the concept of landform sensitivity. The term sensitivity has been defined by different investigators in different ways. For our purposes, it is defined after Brunsden and Thornes (1979) as "the likelihood that a given change in the controls of the system will produce a sensible, recognizable, and persistent response [in the landform of interest]." Inherent in this definition is the tendency for a stream, stream reach, or other landform to respond to an environmental disturbance by going through a period of disequilibrium until a new equilibrium state is achieved (Germanoski and Miller 2004).

Conceptually, sensitivity is thought to involve several distinct components, two of which are (1) the propensity for change as governed by a set of driving and resisting forces, and (2) the capacity of the system to absorb change and remain in an equilibrium state (Downs and Gregory 1993). The rate of change also is important because while a stream or stream reach may be unstable (that is, in a disequilibrium state), it may exhibit a low propensity for change if the driving and resisting forces are such that adjustments occur at a slow rate. Germanoski and Miller (2004) show that for upland watersheds in central Nevada, each of these three components is important. For example, all of the examined basins were found to have incised in response to changes in climate and other perturbations following a major aggradational event between approximately 1980 and 2580 YBP. Watersheds such as Barley (Group 2, table 2.1) quickly adjusted to a new equilibrium state. This process involved rapid incision and profile adjustment with limited influence by side-valley fans. Group 2 channels now possess a low to moderate propensity for change because they have already attained a relatively stable state in comparison to other watersheds in the region. Presumably, they also are better able to absorb the potential effects of future disturbances. Other watersheds also exhibited a low to moderate sensitivity to change (Group 3, table 2.1). However, in contrast to Group 2 basins, the likelihood of change in Group 3 basins is limited by the inability of the driving forces to overcome the forces that resist change at side-valley fans. This is in spite of the stair-step-like nature of the channel's longitudinal profiles (caused by side-valley fans) that place the channels in an inherently unstable condition. Thus, the low to moderate

sensitivity of the catchments in Group 3 is based on the very slow rate of change that occurs there.

The concept of sensitivity can be a powerful management tool as it provides insights into (1) the likelihood that a given river or meadow will respond to future disturbances; (2) the timing, duration, rate, and nature of the response; and (3) the potential for a given system to be stabilized or restored (Downs and Gregory 2004; Germanoski and Miller 2004). The concept not only applies to geomorphology but also to system hydrology and biota. In this chapter, we examine the sensitivity of meadow complexes within upland basins of central Nevada in terms of site geomorphology and hydrology.

Geomorphic Sensitivity

Overview

The most important geomorphic processes within meadow ecosystems are incision, gully development and its associated headcut migration, groundwater sapping, and avulsion (Chapter 3). The rate, magnitude, and frequency of these processes are governed by numerous factors that must be considered in the analysis of meadow sensitivity to disturbance. Quantification of the combined effects of these processes for the purposes of creating predictive models of meadow sensitivity is a complicated and difficult task that must be undertaken on a meadow-by-meadow basis. These complications result from the following factors:

(1) The parameters that control meadow sensitivity function over different temporal and spatial scales. Incision, for instance, is closely tied to both sediment supply and the ability of flood flows to entrain and transport sediment. Thus, the geomorphic sensitivity of a meadow is closely related to the magnitude of runoff for a given frequency of event. The magnitude of runoff is associated with the amount and rate at which water can be funneled through the drainage network to a meadow and is influenced by factors like upstream basin area, relief, absolute elevation, ruggedness, drainage density, geology, and vegetation cover. If no other controls were present, meadow sensitivity would likely decrease from Group 1 to Group 5 (table 2.1) and could be fully characterized by basin morphometry and its effects on precipitation-runoff relations. However, local factors including channel gradients, valley slope and widths, and localized groundwater discharge via springs and bank seepage may either increase or decrease the geomorphic sensitivity of meadows (see

Chapters 3 and 4 for a discussion of the parameters that control these factors). Quantification of meadow sensitivity therefore requires the integration of processes that operate over spatial scales ranging from the entire basin to a channel cross section, a process that is conceptually and mathematically challenging.

(2) Sensitivity is controlled by the interaction of multiple reach-scale parameters that produce non-linear variations in process rates. Moreover, an increase or decrease in one variable may or may not have a strong influence on meadow sensitivity, depending on the nature of other parameters. Take, for instance, channel slope. A 2 percent increase in slope immediately downstream of a meadow (as is commonly found) tends to promote channel incision because higher gradients increase the erosive capability of flood flows, provided the other controlling factors are equal. However, in addition to slope, meadow sensitivity depends on such factors as bed material size and composition, water availability, and the frequency and magnitude of runoff events. Thus, meadow sensitivity cannot be determined on the basis of a single parameter, such as slope, but must include an analysis of multiple parameters and their interactions.

(3) Geomorphic processes that are of most importance in dictating meadow sensitivity are controlled by multiple mechanisms of landform change, which vary spatially over the meadow complex. For example, incision typically involves the grain-by-grain entrainment and transport of sediment as well as the development and migration of knickpoints or headcuts. The rate, magnitude, and nature of these processes vary along the meadows, in part, as a function of the underlying composition of the valley fill. Thus, quantitative predictions of future incision require detailed analyses of both mechanisms of incision and

their interactions for a given material type, a particularly difficult task given that the sediments that underly meadows often change unpredictably.

(4) Meadows are subjected to abrupt shifts through time in the predominant geomorphic processes operating at the site. These process shifts cannot be easily predicted and are dependent on the timing and frequency of major hydrologic events. For example, unincised valley floors were observed to be initially dissected by the erosion of individual particles. As gully depth increased, there was often an abrupt change in the mechanism of incision from the entrainment of individual clasts to one of headcut migration controlled by groundwater-influenced, mass wasting processes. Additional shifts in process occurred during extreme flood events as groundwater-controlled headcut advancement was overridden by plunge pool development, headcut undermining and failure, and sediment removal by surface flows.

Given the above considerations, a *quantitative* assessment of meadow sensitivity to geomorphic change is challenging and requires a detailed analysis of the meadow system. However, as pointed out by Pilkey and Pilkey-Jarvis (2007), a *qualitative* understanding of the physical processes that are operating in a system often can be used to more effectively develop sound management strategies than quantitative models that may dramatically simplify the system or represent outliers of developed empirical trends.

Here, we highlight the primary factors that control meadow sensitivity and how a qualitative analysis of those factors (summarized in fig. 5.1 and table 5.1) can be used to predict the overall geomorphic sensitivity of meadows. The intent is not to develop a system that can replace the need for detailed geomorphic, hydrologic, or biotic analyses of a site. Rather, the goal is to provide a checklist of parameters that

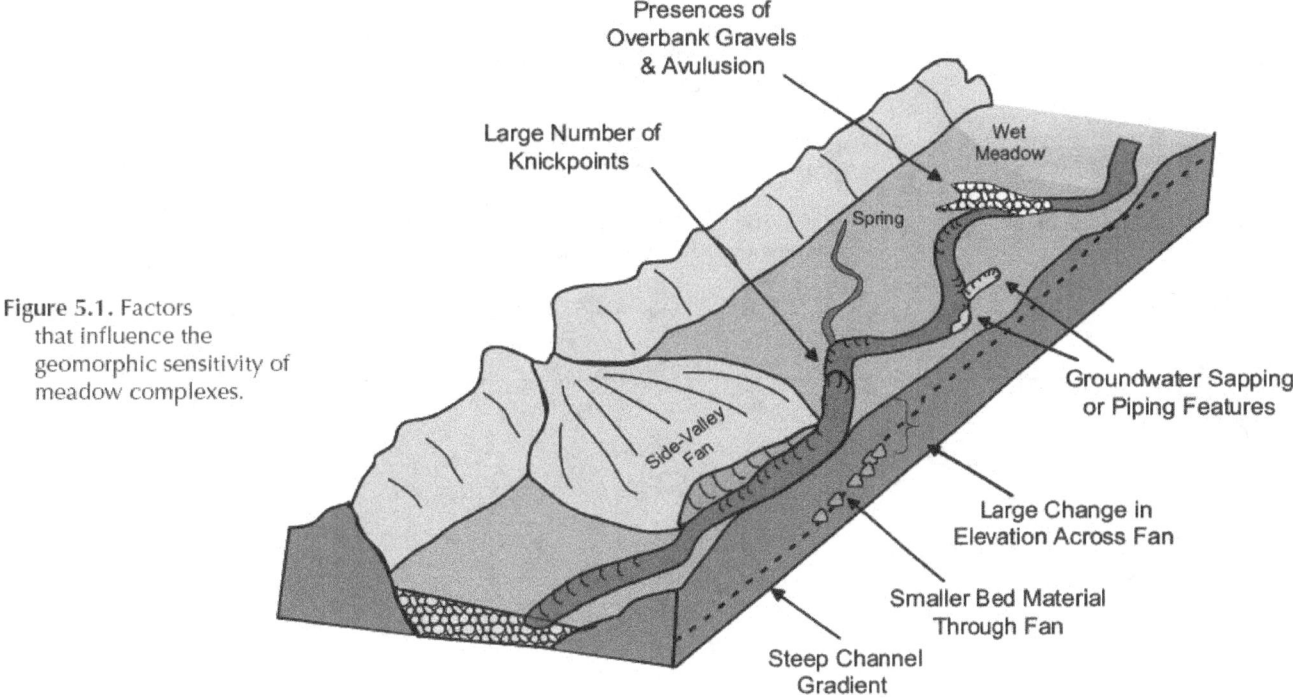

Figure 5.1. Factors that influence the geomorphic sensitivity of meadow complexes.

Presences of Overbank Gravels & Avulusion

Large Number of Knickpoints

Wet Meadow

Spring

Side-Valley Fan

Groundwater Sapping or Piping Features

Large Change in Elevation Across Fan

Smaller Bed Material Through Fan

Steep Channel Gradient

USDA Forest Service Gen. Tech. Rep. RMRS-GTR-258. 2011.

69

Table 5.1. Factors influencing the geomorphic sensitivity of meadow systems.

Factors	Factors Contributing to Sensitive Meadows
Sensitivity to incision, headcut migration, and groundwater sapping	
Water availability	
–Basin characteristics	Large basins, high relief, significant catchment area at high elevations (>3000 m), high ruggedness numbers and drainage densities, impermeable geological materials such as volcanic rocks
–Groundwater discharge	Numerous, high discharge springs feeding spring channels; upward flow gradients and artesian conditions
Flow convergence	
–Valley width	Narrow valleys that abruptly decrease in width down-valley causing groundwater and surface water convergence
–Anthropogenic structures	Berms, dams, and other features that may lead to highly concentrated (channelized) flow on meadow surface
–Linear features	Cattle trails, roads, and other linear features that are devoid of vegetation and may capture and concentrate runoff
Gradients	
–Profile convexities	Occurrence of large convexities in long profile, which cause channel instabilities
–Channel/valley floor	Abrupt increases in channel or valley gradient, particularly through side-valley fans or other profile convexities
Composition of valley fill	
–Channel	Decrease in size of the channel bed material; an exception is the occurrence of highly resistant, clay-rich units commonly associated with paleosols
–Undissected valley floors	Valley fill composed of coarse sand and granules (grus) commonly associated with quartz monzonites and diorites; highly susceptible to erosion and groundwater sapping during rare, high-magnitude runoff events
Knickpoints/headcuts	
–Occurrence	Frequent knickpoints or headcuts, particularly within meadow
–Advancement mechanism	Knickpoints or headcuts advancing by plunge-pool formation, undermining, and failure (most sensitive); groundwater driven mass wasting; sapping (seepage erosion), especially where valley fill is highly permeable
–Surface flow	High probability of receiving surface flows; headcuts fed by shallow channels, roads, cattle trails, or other flow concentrators
–Groundwater; seepage	Higher water tables and pore pressures; layered stratigraphy containing units of highly contrasting permeabilities
–Material composition	Sandy units with higher rates of headcut retreat; clay-rich units sensitive to groundwater piping and locally extensive surface incision of meadows

 USDA Forest Service Gen. Tech. Rep. RMRS-GTR-258. 2011.

Table 5.1. *Continued.*

Factors	Factors Contributing to Sensitive Meadows
Sensitivity to avulsion	
Sediment availability –Geomorphic instabilities	Numerous zones of upstream sediment influx to channel, including areas of mass wasting on hillslopes or trenching of side-valley fans
–Beaver dams	Numerous beaver dams, storage of large volumes of coarse (gravel-sized) sediment
–Anthropogenic features	Anthropogenic features such as roads that may supply and funnel large volumes of sediment to channel; physical connectivity to channel is very important to sediment delivery
Gradients/transport capability	Low-gradient zones, particularly where gradients decrease abruptly or where loss of water results in a loss of flow competence
Channel depths	Shallow channels or zones characterized by distributary network as upstream channels enter meadows
Resistance to flow (roughness) –Vegetation	Increases in roughness associated with riparian or in-channel vegetation, particularly willows
–Structures	Downstream increases in roughness associated with the construction of in-stream structures or other features
Spring channels	Increases in frequency of spring channels which may capture overbank flood waters and promote channel capture

can be rapidly evaluated by land managers to identify the sensitivity of meadows that may or may not be suitable for treatments aimed at reducing the magnitude or rate at which a given geomorphic process negatively impacts a meadow. Those meadows where mitigating the impacts of geomorphic processes appears plausible in terms of their sensitivity to change will require more detailed assessments prior to the selection and implementation of any physical treatment method (e.g., the installation of in-stream structures, bank protection devices, or channel reconstructions).

Geomorphic Sensitivity to Incision

Longitudinal profiles along trunk valleys of upland watersheds show that axial streams possess a stair-step-like morphology in which low-gradient reaches form the step tread and high-gradient reaches form the riser (fig. 5.2). Meadows are frequently located along the low-gradient

reaches or tread of these topographic steps (figs. 5.2). These steps or convexities in the profile form zones of instability that are prone to incision or gully development (Chapter 3). If a convexity exists, the meadow will likely incise at some time in the future. The potential magnitude of incision is dictated by the size (height) of the convexity, which is defined by the difference in elevation between the channel bed (or valley floor) and a uniformly sloping profile that is projected along the upstream channel bed (or valley floor) through the convexity at the downstream terminus (fig. 5.2). However, the existence of a convexity, even one of considerable size, does not necessarily guarantee that a meadow is highly sensitive with respect to channel bed lowering or meadow dissection. The typical runoff event may not be capable of entraining and transporting the material found along the channel bed, thereby inhibiting incision with small to moderate runoff events. In fact, the existence of the stepped profile indicates that incision has not occurred at a rapid rate

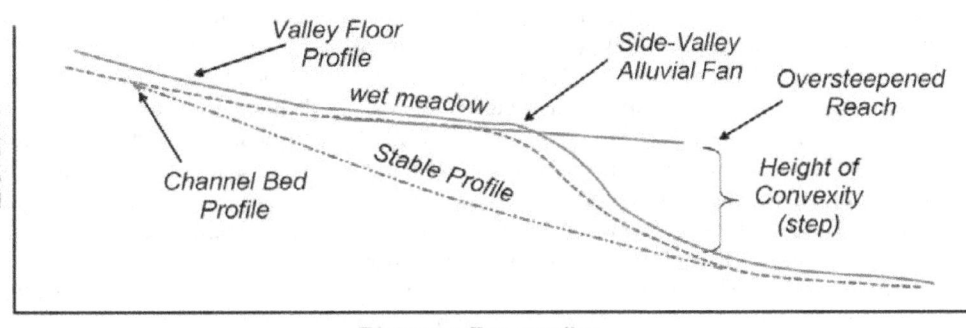

Figure 5.2. Topographic convexity and definition of step height.

Distance Downvalley

USDA Forest Service Gen. Tech. Rep. RMRS-GTR-258. 2011.

71

during approximately the past two millennia, at least where channel profiles are influenced by sediments deposited at the mouth of tributaries (Miller and others 2004). Thus, meadow sensitivity with respect to incision is strongly controlled by the magnitude and frequency of flood flows that are capable of eroding channel bed material, thereby elevating the stepped profile.

Incision is promoted by the ability of a basin to collect and effectively funnel water to meadows. Factors that influence the erosive capability of runoff events include basin elevation and the amount of snowpack accumulation in upland areas, and basin morphometric parameters such as size, relief, and ruggedness upstream of the meadow (Germanoski and Miller 2004). Once runoff water reaches the meadows, the erosive ability of water is modified by local conditions. Thus, while an abundant supply of water may be required for incision, it does not automatically indicate that incision will occur. Local factors that promote incision are: (1) narrow valleys that concentrate overland flood flows; (2) extensive subsurface discharge via springs and bank seepage; and (3) steep channel gradients, both within the meadow and along stream segments that are located immediately downstream of the meadow (Chapter 3). Incision along the downstream reach is important because lowering of the channel's base level in these areas tends to produce localized incision that propagates upstream through the meadow complex (Chapter 3). The rate of incision, and therefore meadow sensitivity, also is strongly influenced by size of the channel bed material, which must be entrained and transported downstream. Put differently, it is influenced by the resistance of the channel bed to erosion.

The traditional and most widely used approach to assessing particle motion and, therefore, the potential for incision is based on the Shields (1936) criterion. The Shields criterion was developed using flume data and evaluates the shear stress near the channel bed that is required to get a particle into motion by moving it up and over its downstream neighbor. The method was constructed for particles of uniform size and yielded the expression:

$$\tau_c = \rho d_w S = 0.06 (\rho - \rho_s) g D \qquad (5.1)$$

where τ_c is the critical shear stress at which particle motion begins; ρ and ρ_s are the densities of the fluid and particle, respectively; g is the gravitational constant; S is the slope of the water surface; and D is the diameter of the particle of interest (which is assumed to be similar to the surrounding particles).

More recent studies have shown that the Shields criterion is valid only for channels where the bed material is of nearly uniform size (Reid and Dunne 1996). In the case of gravel-bed rivers where bed sediment may range from sand to boulders, the equation requires modification for several reasons. First, larger, surrounding neighbors hide or protect smaller particles from the flow. These smaller particles require higher shear stresses than predicted by the original Shields equation in order to initiate motion. In contrast, particles that are larger than average project above surrounding clasts, are readily exposed to the flow, and require lower shear stresses for particle motion than predicted for uniform grains. Other factors of importance to gravel-bed rivers are the binding together of particles of differing size and shapes as they are packed into the stream bed, formation of bedforms, and development of vertical layers of differing grain size distributions in the channel bed (e.g., pavements and subpavements). At present, there is no consensus as to the degree of reduction in shear stress that occurs in gravel-bed rivers (or streams) (Reid and Dunne 1996). A wide range of equations has been developed to describe the initial motion of large particles (table 5.2). The differences among these equations are partly related to differences in the datasets used to create them and the definitions of initiation of motion and shear stress (Reid and Dunne 1996).

One way of using the equations (table 5.2) to assess the probability of incision is to estimate the percent of the channel bed that is likely to be mobilized at a given shear stress. The shear stress required to transport particles that comprise different percentages of the pavement can be calculated using the various equations shown in table 5.2 and plotted in figure 5.3 for the Snoqualmie River, Washington (which has median particle sizes of 56 and 17 mm in the pavement and subpavement, respectively) (Reid and Dunne 1996). These curves can then be compared to the shear stresses that are likely for varying flow depths within the channel. Changes in shear stress as a function of flow depth can be easily estimated using the equation:

$$\tau = \gamma RS \qquad (5.2)$$

where γ is the specific weight of the fluid, R is the hydraulic radius of the channel, and S is the slope of the water surface. An advantage of this simplified approach is that data required for these calculations can be easily collected during a single visit to the site.

Given the approximate nature of the estimates of shear stress required to initiate motion by the equations in table 5.2, predictions of particle entrainment and the potential for channel bed incision must be used with a strong degree of skepticism. The probability of incision is further complicated by the presence and advancement of knickpoints. Nevertheless, this approach (which determines the likelihood for particle entrainment for a given set of flow conditions will provide valuable insight into whether the bed material exhibits a low, moderate, or high degree of mobility. It may be particularly useful to apply these equations to large clasts found along the relatively high-gradient reaches of the channel steps to determine if particle entrainment of the materials controlling the local base level is likely.

Assessment of meadow sensitivity to incision by means of knickpoint or headcut migration is a more difficult task. Meadow development is highly variable from basin to basin and depends on both surface and groundwater conditions. The spatial distribution of headcuts shows that they tend to develop in areas of steep valley gradients, abundant water, and concentrated flow. These parameters often coincide along reaches of the valley floor that are prone to incise by means of knickpoint or headcut advancement. For example, many meadows occur on wide segments of the valley that

Table 5.2. Selected equations used to predict the initiation of motion. Critical shear stress (τ_c in dynes/cm²) is calculated for individual particles of size D_i (cm) positioned within the channel bed material with a median grain diameter (D_{50}, in cm) for geometric mean diameter (D_g, in cm). Modified from Reid and Dunne (1996).

Reference	Equation	Definition of Motion[1]
Shields (1936)	$\tau_c = 0.056\,(\rho_s-\rho)gD_i$	
Miller and others (1977)	$\tau_c = 0.045\,(\rho_s-\rho)gD_i$	
Parker and others (1982)	$\tau_c = 0.09\,(\rho_s-\rho)gD_{50}$	Bedload
Diplas (1987)	$\tau_c = 0.087\,(\rho_s-\rho)gD_i^{0.06}D_{50}^{0.94}$	Bedload
Parker (1990)[2]	$\tau_c = \tau_{rg}\,(\rho_s-\rho)gD_i^{0.10}D_{50}^{0.90}$	Bedload
Komar (1987)[3]	$\tau_c = 0.045\,(\rho_s-\rho)gD_i^{0.35}D_{50}^{0.65}$	Clast
Andrews (1983)	$\tau_c = 0.083\,(\rho_s-\rho)gD_i^{0.13}D_{50}^{0.87}$	Clast
Ashworth and Ferguson (1989)	$\tau_c = 0.072\,(\rho_s-\rho)gD_i^{0.35}D_{50}^{0.65}$	Bedload
	$\tau_c = 0.054\,(\rho_s-\rho)gD_i^{0.33}D_{50}^{0.67}$	Bedload
	$\tau_c = 0.087\,(\rho_s-\rho)gD_i^{0.08}D_{50}^{0.92}$	Bedload
Komar and Carling (1991)	$\tau_c = 0.059\,(\rho_s-\rho)gD_i^{0.36}D_{50}^{0.64}$	Clast
	$\tau_c = 0.039\,(\rho_s-\rho)gD_i^{0.13}D_{50}^{0.82}$	Clast
Costa (1983)	$\tau_c = 26.6D_i^{1.21}$	Deposit
Williams (1983)	$\tau_c = 12.9D_i^{1.34}$	Deposit

[1] Method with which particle motion is defined; Bedload—initiation of motion defined by occurrence of a small but finite amount of transport; Clast—initiation of motion defined by largest particle moving at a given τ; Deposit—initiation of motion defined from the largest particles deposited during an event with a given τ at crest stage.

[2] D_g is the surface geometric mean diameter of the clast, which is calculated as $lnD_g = \Sigma\,F_i LnD_{i}$, where Fi is the ith particles size class and has a geometric mean of D_i, and $\tau_{rg} = 0.836(D_g/D_{50}sub)-0.905$ is the reference dimensionless shear stress for D_g.

[3] Equation based on surface grain parameter but used for subsurface.

are characterized by low gradients (Chapter 3). During flood events, overland flows are concentrated by a reduction in valley width and are augmented by groundwater discharge. In addition, the erosive capability of the flow is enhanced by increases in gradient, thereby creating the ideal situation for gully/headcut formation. Once produced, the headcuts have the potential to migrate upvalley into the meadow system. Thus, variations in valley width, gradients, and zones of

groundwater discharge are important factors that influence the degree of channel incision within the meadows.

The existence of a knickpoint or headcut indicates that the channel or valley floor is unstable and subject to entrenchment. However, a knickpoint or headcut does not necessarily mean that the meadow is highly sensitive to incision as these features may not migrate upstream at a significant rate (that is, within 10^0 to 10^2 years). Insights concerning the rates of knickpoint or headcut migration into and/or through a meadow can be obtained by examining (1) the source and availability of water to the feature and (2) the processes through which the features advance upvalley (Chapter 3). For knickpoints within a well-defined channel of a meadow complex, field surveys demonstrated that the primary mechanism of advancement is by means of knickpoint retreat associated with plunge pool formation, material undercutting, and failure of the knickpoint face. When combined with a concentrated and continuous supply of water from upstream, the knickpoints generally move quickly through the meadow (as in the case of Kingston 3 meadow, Chapter 3) unless migration is hindered by dense resistant roots, such as those associated with willows (as is the case in Birch Creek; fig. 1.7). Thus, where these types of knickpoints exist, meadows are moderately to highly sensitive to incision through continued knickpoint migration.

Rates of headcut migration into previously undissected meadows are more variable, both between meadows and through time at a given meadow. Although quantitative data on rates of migration are limited, they range from a less than 1 m per year to tens of meters per year during high

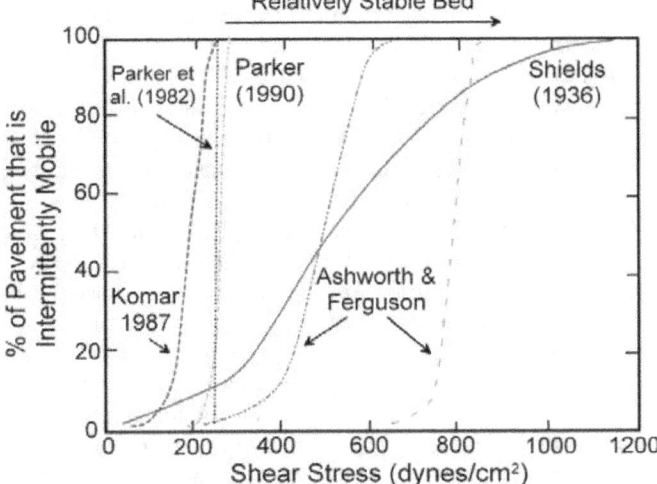

Figure. 5.3. Percent of channel bed clasts that are mobile, as calculated using equations in table 5.2. Data for Snoqualmie River, Washington. Figure from Reid and Dunne (1996).

USDA Forest Service Gen. Tech. Rep. RMRS-GTR-258. 2011.

73

magnitude events such as occurred in 1982 and 1983. In general, headcut retreat that is driven by seepage erosion or groundwater-related mass wasting processes (as observed in Indian Valley and Corcoran Canyon, fig. 1.7) proceeds rather slowly—less than approximately 1 m per year. These rates are unlikely to change significantly from one runoff year to the next if the available surface water is limited due to a small upstream catchment area of low relief or altitude or a wide valley that is incapable of concentrating flow. For example, in Cahill Canyon (fig. 1.7), a low-relief headcut is advancing into a small meadow located near the headwaters of the drainage. Although the headcut is positioned along a slightly oversteepened reach of the valley floor and is developed in fine-grained sediments, the likelihood of rapid advancement is small because both surface and groundwater flow to the headcut is limited. In contrast, headcut advancement by means of plunge pool development and failure associated with overland flows can occur much more rapidly. In Indian Valley, for example, the diversion and concentration of flow onto a previously undissected portion of the valley floor led to extremely high rates of upstream headcut migration—several to tens of meters per year—between 1961 and 1982 (fig. 3.15).

The mechanisms of headcut migration can change through time. Temporal changes are associated with rare, high magnitude runoff events and anthropogenic activities that concentrate flow on the valley floor; remove the existing vegetation; and, reduce the erosive resistance of the valley fill. Examples of anthropogenic activities include development of roads, drainage diversions, or berms. Livestock, which often produce trails capable of concentrating flow and funneling it to the top of headcuts, may also exacerbate upvalley headcut migration (for example, Indian Valley, fig. 3.19).

A rapid and effective method of assessing meadow sensitivity to headcut advancement is to determine the rates of upstream headcut migration by comparing the position of headcuts on aerial photographs of differing ages. If multiple sets of photos are examined, the average rates of migration can be determined for the period bracketed by the aerial photographs. The estimated rates, determined for multiple photographic pairs, can then be compared to local precipitation records to determine rates of advancement associated with the period's precipitation/runoff magnitudes. In addition, it may be possible to obtain a qualitative understanding of the frequency with which flood flows cause rapid upstream headcut migration. The analysis also can provide insight into the portions of the meadow that may be sensitive to current or future incision by headcut migration and into the causes of instability such as diversion of surface flows to a new area of the meadow or valley floor.

Meadows that are extremely sensitive to incision by groundwater sapping processes are those that are underlain by highly permeable sediments such as the grus-dominated valley fill in Marshall Canyon. Erosion of small, discontinuous channels during low to moderate runoff events may lead to a shift in the dominate erosion process to groundwater sapping during major floods, particularly where flows from tributaries and springs converge. As a result, headcuts can form and migrate tens of meters in a few days (fig. 3.7), making these meadows extremely sensitive to disturbance (see discussion on Marshall Canyon, Chapter 3).

Geomorphic Sensitivity to Avulsion

The geomorphic processes that affect wet meadow ecosystems are incision, localized aggradation, and avulsion (Chapter 3). Avulsion events can significantly alter meadow complexes by (1) delivering coarse gravel-sized materials to the valley floor; (2) creating high, linear ridges within the meadow that exhibit relatively deep water tables; and (3) leading to development and enlargement of new channels, which are often prone to incision and localized groundwater lowering (fig. 3.22).

Avulsion is caused by the interaction of several factors that lead to a threshold crossing event. While it is extremely difficult to predict the probability that a meadow will experience an avulsion during a given period, the primary controlling factors can be evaluated to assess whether a meadow has a high, moderate, or low risk of channel shifting and abandonment. For example, avulsion within a meadow is primarily driven by the rapid influx or release of coarse sediment from an upstream reach and the subsequent deposition of that sediment within the channel as it traverses the meadow complex. Thus, the likelihood of avulsion is closely tied to upstream sediment sources, which may periodically deliver large quantities of coarse material to the drainage network. Without these sources and the influx of coarse sediment, avulsion will not occur. Thus, any evaluation of the future stability of a meadow should involve the identification of upstream sediment supplies. Potential supplies are: (1) beaver dams and ponds that store large volumes of course debris that can be released upon dam failure; (2) unstable hillslopes that are characterized by mass wasting scars, which can deliver sediment directly to the channel; (3) steep roads that cross or lie immediately adjacent to the channel and have the potential to be extensively gullied; and (4) steep side-valley alluvial fans that are or may become trenched, thereby supplying sediment to the drainage system. Each of these sources can be mapped on topographic sheets, and their potential to supply debris to the drainage network can be evaluated.

The influx of coarse sediment to the channel does not always lead to avulsion as the material may be transported downstream through the meadow complex. It is therefore necessary to examine the local factors that may lead to avulsion within the meadow. One factor that promotes avulsion is a reduction in the capacity of the channel to contain moderate to large flood events. Decreases in channel capacity are frequently related to stream bed aggradation produced by a decline in channel gradient near upstream meadow segments. Reductions in stream gradients are common (fig. 3.21) and result in a lowering of both channel capacity

74

USDA Forest Service Gen. Tech. Rep. RMRS-GTR-258. 2011.

and competence. Other factors that lead to aggradation are an increase in roughness (resistance to flow) caused by riparian vegetation, particularly willows, and in-stream obstructions to flow, including erosion control structures.

Ongoing stream aggradation can be identified along meadow channels in the form of longitudinal bars on terraces and other low-lying surfaces next to the stream (fig. 3.21) or as thick accumulations of gravel within the channel bed, which are often accompanied by reductions in channel depth. Whether or not these zones of aggradation ultimately result in avulsion depends on the loss in channel capacity and depth and the nature of adjacent meadow topography. In a review of the causes of avulsion, Jones and Schumm (1999) found that avulsion was promoted by steep floodplain gradients in comparison to the pre-avulsion channel. In central Nevada, meadow surfaces are most likely to exhibit gradients that are greater than those of the channel in areas where the stream is highly sinuous. Highly sinuous channels exhibit a higher likelihood of avulsion than straight channels, provided other controlling factors are similar. Another control on the likelihood for avulsion is the occurrence of linear depressions, which are often associated with paleochannels within the meadow complex. These depressions may be intersected by the modern channel. Where they intersect, channel depths and, therefore, capacities are relatively low, allowing flood waters to spill over into the depression before inundating other portions of the meadow's surface. Spring channels also serve as preferential routes of flood flow. The fine-grained nature of sediments at the surface of depressions and lining the perimeter of spring channels often allows them to be scoured, producing topographic conduits with a bed below the adjacent channel floor. As a result of the differing channel bed elevations, the newly scoured channel can eventually capture the entire upstream flow. For example, in the Birch Creek 1 meadow (fig. 1.7), aggradation and a loss in channel capacity presumably led to a recent increase in overbank flooding. The flood flows were concentrated in the spring channel, which over time incised and widened to become the new truck channel, leaving the aggraded reach as an abandoned segment. Localized aggradation of an unincised reach farther upstream and subsequent willow colonization suggests that the meadow remains highly sensitive to avulsion processes because (1) channel capacity is likely to be decreased by the deposition of coarse-sediment within the channel, resulting in overbank flows, and (2) the overbank flows may be routed into existing spring channels.

Man-made structures often increase hydraulic roughness and can, therefore, lead to stream bed aggradation and a loss in channel capacity if there is a supply of coarse sediment to the reach. If the loss in channel capacity is significant, the result may be avulsion. Thus, care must be taken to ensure that structures that are used to inhibit channel incision while coarse sediment influx is limited do not lead to aggradation and avulsion during large events when bedload transport rates are high. In other words, in-stream structures or other forms of bed and bank modifications may simply shift the zone of incision to a new location.

Possible approaches to limit the effects of these structures are to design structures to fail during high magnitude events, thereby reducing their ability to cause intense, localized aggradation, and to restrict their use where coarse sediment is likely to be input to the meadow.

Geomorphic Sensitivity Summary

Numerous factors promote and resist geomorphic change within meadow complexes (table 5.1). The challenge for land managers is to determine whether interactions of these factors at a particular meadow have produced a system that is relatively stable and has the potential to be effectively managed or a system that is highly sensitive to change. Determining outcomes of interacting factors is difficult. Nevertheless, an evaluation of whether the factors (table 5.1) contribute to meadows of high, moderate, or low sensitivity informs the likelihood of future change. Take, for example, a meadow characterized by a large, upstream basin; a rapidly narrowing downstream valley; and a channel that is characterized by a pronounced convexity, steep downstream gradients, relatively small bed material, and significant groundwater influx. The combined effects of these factors will likely produce a meadow that is highly sensitive to geomorphic change. Thus, a simple checklist evaluation of the primary controlling factors can be used to rank the sensitivity of upland meadows to incision or avulsion. This evaluation can be used to decide if it is necessary to conduct more detailed geomorphic studies of the site with the intent of developing management options or if resources would be more wisely spent on another meadow system.

Hydrologic Sensitivity

Overview

The concept of hydrologic sensitivity of meadows is used here in a manner similar to geomorphic sensitivity. Hydrologic sensitivity describes the propensity for changes in groundwater conditions that result in a decline in the water table depth. Because montane meadow complexes in the central Great Basin are groundwater-dependent ecosystems, the typical response is a shift in vegetation patterns from wet and mesic meadow community types to drier types over part or all of the meadow (Chambers and others 2004). The drivers of change within meadows, in most cases, are related to the processes of channel incision, headcut migration, or avulsion. Drivers of change external to meadows include climatic change and disruption of recharge, routing, or connectivity of source waters that support meadows.

The general relationship between stream incision, lowering of the water table, and vegetation shifts have been described for arid and semi-arid regions (Stromberg and others 1996; Chambers and Miller 2004; Webb and Leake 2006). In some studies, linkages between streams, groundwater levels, and

USDA Forest Service Gen. Tech. Rep. RMRS-GTR-258. 2011.

75

vegetation have been well enough established to develop models to predict vegetation shifts in response to changes in hydrology (Schilling and others 2004; Loheide and Gorelick 2007). However, in many places, hydrogeologic complexity prevents effective use of quantitative models. Variables that limit the value of quantitative models include lack of stratigraphic data, partial penetration of streams into aquifers, transient hydrologic conditions, and characterization of stream bed materials related to exchange of groundwater and stream water (Woessner 2000; Sophocleous 2002; Vidon and Hill 2004; Loheide and others 2009). In some cases, such as in major restoration projects, money- and time-intensive efforts may be warranted to fully evaluate meadow conditions in order to develop accurate quantitative models. However, for most areas, these intensive efforts are seldom feasible. Alternatively, conceptual models based on a process-based understanding can be effective research and management tools (Woessner 2000; Vidon and Hill 2004; Loheide and others 2009).

Hydrologic Processes and the Factors Controlling Sensitivity

Our study of 56 riparian meadows has provided information on meadow processes, linkages between biotic and abiotic systems, and landscape controls. In this section, qualitative factors controlling hydrologic sensitivity are used to assess meadow conditions. The key controls on hydrologic sensitivity are: (1) based on conceptual models that have been validated through our research, (2) observed in other riparian systems, and (3) founded on established principles of hydrogeology.

The individual hydrologic characteristics of meadows are wide ranging, but sufficient generalizations can be made to provide a foundation for analyzing hydrologic sensitivity. Springs, artesian conditions, and perched water tables in meadows of the central Great Basin indicate the presence of heterogeneous geologic materials and complex groundwater conditions. The typical meadow has a complex geologic setting with complex stratigraphy characterized by strongly contrasting hydraulic conductivities and high hydraulic gradients. The variability in spatial and temporal hydrologic patterns, such as water levels and pathways, also is due to natural climate and weather cycles and the combined influences of mixed groundwater sources. The nature of the connection between groundwater and surface water (Chapter 4) is an especially strong determinant in how the water table and, therefore, vegetation types respond to stream incision. Different parts of meadows have different hydrologic patterns, and changes that are external to the meadow in the recharge regions of the source waters also affect meadow hydrology. Thus, evaluation of meadow sensitivity requires an understanding of each meadow's hydrologic, geomorphic, and vegetation characteristics.

Four groups of factors are used to assess hydrologic sensitivity: (1) meadow hydrology, including groundwater and stream water interactions; (2) meadow stratigraphy;

(3) geomorphic processes and stratigraphic setting; and (4) source waters (table 5.3).

Meadow Hydrology: Groundwater-Stream Water Interactions

The connection of surface water to groundwater along stream channels is recognized for its importance in nutrient transfer and other aspects of stream ecology (e.g., Hayashi and Rosenberry 2002; Sophocleous 2002). The term "connection" is used to describe if and how often stream water is connected to groundwater along the channel perimeter. The type and nature of the channel connection to the groundwater table directly affects the kind and magnitude of groundwater responses (table 5.3a.1; fig. 5.4). Several connection types are recognized: (1) continuous, which requires perennial stream flow and a shallow water table; (2) intermittent or ephemeral, where stream flow or seasonal variations in water table elevation are needed for a connection; and (3) not connected under typical climatic conditions, where stream flows are short-lived and groundwater tables are deep (e.g., Lerner 2003). The connection type does not indicate directly whether the stream segment is gaining or losing.

Channels that are created and fed only by springs, not runoff, tend to be small and do not significantly disrupt the water table geometry (fig. 5.4a). Spring-fed channels tend to have lower width to depth ratios and less variable discharge than runoff-dominated channels (Griffiths and others 2008). Channels that convey runoff are larger and, in general, much more dynamic than spring-fed channels. In some places, channels that convey runoff are perennial, whereas in others, they are ephemeral or intermittent, flowing only during periods of high runoff. Perennial channels that convey runoff and groundwater baseflow intersect the water table, are typically gaining, and cause subsurface flow convergence that results in a lower water table adjacent to the channel (fig. 5.4c). Stream incision of these channels causes further declines in the water table and, consequently, can lead to shifts in plant community types. This response is well documented (see Chambers and others 2004; Shilling and others 2004; Loheide and Gorelick 2007; Loheide and others 2009). Intermittent and ephemeral runoff channels are not connected to the water table for most of the year, and when they do convey flow, they are losing stream segments (fig. 5.4b). Incision of these channels will not cause a decline in the water table unless the channel reaches a depth where it intersects the water table.

Perennial channels that convey runoff are typically gaining streams. However, some of the perennial stream segments in meadows are losing, even though they are connected to the groundwater and convey some runoff (table 5.3a.2). These stream segments can support meadow complexes as indicated by the occurrence of wet or mesic plant communities adjacent to the channel and drier plant communities at distance from the channel (fig. 5.5). Where streams are the primary source of water to meadows, stream incision has the potential to cause a complete loss of shallow groundwater necessary to support wet and mesic vegetation.

Table 5.3. Factors influencing the hydrologic sensitivity of meadow systems.

Factors	Factors Contributing to High Sensitivity of Meadows
A. Sensitivity related to meadow hydrology: groundwater-stream water interaction	
(1) Stream channel connection to groundwater fig. 5.4	Stream channels that intersect groundwater table and are incised deeply enough to cause groundwater flow convergence to channel, typically reflected by vegetation patterns adjacent to channel
(2) Gaining or losing fig. 5.5	Losing streams that are primary water source for meadows, especially in perched systems, because further incision will increase depth of groundwater table in wettest part of meadow and may cut off recharge of shallow, perched system
(3) Relation of groundwater flow direction to position of new channel fig. 5.6	Incision of valley floor on upgradient side of flow will cause drop in groundwater table across remainder of valley floor.
B. Sensitivity related to meadow stratigraphy	
(1) Hydraulic conductivity of meadow sediments adjacent to stream channel fig. 5.7	Incision of high hydraulic conductivity materials will cause more of a widespread drop in the water table than finer-grained materials.
(2) Key hydrostratigraphic units and stratigraphic complexity figs. 5.8 and 5.9	Areas with complex stratigraphy, especially with perched and artesian conditions, are most likely to change significantly (unpredictably) with incision or new channels. In extreme cases, incision of a key confining layer may cause widespread drop in water table and loss of entire wet meadow complex.
(3) Resistance of stratigraphic units to erosion fig. 5.10	Pervasive fine-grained, noncohesive sediments are more prone to erosion, causing lowering of water table
C. Sensitivity related to geomorphic processes and stratigraphic setting	
Hydrogeomorphic condition after incision or new channels fig. 5.11	Incision or new channels that do not create new, lower-elevation meadow complexes result in a greater net loss of meadow area.
D. Sensitivity related to source waters	
Source waters and their connectivity to meadows figs. 5.12 and 3.18	Meadows supported by source waters with limited recharge areas, a limited recharge period, and variable connectivity to the meadow hydrology are susceptible to change due to upland changes in land cover, climate, and stream channels.

The sensitivity of this type of system is well documented in meadows 1 through 5 in Corcoran Canyon (figs. 1.7 and 4.2), which occur on step-shaped profiles. The string of five meadows are separated by non-meadow zones, where the stream channel is incised to depths greater than 0.5 m (table 4.2d).

The hydrologic sensitivity of a meadow can be directly influenced by the geomorphic sensitivity, especially when new channels are formed, such as by headcut migration or avulsion. The locations of new channels with respect to the direction of groundwater flow along a valley floor can have marked effects on groundwater. In some cases, new channels can capture all shallow groundwater flow (table 5.3a.3).

Capture of shallow groundwater flow is most pronounced where orientation of the stream channel is perpendicular to the direction of groundwater flow (fig. 5.6). This aspect of hydrologic sensitivity is seen in Indian Valley, where a network of headcut trenches, driven by groundwater sapping, migrated into a previously wet meadow complex with no channels. As shown in fig. 5.6d, wet to mesic plant communities persist across much of the valley floor where a new channel trench developed on the downgradient side of the valley with respect to groundwater flow (see the yellow arrow). This is in contrast to another segment of the valley floor that is now void of wet-mesic plant communities, where headcut migration on the upgradient side of the valley

USDA Forest Service Gen. Tech. Rep. RMRS-GTR-258. 2011.

77

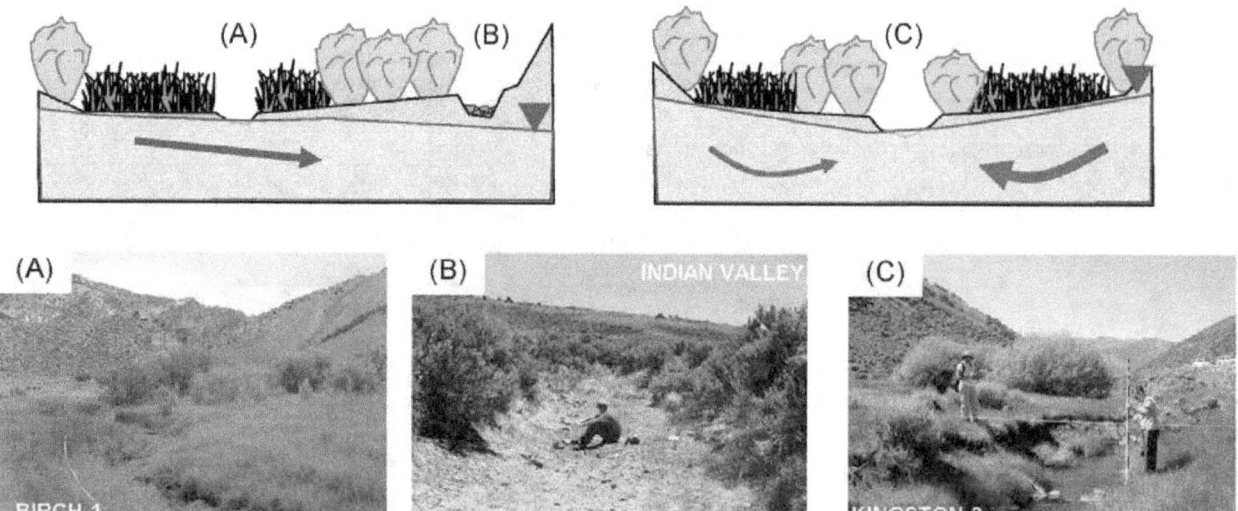

Figure 5.4. Diagrams at top depict three broad types of connections between stream channels and groundwater. These diagrams are generalized to show general topography, groundwater table and flow, wet vegetation, and dry vegetation. The photographs below show the same channel types, indicated by the corresponding letter, in the study meadows. The left diagram (a) shows a spring-fed channel and (b) shows an intermittent runoff channel. Though the spring channel intersects the groundwater table, it does not significantly alter the groundwater table. The runoff channel (b) does not cause lowering of the groundwater table. Gaining, perennial meadow streams, as shown in (c), are connected to groundwater and cause flow convergence and a decline in water table.

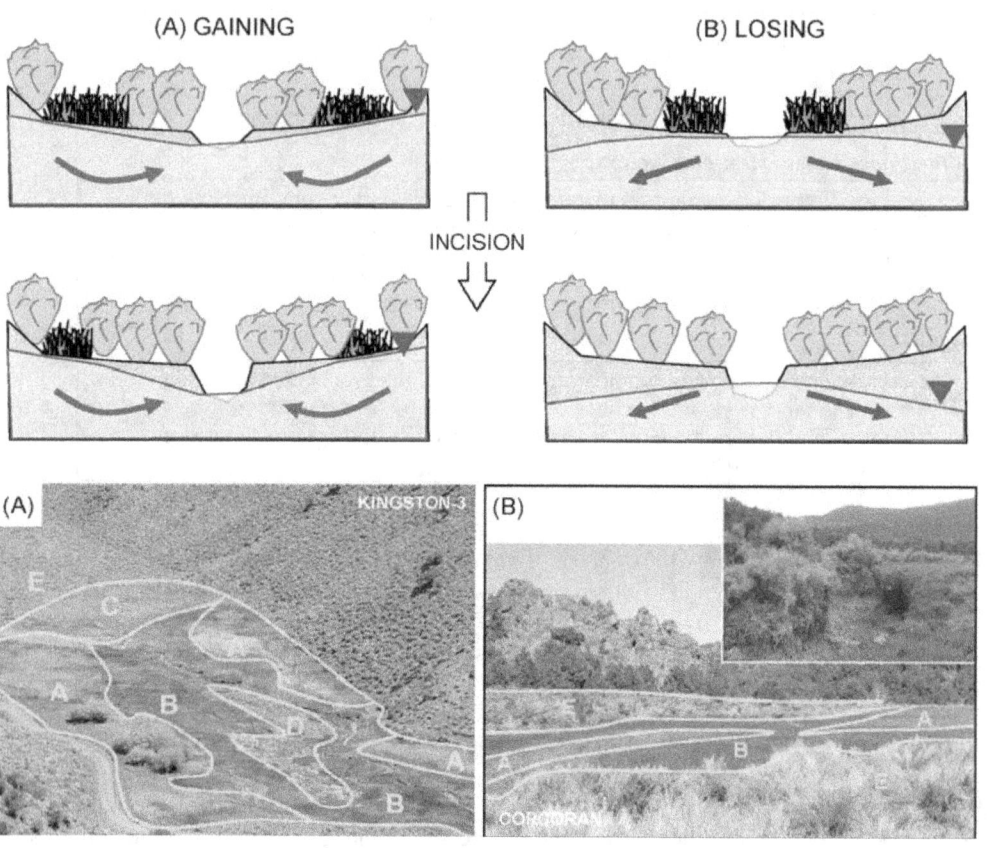

Figure 5.5. Diagrams at the top depict likely response of a gaining stream and a losing stream channel to incision. (a) Incision of a gaining stream, where sustaining water of the meadow complex is not stream water, will result in a limited water table drop adjacent to the channel (a2). (b) Incision of a losing stream, where the stream water supports a meadow complex, may result in loss of wet meadow complex (b2). Plant community patterns in Kingston 3 and Corcoran reflect stream type, as discussed in Chapter 5, with wet to mesic plants at valley margins in a gaining system (a3) and adjacent to the stream in a losing system (b3). Plant community types are A—Wet Meadow (example, Nebraska sedge), B—Mesic Meadow (example, Baltic rush), C—Dry Meadow (example, Nevada Blue Grass), D—Mix: Dry and Sage Meadow, and E—Sage Meadow. Inset photograph (b3) shows a site with sagebrush encroachment into a former wet meadow following incision.

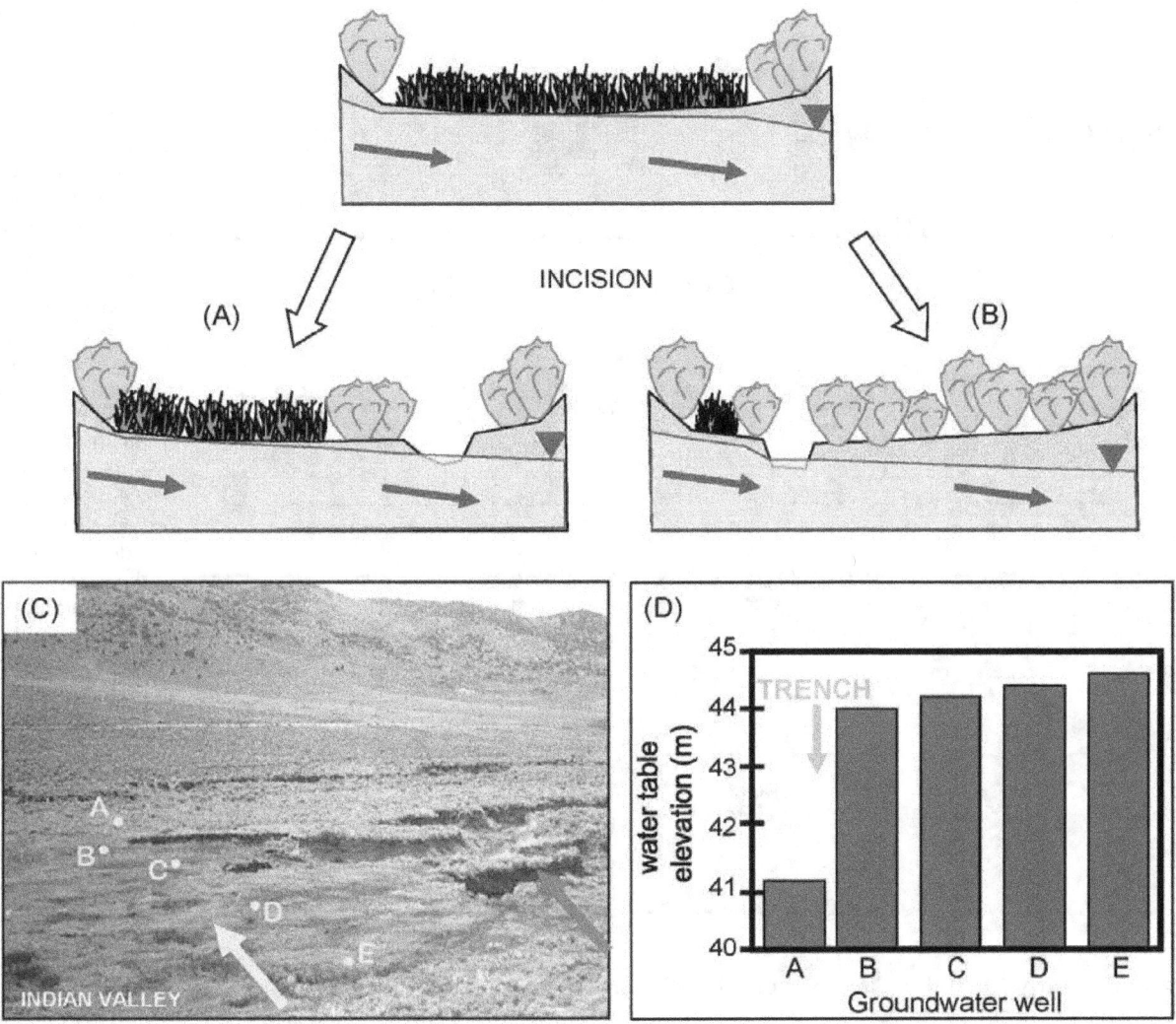

Figure 5.6. (a) New channel incision on unincised valley floor on the down-gradient side of groundwater flow (b) will cause a drop in the groundwater table across only a small portion of valley floor with a minimum loss of wet meadow complex area. In Indian Valley (d—yellow arrow), groundwater wells (A, B, C, D, and E) show cross-valley flow is intercepted by a trench that recently migrated headward due to groundwater sapping, which resulted in a drop of the groundwater table in excess of 2 m (e). Alternatively, (c) channel incision on the upgradient side of the valley floor will cause a water table drop across the remainder of the valley floor within a large loss of wet meadow complex area. The valley floor is all sage meadow in Indian Valley (d) where trenches have intercepted almost all shallow groundwater flow (d—red arrow).

intercepted and lowered the groundwater table across the entire valley floor (see the red arrow). In the meadows of the central Great Basin, it is common for groundwater flow directions to have a strong cross-valley component, especially where side-valley alluvial fans are present (e.g., Kingston 3 meadow). With respect to sensitivity and groundwater, special attention should be given to potential new channels created either by headcut migration or avulsion on the up-gradient side of the valley.

Meadow Stratigraphy

The distinction between meadow hydrologic and stratigraphic controls on sensitivity is somewhat arbitrary because the factors are interdependent. The characteristics of a stratigraphic unit or sequence either support the shallow groundwater system or determine how meadow subsurface hydrology responds to channel incision. Hydraulic conductivity of the sediments surrounding the stream channel (table 5.3b.1) can influence the rate and extent of incision. Incision by a stream that is connected to groundwater (i.e., intersecting the water table) into a coarser-grained, high hydraulic conductivity stratigraphic unit will cause a more extensive drop in the water table than incision into a finer-grained unit (figs. 5.7a and b) (Vidon and Hill 2006). Immediately adjacent to the stream channel, however, the amount of water table drop may be greater in finer-grained material than in coarser-grained material. The principles that underlie this phenomenon are analogous to those used to predict the response of the groundwater table to a pumping well. Aquifer hydraulic conductivity, thickness, and porosity are key factors that control the amount and extent of drawdown

USDA Forest Service Gen. Tech. Rep. RMRS-GTR-258. 2011.

79

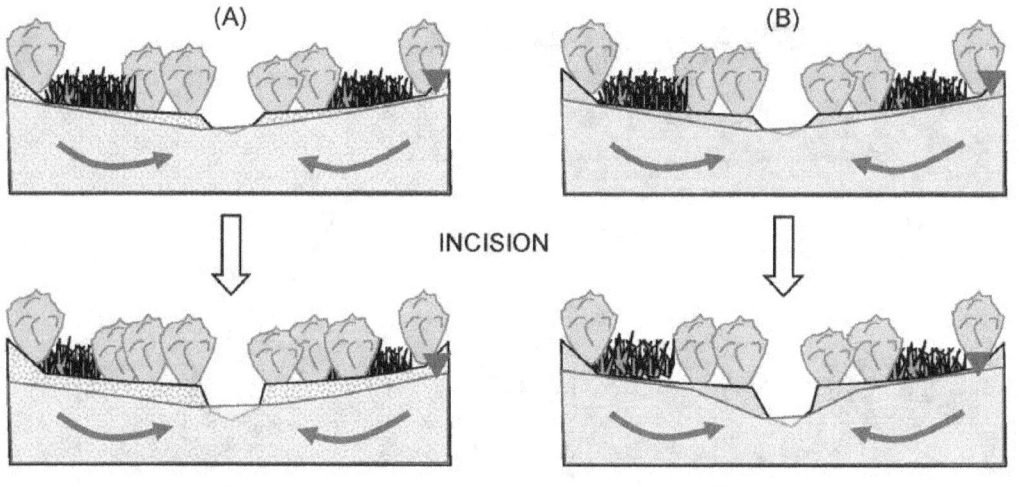

INCISION

Figure 5.7. Diagrams depict response of meadow to incision of a channel into sediment with (a) high permeability (high hydraulic conductivity) versus (b) low permeability. The drop in the water table will be more widespread in sediments of high hydraulic conductivity. At the Kingston 3 meadow (c), incision of the channel caused a greater drop in the water table on the far side of the creek (see the sagebrush area in the photographs). The sediments at this site are part of an avulsion deposit (fig. 5.1). Analysis of sediment cores (white arrow) showed that two horizons in the upper 1 m contained more than 50 percent gravel.

(Freeze and Cherry 1979). The direct role of hydraulic conductivity on the decline of the water table in response to incision is apparent at the Kingston 3 meadow (Lord and others 2007). Stream incision caused a widespread drop in the water table where it intersected a sandy gravel avulsion deposit (fig. 5.7c), and it caused encroachment of sagebrush. Finer-grained sediments on the opposite side of the stream prevented a wide-spread drop in the water table.

The stratigraphy of most meadow systems is complex, which largely explains why perched water tables, springs, and artesian conditions are so common (Chapter 4). In some cases, the shallow meadow water table is supported by a single hydrostratigraphic unit, typically a low-permeability sedimentary layer that sustains the meadow (table 5.3b.2). In Barley Canyon, a wet and mesic meadow complex was supported by a fine-grained, low-permeability unit overlying a sandy unit of high hydraulic conductivity (fig. 5.8). The stream at this site incised about 2 m wide and breached a confined aquifer that maintained a shallow water table. Once breached, the aquifer drained directly to the stream. The water table drop was so significant that wet and mesic plant communities were replaced by sagebrush and other drier meadow plants. Stream incision or creation of new channels in complex stratigraphic settings is likely to disrupt hydrologic conditions, locally resulting in loss of artesian flow or a perched water table (Shilling and others 2004), both of which would adversely impact the meadow.

Resistance of stratigraphic units is important to stream channel sensitivity and has direct implications to hydrologic sensitivity (table 5.3; fig. 5.9). In streams connected to the groundwater, depth of the channel determines depth of the water table. Where stream incision is inhibited by a resistant layer (such as a gravel-rich layer or a cohesive, fine-grained unit), the layer will prevent further decline in the water table. This controlling factor is demonstrated in many meadows where resistant gravel units that are deposited by side-valley alluvial fans at the downstream end of meadows have prevented or slowed incision (fig. 5.10).

Influence of Gully and Headcut Advancement

Incision results in varying degrees of loss of meadows that are dominated by wet and mesic plant communities regardless of whether incision occurs by individual particle entrainment or by knickpoint processes (Chapter 3). Loss of meadows can be particularly extensive within broad, low-gradient valleys such as in Indian Valley, where headcuts migrate upstream, enhanced by groundwater sapping, and produce a network of deeply entrenched gullies. However, headcut migration can result in water table levels that are located at or just below the floor of the broad, flat-bottomed trench. This occurs because the trench floor serves as the local base-level control for the water table. The net result is that the newly formed trench floor can support wet-meadow

80

USDA Forest Service Gen. Tech. Rep. RMRS-GTR-258. 2011.

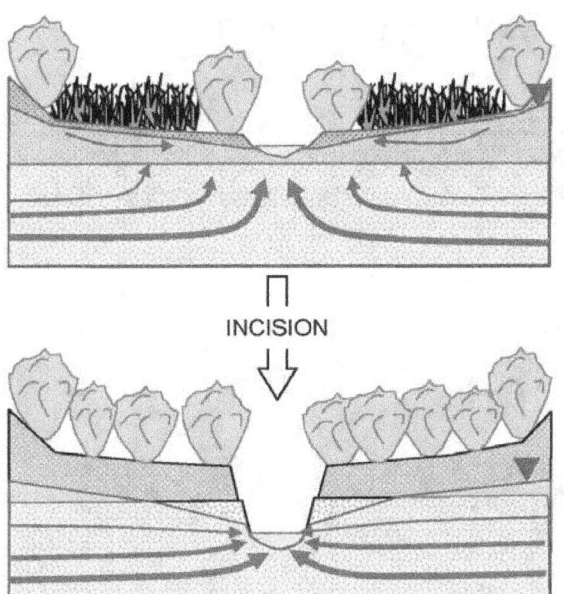

Figure 5.8. Channel incision through a key hydrostratigraphic unit (a and b), such as a low-permeability confining unit, can eliminate the hydrologic framework that supports shallow water tables. In Barley Canyon (c and d), a wet meadow complex was lost when channel incision progressed down through a fine-grained unit into a high-permeability, sandy horizon.

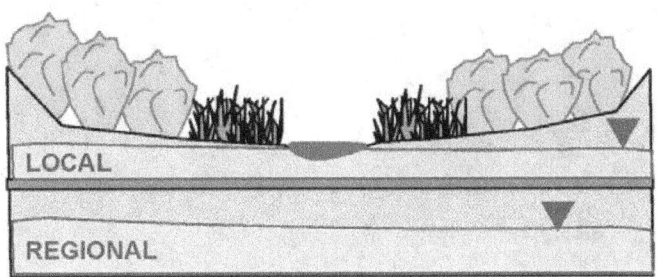

Figure 5.9. Many meadows in the central Great Basin are perched and support perched streams that are underlain by low hydraulic conductivity, confining units. If the water from the perched stream supports the meadow, channel incision through the confining layer would likely result in the loss of wet plant communities, such as is shown in fig. 5.8. The photograph shows the lower portion of the Birch Creek meadow, which is supported by a perched water table.

vegetation (table 5.3c; fig. 5.11) (Jewett and others 2004). In areas where such conditions exist, a new trench-bottomed gully network will offset some of the loss of wet meadow vegetation and the decrease in overall habitat quality.

Influence of Source Waters

The hydrologic sensitivity of meadows is influenced by processes and properties that are external to meadows as well as those within meadows (table 5.3d). Understanding the recharge regions for meadow source waters is critical for effective management of ecological functions controlled by hydrology (Winter and others 2001; Loheide and others 2009). The seasonal patterns of water table levels, or hydroperiods, in meadow complexes are strongly controlled by recharge characteristics. Source waters can be recharged from single or multiple source areas, can vary in scale from local to regional, can occur as diffuse recharge over broad areas or in concentrated areas as stream channel bed-focused recharge, and can occur over short to long periods of time (e.g., Winter and others 2001; Constantz and others 2007; Prudic and others 2007). The annual recharge of subsurface water levels is largely fed by snow, which usually melts over a short period of time, commonly in about one month (figs. 4.18 and 5.12). The response of water table levels in meadows will vary with location of the snowpack, pathway from snowmelt to meadow groundwater, and nature of the connections between surface water and groundwater. In meadows with complex hydrogeology, different parts of the same meadow complex may have different source waters and hydroperiods. These different sources or pathways of water can result in divergent groundwater-level trends within the same meadow—such as what occurs in the Kingston 3 meadow (fig. 5.12).

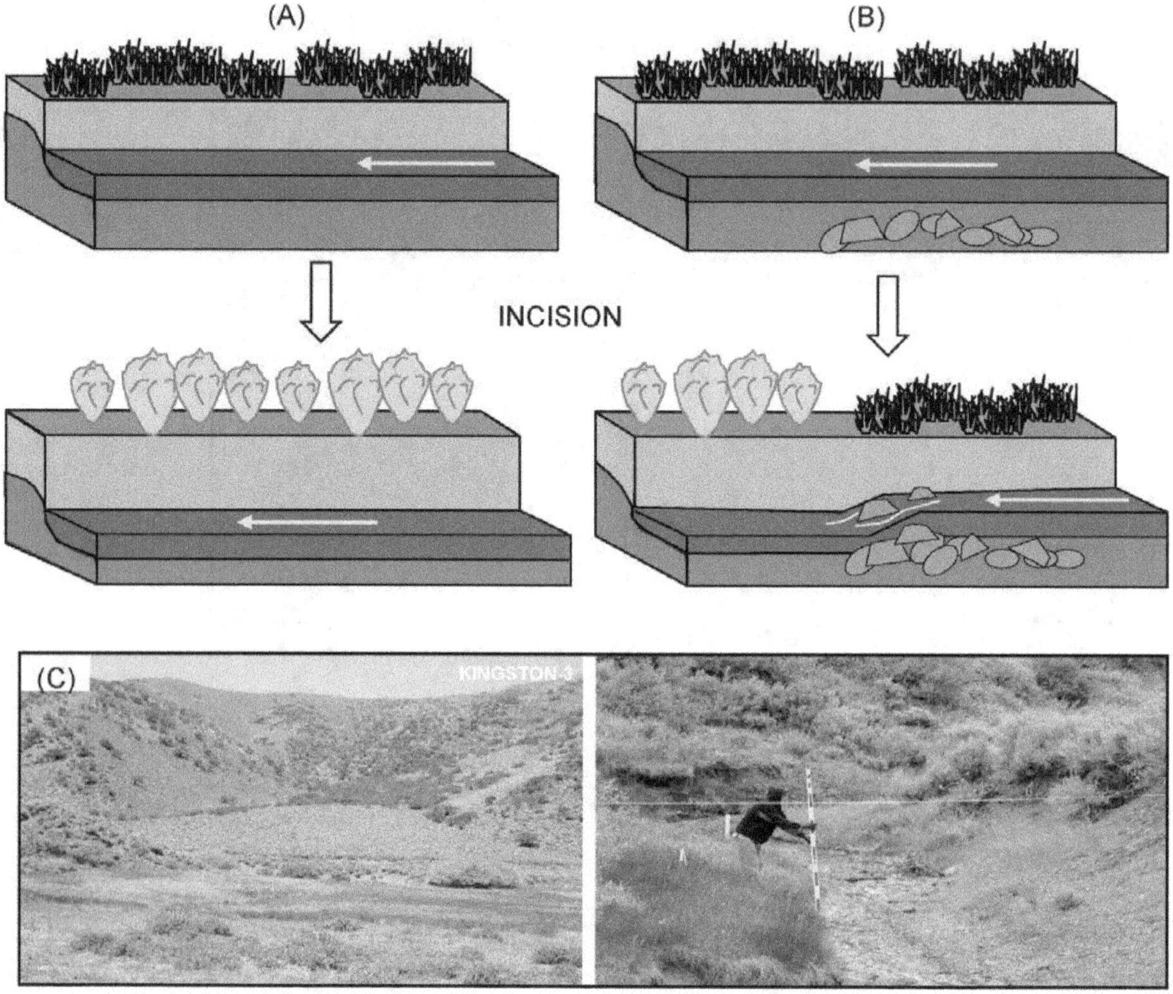

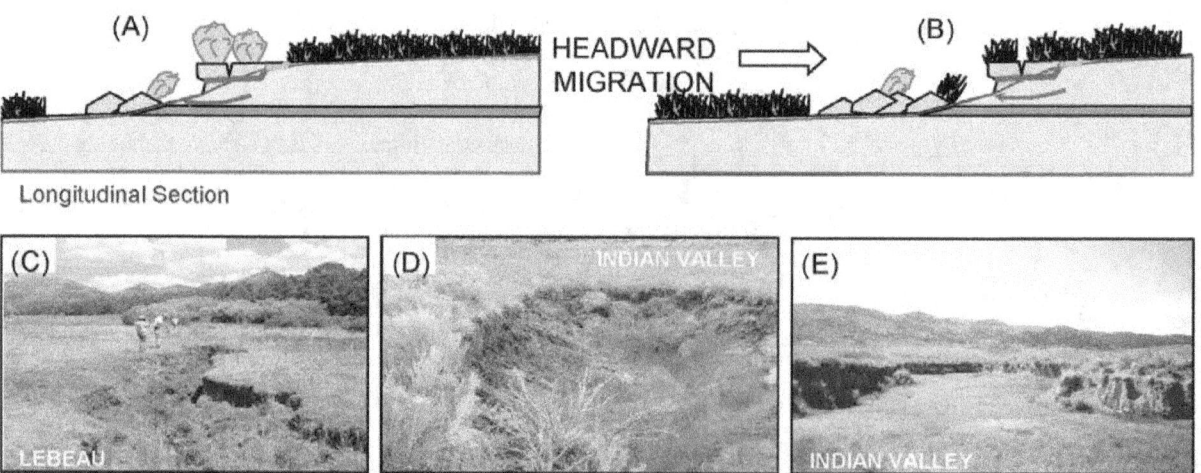

Figure 5.10. Stream incision that is not impeded by resistant stratigraphic units (a) will result in a larger drop in the groundwater table than where a resistant unit is encountered (b) that serves as a local base level control. A cobbly gravel sediment layer deposited by a side-valley alluvial fan at the Kinston 3 meadow serves to stabilize the stream (c) (see fig. 5.1).

Figure 5.11. Headcut migration of gully-trench systems (a and b) occurs at a continuum of scales in generally fine-grained sediments (c, d, and e) and is driven or enhanced by groundwater sapping. The groundwater table drops to the level of the new trench bottom and may intercept cross-valley shallow groundwater flow (fig. 5.6). With enlargement of the trench system, a wet-mesic meadow complex (e) may develop at the new lower elevation.

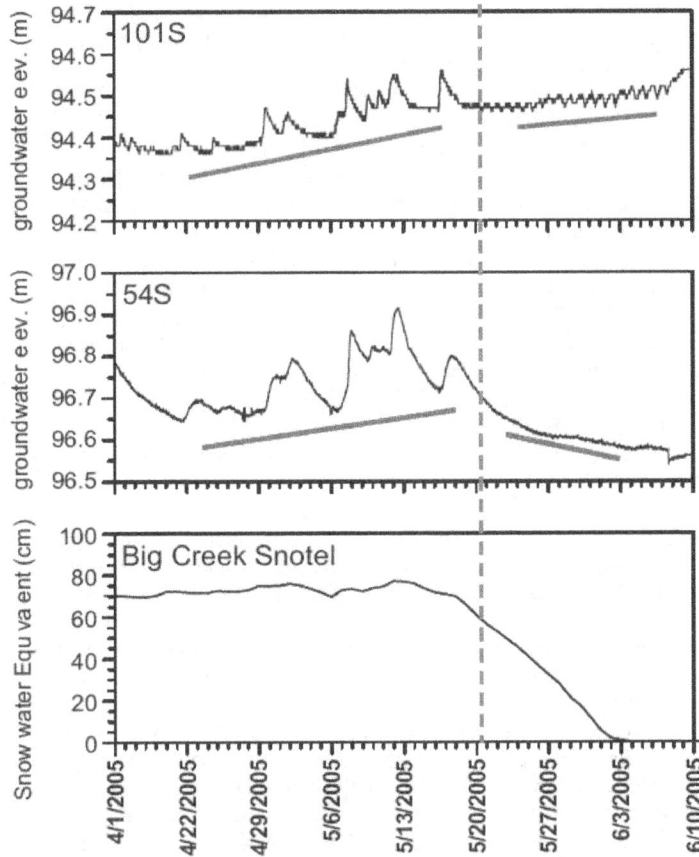

Figure 5.12. Groundwater elevations at two well sites—101S and 54S—in the Kingston 3 meadow show synchronous responses early in the annual, snow-melt driven rise of water levels, but they have divergent responses after May 20th. The lower plot shows snow water equivalent data for the nearby, high-elevation (2650 m) Big Creek SNOTEL site. These divergent responses are explained by stage-dependent differences in connectivity between the source waters and the meadow.

A meadow with a small, source-water recharge area or short recharge period generally will be more sensitive to change than one with a larger recharge area and period. Conversely, meadows with predictable water tables, broad source areas, and long recharge cycles will be less sensitive to natural or anthropogenic change. To understand the hydrologic sensitivity of the system, the source of meadow groundwater needs to be identified and monitored. In lieu of or in addition to monitoring source waters, gathering continuous groundwater and stream water level data should be a management goal to at least understand the timing and patterns of recharge cycles.

Hydrologic Sensitivity Summary

The sensitivity of meadow complexes in the central Great Basin is controlled by numerous physical and biotic factors. The areas that are most naturally sensitive are most likely to change in response to anthropogenic activities. These

meadow ecosystems require shallow water tables; therefore, understanding hydrogeologic controls on overall sensitivity is critical. Hydrologic sensitivity is controlled largely by meadow hydrogeology, especially by the interaction of groundwater and stream water, stratigraphy, geomorphic processes, and the area and timing of groundwater recharge. While all of the variations in these controls cannot be readily quantified, there are traits associated with different degrees of sensitivity. High hydrologic sensitivity is indicated by: (1) a meadow stream channel that has a continuous connection between groundwater and stream water, especially if the stream water recharges the groundwater; (2) complex stratigraphy, including highly permeable layers; (3) an active stream with high geomorphic sensitivity; and (4) source waters that recharge groundwater over limited space and over short periods of time. In contrast, low hydrologic sensitivity is indicated by meadows that: (1) are not intersected by stream channels that convey runoff; (2) are supported by regional groundwater discharge; (3) have simple stratigraphic sequences; and (4) have source waters of wide areal extent that recharge over extended periods of time.

The task of assessing sensitivity of meadow complexes can be difficult, but much can be learned by first identifying the processes and properties that control hydrologic and geomorphic sensitivity by assessing characteristics described in this chapter (tables 5.1 and 5.3). A preliminary grouping of meadows by sensitivity traits is an important first step in management of meadow systems, even though it must be followed by more detailed studies of target meadows. The discussions in Chapter 9 on meadow management and treatment options broaden this discussion by describing how sensitivity can be used as part of a strategy for resource scientists to monitor, manage, and restore meadow complexes.

References

Brunsden, D.; Thornes, J.B. 1979. Landscape sensitivity and change. Transactions, Institute of British Geographers. 4: 463-484.

Downs, P.; Gregory, K. 1993. The sensitivity of river channels in the landscape system. In: Thomas, D.S.G.; Allison, R.J., eds. Landscape Sensitivity. Chichester, United Kingdom: John Wiley and Sons: 15-30.

Downs, P.; Gregory, K. 2004. River Channel Management: Towards Sustainable Catchment Hydrosystem. London, United Kingdom: Hodder Arnold. 395 p.

Chambers, J.C.; Miller, J.R., eds. 2004. Great Basin Riparian Ecosystems—Ecology, Management and Restoration. Covello, CA.: Island Press. 303 p.

Chambers, J.C.; Tausch, R.J.; Korfmacher, J.L.; Miller, J.R.; Jewett, D.G. 2004. Effects of geomorphic processes and hydrologic regimes on riparian vegetation. In: Chambers, J.C.; Miller, J.R., eds. Great Basin Riparian Ecosystems—Ecology, Management and Restoration. Covelo, CA: Island Press: 196-231.

Constantz, J.; Adams, K.S.; Stonestrom, D.A. 2007. Overview of ground-water recharge study sites—Chapter C. In: Stonestrom, D.A.; Constantz, J.; Ferré, T.P.A.; Leake, S.A. Ground-water recharge in the arid and semiarid southwestern United States. U.S. Geological Survey Professional Paper. 1703: 61-82.

USDA Forest Service Gen. Tech. Rep. RMRS-GTR-258. 2011.

83

Freeze, R.A.; Cherry, J.A. 1979. Groundwater. Englewood Cliffs, NJ: Prentice-Hall Inc. 604 p.

Germanoski, D.; Miller, J.R. 2004. Basin sensitivity to channel incision in reponse to natural and anthropogenic disturbance. In: Chambers, J.C.; Miller, J.R., eds. Great Basin Riparian Ecosystems—Ecology, Management and Restoration. Covello, CA: Island Press: 88-123.

Griffiths, R.E.; Anderson, D.E.; Springer, A.E. 2008. Morphology and hydrology of small spring-dominated channels. Geomorphology. 102: 511-521.

Hammersmark, C.T.; Rains, M.C.; Mount, J.F. 2008. Quantifying the hydrologic effects of stream restoration in a montane meadow, northern California, USA. River Research Applications. 24: 735-753.

Hayashi, M.; Rosenberry, D. 2002. Effects of ground water exchange on the hydrology and ecology of surface water. Ground Water. 40(3): 309-316.

Jewett, D.G.; Lord, M.L.; Miller, J.R.; Chambers, J.C. 2004. Geomorphic and hydrologic controls on surface and subsurface flow regimes in riparian meadow ecosystems. In: Chambers, J.C.; Miller, J.R., eds. Great Basin Riparian Ecosystems—Ecology, Management and Restoration. Covello, CA: Island Press: 124-161.

Jones, L.S.; Schumm, S.A. 1999. Causes of avulsion: an overview. Special Publications in Association of Sedimentology. 28: 171-178.

Lerner, D.N. 2003. Surface water-groundwater interactions in the context of groundwater resources. In: Xu, Y.; Beekman, H.E., eds. Groundwater recharge estimation in Southern Africa. IHP Series No. 64. UNESCO, Paris: 91-107, ISBN 92-9220-000-3.

Loheide, S.P.; Deitchman, R.S.; Cooper, D.J.; Wolf, E.C.; Hammersmark, C.T.; Lundquist, J.D. 2009. A framework for understanding the hydroecology of impacted wet meadows in the Sierra Nevada and Cascade Ranges, California, USA. Hydrogeology Journal. 17: 229-246.

Loheide, S.P., II; Gorelick, S.M. 2007. Riparian hydroecology: a coupled model of the observed interactions between groundwater flow and meadow vegetation patterning. Water Resources Research 43, W07414, doi: 10.1029/2006WR005233.

Lord, M.; Jewett, D.; Miller, J.; Germanoski, D.; Chambers, J.; Sturtevant, K.; Baker, G. 2007. Hydrology of central Great Basin meadow ecosystems—effects of stream incision: Abstract Volume. Sixtieth annual meeting of the Society for Range Management, Reno, NV.

Miller, J.R.; House, K.; Germanoski, D.; Tausch, R.J.; Chambers, J.C. 2004. Fluvial geomorphic responses to Holocene climate change. In: Chambers, J.C.; Miller, J.R., eds. Great Basin Riparian Ecosystems—Ecology, Management and Restoration. Covelo, CA: Island Press: 49-87.

Pilkey, O.H.; Pilkey-Jarvis, L. 2007. Useless Arithmetic: Why Environmental Scientists Can't Predict the Future. New York, NY: Columbia University Press. 230 p.

Prudic, D.E.; Niswonger, R.G.; Harrill, J.R.; Woods, J.L. 2007. Streambed infiltration and ground-water flow from the Trout Creek Drainage, an intermittent tributary to the Humboldt River, north-central Nevada—Chapter K. In: Stonestrom, D.A.; Constantz, J.; Ferré, T.P.A.; Leake, S.A. Ground-water recharge in the arid and semiarid southwestern United States. U.S. Geological Survey Professional Paper. 1703: 313-351.

Reid, L.M.; Dunne, T. 1996. Rapid Evaluation of Sediment Budgets. Reiskirchen: Germany: Catena Verlag. 164 p.

Schilling, K.E.; Zhang, Y.K.; Drobney, P. 2004. Water table fluctuations near an incised stream, Walnut Creek, Iowa. Journal of Hydrology. 286: 236-248.

Schilling, K.E.; Zhongwei, L.; Zhang, Y. 2005. Groundwater-surface water interaction in the riparian zone of an incised channel, Walnut Creek, Iowa. Journal of Hydrology. 327: 140-150.

Shields, A. 1936. Anwendung der Ahnlichkeitsmechanik und Turbulenzforschung auf die Geschiebebewegung. Report 26, Berlin: Mitteil. Preuss. Versuchsant. Wasserbau und Schiffsbau. 24 p.

Sophocleous, Marios. 2002. Interactions between groundwater and surface water: the state of the science. Hydrogeology Journal. 10: 52-67.

Stromberg, J.C.; Tiller, R.; Richter, B. 1996. Effects of groundwater decline on riparian vegetation of semiarid regions: the San Pedro, Arizona. Ecological Applications. 6(1): 113-131.

Vidon, P.G.; Hill, A.R. 2004. Landscape controls on the hydrology of stream riparian zones. Journal of Hydrology. 292: 210-228.

Vidon, P.G.; Hill, A.R. 2006. Landscape-based approach to estimate riparian hydrological and nitrate removal functions. Journal of the American Water Resources Association. 42(4):1099-1112.

Webb, R.H.; Leake, S.A. 2006. Ground-water surface-water interactions and long-term change in riverine vegetation in the southwestern United States. Journal of Hydrology. 320: 302-323.

Williams, G.P. 1983. Paleohydrological methods and some examples from Swidish fluvial environments. Geografiska Annaler. 65A: 227-244.

Winter, T.C.; Rosenberry, D.O.; Buso, D.C.; Merk, D.A. 2001. Water source to four U.S. wetlands: implications for wetland management. Wetlands 21(4): 462-473.

Woessner, W.W. 2000. Stream and fluvial plain ground water interactions: rescaling hydrogeologic thought. Ground Water. 38(3): 423-429.

84

USDA Forest Service Gen. Tech. Rep. RMRS-GTR-258. 2011.

Chapter 6:   Meadow-Stream Processes and Aquatic Invertebrate Community Structure

Chris A. Jannusch, Sudeep Chandra, Tom Dudley,
Jeanne C. Chambers, and Wendy Trowbridge

Introduction

Riparian areas make up less than 1 percent of the total area of the Great Basin, yet they provide many critical ecosystem services, and they support a disproportionately large percentage of the regional biodiversity (Hubbard 1977; Saab and Groves 1992). Jenson and Platts (1990) estimate that over 50 percent of the riparian areas in the Great Basin are in poor ecological condition due to various forms of disturbance and climate change (Chambers and Miller 2004). Ongoing stream incision in the region and progressive degradation of riparian meadow complexes make meadow systems a management priority (Chambers and Miller 2004). Understanding the connections between benthic macroinvertebrate (BMI) communities and meadow-stream environmental characteristics provides managers with important information about the effects of this degradation.

Biological surveys of BMI communities have been used along with water chemistry analyses to indicate environmental conditions in other lotic ecosystems (Yoder and Rankin 1998; Karr and Chu 1999). Benthic invertebrates are relatively long-lived, diverse, and ubiquitous (Linke and others 1999). Due to these factors and because their response to disturbance is broad, they are good indicators of system changes.

Previous ecological research in Great Basin streams of Nevada has focused on links between riparian condition and aquatic invertebrate community structure (Kennedy and others 2000); invertebrate community responses to spring disturbance (Sada and others 2005); and assemblage clustering driven by natural environmental gradients (Myers and Resh 2002). Our study builds, in part, upon the work of Kennedy and others (2000), who found that community composition was strongly related to a number of environmental parameters such as total dissolved residue, fish diversity, and percent silt. Since relationships between landscape and benthic composition have been demonstrated, we sought to examine whether such relationships could be shown using common benthic measurements.

While there have been studies of the nutrient dynamics of central Great Basin streams, little research has documented the temporal and spatial patterns of environmental characteristics and the resulting implications for aquatic invertebrate communities in meadow reaches. Amacher and others (2004) demonstrated that catchment lithology is an important driver of stream water chemistry in Kingston Creek and other upland Toiyabe streams. Mast and Clow (2000) showed that early season snowmelt can dilute aqueous nutrients derived from catchment lithology.

In 2005, we initiated a study to determine if multimetric bioassessment methods that are commonly used by management agencies in the United States are sensitive to riparian meadow influences on benthic communities at Kingston Creek. Comparing multimetric and multivariate methods, we investigated whether a meadow environment affects community structure by sampling invertebrates and environmental characteristics at finer spatial and temporal scales than in previous work.

Methods

Data Collection

We collected invertebrates and environmental data at 12 sites upstream, within, and downstream of Kingston 3 meadow (figs. 1.7 and 6.1). There is a 50-m vertical drop across the 2000-m sampled area. The discharges of multiple springs within the meadow merge into two main tributaries that join the main creek at the bottom of the meadow reach. Sampling was conducted in 2005 in late spring (May), early summer (June), mid summer (July), late summer (August), and early fall (October).

All environmental parameters and invertebrate metrics that were measured are listed in table 6.1. Sites were sampled on approximately two-week intervals for environmental parameters. Depth, current velocity, and dominant substrate size were measured at five equidistant points along a stream cross-section transect for each site (Sanders 1998). Velocity was measured with a Marsh-McBirney Flo-mate 2000 current meter, and discharge was calculated using the cross-sectional area method (Sanders 1998). Dissolved oxygen, temperature, and specific conductivity were measured with a handheld probe (YSI-85). Dominant substrate size was categorized as fine sediment, sand, gravel, cobble, or boulder. Seasonal cover of vegetation over the stream was measured at the center of each transect using a densiometer (Barbour and others 1999). A water sample was obtained at each site using the depth-integrated equal-transit-rate-equal-width-increment method (Amacher and others 2004). Water samples were kept in refrigerated, dark conditions until processing. A mixed subsample was filtered using GF/F filters (0.7 μm) and measured for dissolved nutrients (nitrate, ammonium, soluble reactive phosphorous, and total dissolved phosphorous) and total phosphorus at the Aquatic Ecosystems Analysis Laboratory (AEAL) at the University of Nevada, Reno, and at the High Sierra Water Lab using standard methods (Hunter and others 1993).

USDA Forest Service Gen. Tech. Rep. RMRS-GTR-258. 2011.

85

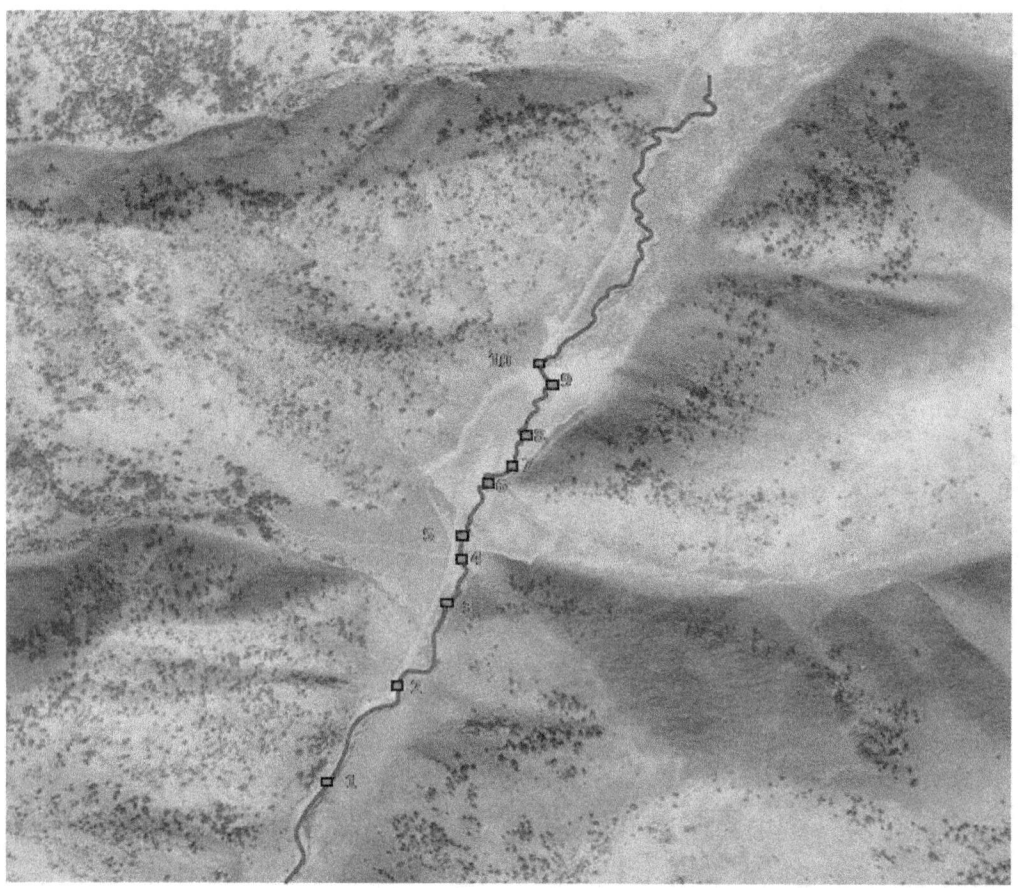

Figure 6.1. Kingston 3 meadow and sampling locations. This meadow lies at an approximate elevation of 2325 m. These sites encompassed close to 50 m in vertical gain and spanned nearly 2000 m of the creek. Sites 1 through 4 (below meadow) and 5 through 9 (meadow) had sufficient stream depths for sampling throughout the sampling season. Sites 10 through 12 (above meadow) were dropped from analysis.

Table 6.1. Environmental variables measured and bioassessment metrics calculated for Kingston Creek. EPT = Ephemeroptera, Plecotera, and Trichoptera.

Environmental parameters	Invertebrate metrics
Stream Discharge	Abundance
Substrate Size	Total Taxa
Percent Vegetative Cover	EPT Abundance
Specific Conductivity	Diptera Richness
Dissolved Oxygen (DO)	EPT Richness
Nitrate (NO_3)	Percent Tolerant Taxa
Ammonium (NH_4)	Percent Intolerant Taxa
Soluble Reactive Phosphorous (SRP)	Percent Dominance
Total Dissolved Phosphorous (TDP)	Percent Non-insect Taxa
Total Phosphorus (TP)	Percent EPT Richness
	Percent EPT Abundance
	Ephemeroptera Richness
	Plecoptera Richness
	Trichoptera Richness
	Percent Chironomidae Richness
	Hilsenhoff Biotic Index (modified)
	Shannon Diversity Index
	Percent Shredders
	Percent Scrapers
	Percent Filterer-Collectors
	Percent Gatherer-Collectors
	Percent Predators

USDA Forest Service Gen. Tech. Rep. RMRS-GTR-258. 2011.

BMI sampling and habitat characterization took place approximately every four weeks. Two invertebrate samples were taken at each site. U.S. Environmental Protection Agency (USEPA) protocols (Barbour and others 1999), UC-Sierra Nevada Aquatic Research Lab protocols (Herbst and Silldorff 2006), and California Department of Fish and Game protocols (CA DFG 2003) were modified for this study. Two BMI samples were obtained from each site using a Hess-type surber sampler (0.105 m², 247 µm mesh size). In order to obtain a more accurate representation of community structure within each site, samples were taken from the different microhabitat types that were present (Kerans and others 1992)—one from the thalweg and one from the stream edge. Data from thalweg and edge samples were then combined for each site because effects of environmental parameters on invertebrates are detectable across microhabitats (Parsons and Norris 1996; Rehn and others 2007). Samples were preserved in the field using 70 percent ethanol. Invertebrates were picked from substrate at the AEAL under dissecting microscopes. Invertebrates, excluding early instars, were enumerated and identified to genus—except for oligochaetes and water mites, which were identified to order, and chironomidae, which were identified to sub-family—using Merritt and Cummins (1996), Wiggins (1996), Stewart and Stark (2002), Thorp and Covich (1991), and Post (2005). The California Department of Fish and Game's Aquatic Biology Laboratory at Chico State University verified taxa.

Data Analysis

Cross-sectional stream discharge varied from 0.01 to 0.26 m³/sec and stream depths ranged from 2 to 34 cm. Over the course of the study, the farthest upstream sites dried up. At sites where stream depths dropped below our ability to sample (5 cm), the sites were removed from our analysis. This threshold eliminated the three sites above the meadow and gradually reduced our meadow sites from six to three over the course of the field season. In addition, the earliest sample points—late spring and early summer—were removed from analysis because invertebrate totals (<500 individuals) were insufficient to meet standard USDA Forest Service/USEPA and California bioassessment criteria (Barbour and others 1999; Herbst and Silldorff 2006). Therefore, we analyzed the remaining two reaches—meadow and below meadow— in mid summer, late summer, and early fall.

For each of the three time periods, we compared invertebrate communities between the two reaches with multi-response permutation procedures (MRPP). Groups were defined by reach (meadow or below meadow) and we examined species composition at each site. The Sørensen distance method (also known as Bray-Curtis) was used in this procedure since it performs well with ecological data (McCune and Grace 2002). MRPP was used for a number of reasons. It is a nonparametric method that was developed for testing group differences (McCune and Grace 2002). It is closely related to non-parametric multivariate analysis of variance (MANOVA) used by Sada and others (2005) for

assessing aquatic invertebrate community similarity across disturbance gradients in the Great Basin. Zimmerman and others (1985) applied a variant of MRPP to examine vegetation community differences in the Great Basin.

Stream reaches that MRPP demonstrated to be biologically distinct from one another (p<0.05) at the community scale within a given season were analyzed further for reach-specific relationships among invertebrate metrics, invertebrate taxa, and environmental variables. Abundances of individual taxa were compared between reaches using analysis of variance (ANOVA) to illustrate taxon-driven community differences. Dominant taxa were also examined for their possible role in contributing to the differences between reaches and over time.

For the multimetric analysis, we calculated 22 invertebrate metrics based on Herbst and Silldorff's (2006) benthic index of biotic integrity (B-IBI) for the eastern Sierra and western Great Basin (table 6.1). Hilsenhoff biotic index values for individual taxa that indicate tolerance/intolerance to organic pollution were taken from EPA's northwest assessment (Barbour and others 1999). Metric values were aggregated and scaled to 0 to 10 (Barbour and others 1999). B-IBI values were created from composites of scaled biological metrics (Herbst and Silldorff 2006) for each reach by season (table 6.2). We evaluated the B-IBI values for each reach over time and compared reaches. Like MRPP, this approach is designed to illustrate spatio-temporal changes in community composition (Barbour and others 1999).

Environmental variables (table 6.1) were sampled approximately every two weeks—twice as frequently as invertebrate—during mid summer and late summer. During those two seasons, environmental data were averaged from two dates within each season. One sample was taken during early fall. We performed individual ANOVAs for each environmental variable to test whether they differed across reaches. Environmental variables were assessed for normality (skew<2 standard deviations) in PC-ORD. Non-normal distributions were monotonically log transformed. To identify relationships over time, Pearson's coefficients were calculated using invertebrate metrics and environmental data for each season (Myers and Resh 2002). We defined highly correlated relationships as those with r-values greater than |0.90| (Myers and Resh 2002). Linear relationships between environmental variables and invertebrate metrics would indicate the potential of fine-scale biotic and abiotic interactions.

Results

Seventy-two taxa (table 6.3) and 40,494 invertebrates were identified. The multivariate (MRPP) and multimetric (B-IBI) methods we used to compare the meadow and below-meadow communities provided differing results. MRPP indicated that significant community-level differences existed between reaches during mid summer (p = 0.04, n = 9) and late summer (p = 0.02, n = 8). No measurable community difference was detected between reaches in early fall (p = 0.53, n = 6). B-IBI scores, however, were identical

USDA Forest Service Gen. Tech. Rep. RMRS-GTR-258. 2011.

87

Table 6.2. Taxa list for Kingston Creek upper meadow-stream. Taxa with an asterisk are predators found in early fall. EPA tolerance values assessed for Idaho were used.

Order/Suborder	Family	Genera
Trombidformes/Hydracarina		
Amphipoda	Crangonyctidae	Crangonyx
	Gammaridae	Gammarus
	Pontoporeiidae	Monoporeia
	Gastropoda	Gastropoda
Nematoda		
Nematomorpha		
Bivalvia		
Oligochaeta		
Ostracoda		
Ephemeroptera	Baetidae	Baetis
		Acerpenna
	Ephemerellidae	Drunella
	Heptageniidae	Cinygmula
		Epeorus
	Sipholonuridae	Parameletus
Plecoptera	Chloroperlidae	Haploperla
	Nemouridae	Malenka
		Zapada
Trichoptera	Brachycentridae	Micrasema
		Brachycentrus
	Glossosomatidae	Glossosoma
	Hydropsychidae	Parapsyche*
		Arctopsyche
		Leptonema
		Hydropsyche
	Hydroptilidae	Hydroptila
		Orthotrichia
		Metrichia
	Lepidostomatidae	Lepidostoma
		Psycopglypha
	Limnephilidae	Limnephilus
		Hesperophylax*
		Clostocea
	Odontoceridae	Namamyia
	Philopotamidae	Dolophilodes
	Polycentropodidae	Polycentropus*
	Rhyacophilidae	Rhyacophila*
Diptera	Ceratopogonidae	Leptoconops
		Culicoides
		Probezzia*
	Chironomidae	Orthocladinae
		Diamesinae
		Chironomini
		Tanypodinae
		Tanytarsini
	Dixidae	Dixa
	Psychodidae	Pericoma/
		Telmatoscopus
	Simuliidae	Simulium
		Prosimulium
	Tipulidae	Antocha
		Dicranota*
		Pedicia
Coleoptera	Dytiscidae	Dytiscus
	Elmidae	Stenelmis
		Atractelmis/
		Cleptelmis
		Zaitzevia
		Optioservus
		Gonielmis
		Heterlimnius
		Narpus
		Ordobrevia
		Ampumixis
	Hydrophilidae	Helobata
		Laccobius
Lepidoptera	Pyralidae	Pyralidae

during mid summer, late summer, and early fall, indicating no substantial metric level difference between the reaches (table 6.2). While the index scores were identical across reaches within season, the scores gradually increased from three to five from mid summer to early fall (table 6.2). To investigate patterns in the taxon-driven distinctions between reaches, we used ANOVA to examine dynamics in individual taxa beginning with the dominant taxa.

The midge subfamily *Orthocladiinae* was the dominant taxon for all sites, regardless of reach, during mid summer (range 43 to 85%). The mayfly *Baetis* dominated sample composition for all sites during late summer (range 45 to 86%). In mid summer, the mayfly *Drunella* and *Orthocladiinae* were found in higher numbers in the meadow reach compared to below meadow, though at marginally significant values ($p = 0.056$ and $p = 0.063$, respectively). During late summer, the mayfly genus *Baetis* occurred in significantly higher numbers at the meadow reach compared to below meadow ($p = 0.042$). Environmental variable comparisons provide additional context for variations found in the invertebrate community.

By fall, there is no flow above the meadow, and the flow within and below the meadow is supported by groundwater inputs. Consequently, discharge was greater at the below-meadow reach during both mid summer and late summer (table 6.4). In mid summer, substrate size was greater at the below-meadow reach of the stream (table 6.4). Specific conductivity values ranged from 353 to 467 µS/cm. Dissolved oxygen levels varied between 4.77 and 7.36 mg/l. Aquatic nutrient ranges are illustrated in fig. 6.2. Specific conductivity and total phosphorous were greater in the meadow reach than below the meadow during late summer (table 6.4; fig. 6.3). This pattern suggests that the two springs within the meadow have distinct influences on water chemistry, most noticeably on specific conductivity and total phosphorous.

The two spring tributaries had distinct impacts on water quality that varied by season (fig. 6.3). Total phosphorous concentrations in the stream increased downstream of the upper spring tributary during late summer (table 6.4; fig. 6.3). Immediately downstream from the lower spring, specific conductivity dropped in mid summer, stabilized in late summer, and increased during early fall (fig. 6.3). Specific conductivity levels typically increased from mid summer to late summer to early fall as the influence of groundwater increased.

Irrespective of reach, a number of relationships between invertebrate metrics and environmental parameters for mid summer, late summer, and early fall were notable. Correlation patterns of those relationships changed across seasons. The number of highly correlated relationships between environmental parameters and invertebrate metrics (with $r > |0.90|$) increased from zero in mid summer to five in late summer to eight in early fall (tables 6.5 through 6.7). During late summer, discharge, dissolved oxygen (DO), and overstory cover were all correlated with three metrics (table 6.6). Discharge and DO both correlated with the percent of intolerant taxa and percent of shredder taxa. Overstory, however, was correlated with the percent of Ephemeroptera, Plecotera, and

USDA Forest Service Gen. Tech. Rep. RMRS-GTR-258. 2011.

Table 6.3. Scaled metric values and index scores for meadow and below-meadow reaches during three seasons.

	Mid summer		Late summer		Early fall	
	Below-meadow	Meadow	Below-meadow	Meadow	Below-meadow	Meadow
Density	0	3	1	4	3	3
Total Taxa	5	6	4	5	8	7
EPT Richness	2	3	2	3	8	7
EPT Abundance	0	1	1	5	3	2
Diptera Richness	6	8	5	6	6	6
Percent Dominance	8	7	8	8	6	6
Percent Non-insect	1	1	1	1	1	6
Shannon Index	6	6	5	5	8	7
Percent EPT Richness	3	4	5	4	9	8
Percent EPT Abundance	1	1	8	8	7	7
E. Richness	5	7	4	4	6	6
P. Richness	1	0	4	6	5	8
T. Richness	1	2	1	1	8	5
Percent Chironomid Richness	5	4	6	6	3	3
Percent Intolerant Taxa	0	0	1	2	5	5
Percent Tolerant Taxa	1	1	0	0	1	5
Percent Shredders	0	0	1	2	2	5
Percent Scrapers	3	0	0	0	1	1
Percent Filterer-Collectors	1	4	2	2	6	1
Percent Gatherer-Collectors	9	8	9	8	6	8
Percent Predators	2	2	2	1	7	2
Hilsenhoff Biotic Index	7	8	8	8	7	8
Index scores	**3**	**3**	**4**	**4**	**5**	**5**
	n = 4	n = 5	n = 4	n = 4	n = 4	n = 2

Table 6.4. Results from ANOVA among variables between meadow and below-meadow reaches for each season. Single asterisks indicate transformed distributions. Numbers in bold are significant at p<0.05. See table 6.1 for abbreviated variables.

Variables	Mid summer	Late summer	Early fall
Discharge (m3/s)	**<0.01**	**<0.01**	0.46
DO (mg/L)	0.61	0.71*	0.22
Specific Conductivity (µS/cm)	0.17	**<0.01**	0.55
TDP (µg/L)	0.06	0.07	0.08
SRP (µg/L)	0.07	0.1	0.07
NH4 (µg/L)	0.36*	0.75	0.54
NO3 (µg/L)	0.96	0.1	0.1
TP (µg/L)	0.37	**<0.01**	0.08
Overstory Cover (percent)	0.89	0.87	0.37
Substrate Size	**0.02**	1	0.2
Number of sites	n = 9	n = 8	n = 6

Trichoptera (EPT) richness. Four environmental variables were found to correlate with six metrics in the early fall (table 6.7). Three environmental variables (discharge, TP, and NH4) were highly correlated with multiple invertebrate metrics. These results reveal that correlations between environmental variables and community metrics increase from mid summer to early fall. Only in early fall did we see aquatic nutrients correlate with invertebrate metrics. Total phosphorous, ammonia, and nitrate correlated with percent EPT, non-insect abundance, plecoptera richness, percent shredder taxa, and tolerant/intolerant taxa. Pearson's coefficient calculations examined data on a site-by-site basis, indicating the influence of the environmental variables on community structure, irrespective of possible meadow effects.

Discussion

The degradation of central Great Basin meadow ecosystems presents an important management challenge. These meadows are highly productive habitat islands (Sada and others 2005) but they are prone to channel incision and desiccation. Understanding the relationship between changing environmental characteristics and BMI communities

USDA Forest Service Gen. Tech. Rep. RMRS-GTR-258. 2011.

89

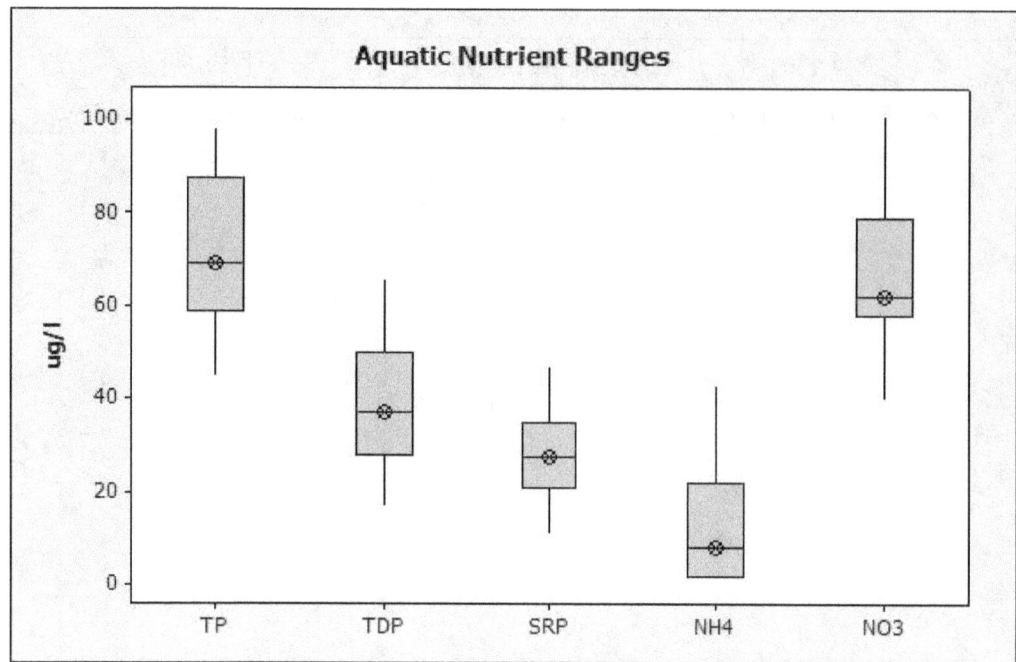

Figure 6.2. Aquatic nutrient ranges for nine sites at Kingston Creek from mid summer through early fall. The 25th and 75th percentiles are shown as a box around the 50th percentile. The error bars represent the highest and lowest values within the upper and lower limits where the upper limit is Q3 + 1.5 (Q3 - Q1) and the lower limit is Q1 - 1.5 (Q3 - Q1).

provides managers with important information about the impact of meadow degradation on aquatic ecosystems. In Kingston Creek, we found strong relationships between environmental characteristics and BMI communities. There were, however, important seasonal differences and differences in the results of the two different analytical methods we used (MRPP and multimetric bioassesments).

The seasonal variation we observed was largely driven by surface water run-off and the relative contribution of groundwater springs. Throughout the season, the water chemistry changed as surface water runoff decreased and the relative contribution of groundwater increased. The two spring tributaries had distinct impacts on water quality that varied by season (fig. 6.3). Total phosphorous concentrations in the stream increased downstream of the upper spring tributary during late summer (table 6.4; fig. 6.3). In addition, Amacher and others (2004) suggest that plant community type may subtly influence water quality on a seasonal basis in these systems. The MRPP analysis illustrated that meadow and below-meadow reaches are biologically distinct from each other during mid and late summer but their populations homogenize during the early fall when surface flows are lowest and the number of correlations between metrics and environmental parameters is greatest. Hannah and others (2007) also found that as spatio-temporal heterogeneity of water sources for mountain streams decreased, invertebrate diversity decreased. Benthic communities in glacial streams also show seasonal variation that is related to the dominant water source (Burgherr and others 2002).

There are several analytical issues that also may have contributed to the fall community homogeneity detected by the MRPP and multimetric method. Two alternative effects may explain this apparent homogeneity. First, because some sites could not be measured in fall, the smaller sample size led to decreased statistical power to detect community

differences. Second, sites that were not measured in the fall may have been driving community variability within the meadow. Though both MRPP and the multimetric method describe population homogeneity in the fall, these other factors may be affecting that observation.

Comparing the results of the two analyses demonstrates that these methods analyze different components of community data. Since multimetric bioassesment is based on indices (i.e., diversity, functional feeding groups, and EPT richness), numeric fluctuations in individual taxa can be masked within the metrics. Conversely, because the MRPP tests for community differences at the taxon scale, it does not detect evenly occurring changes in abundance like multimetric bioassessments. An inspection of the dominant taxa in Kingston Creek shows why the two methods differ. While there were taxonomic differences between the two reaches with more *Orthocladiinae* in the meadow in mid summer and more *Baetidae* in the meadow in late summer, raw percentage values of taxonomic dominance remained unchanged. Functional feeding group and tolerance/intolerance metrics also were unable to recognize the community change since *Orthocladiinae* and *Baetidae* have identical values (filterer-collectors and Hilsenhoff biotic index values of five). However, MRPP does detect differences in composition between the reaches during this time period.

Kennedy and others (2000) examined 19 Great Basin streams in early summer and found that substrate size was one of several in-stream characteristics related to invertebrate indices. The strength of the observed relationships may have been, in part, a function of the season in which the data were collected. Studies of both mountain and desert streams have recognized that spatio-temporal variation of invertebrate communities across seasons are driven by environmental variables (Boulton and others 1992; Robinson and others 2001). Beche and Resh (2007) also documented

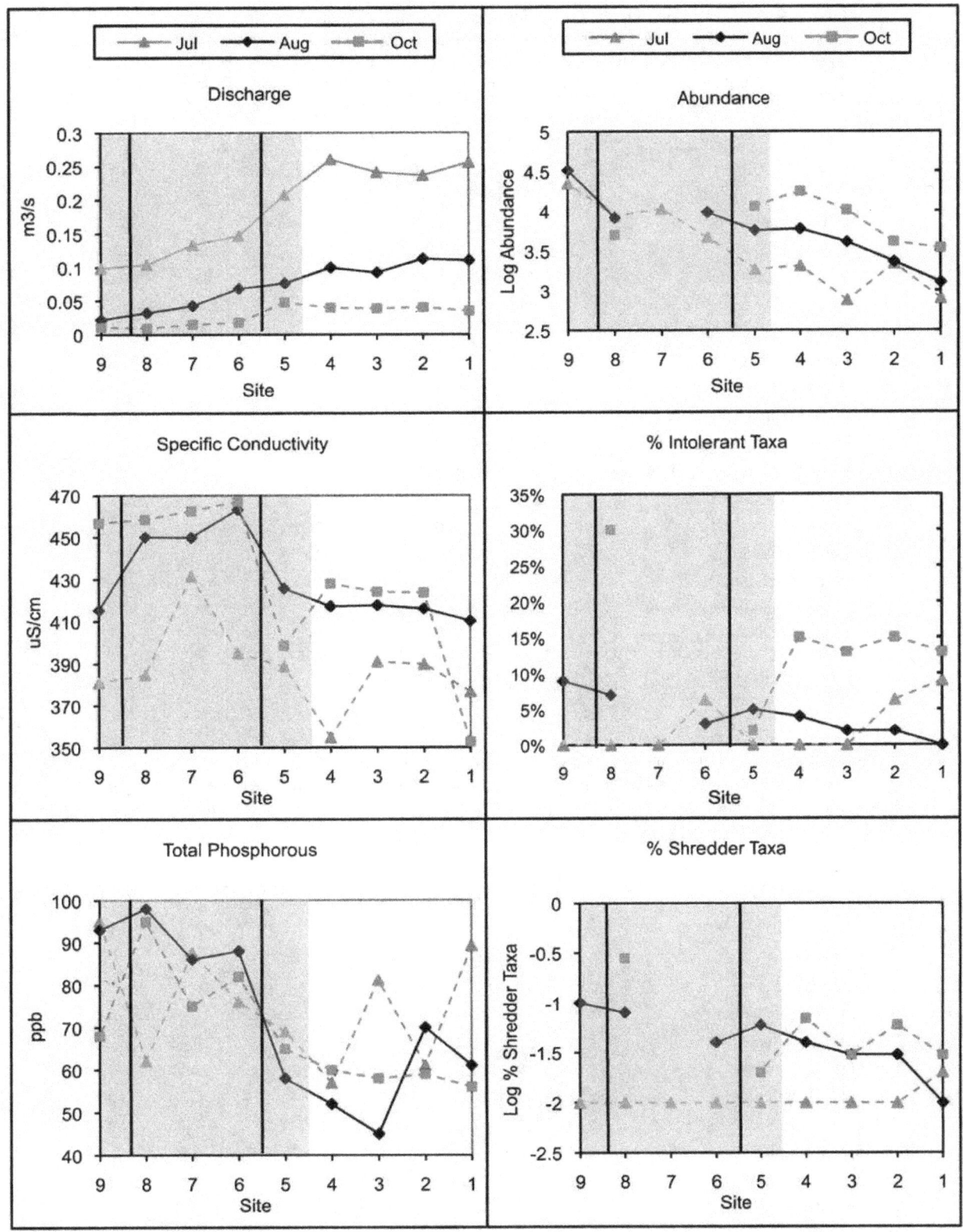

Figure 6.3. Panel illustrating the metrics and environmental variables that were significant in distinguishing meadow and below meadow reaches during late summer. Stream flow is from left to right. Solid trend lines indicate p<0.05. Gray shading represents meadow extent. Vertical lines represent noted springs.

USDA Forest Service Gen. Tech. Rep. RMRS-GTR-258. 2011.

91

Table 6.5. Pearson's Coefficients for metrics and environmental variables for mid summer. Values representing highly correlated relationships (r>|0.90|) between metrics and environmental variables are boxed and bold. Highly correlated relationships increase in number from mid summer to early fall. See table 6.1 for abbreviations of variables.

	Discharge	DO	Specific conductivity	NH4	NO3
Abundance	-0.81	0.18	0.01	-0.33	0.85
Total Taxa	-0.56	0.56	-0.28	0.05	0.68
EPT Richness	-0.43	0.40	-0.09	-0.23	0.58
EPT Abundance	-0.83	0.23	-0.02	-0.29	0.81
Shannon Diversity	-0.10	0.43	-0.08	-0.03	-0.17
Percent Dominant Taxa	0.66	-0.37	-0.03	0.26	-0.17
Percent Non-insect Taxa	0.43	0.44	-0.22	0.11	-0.08
Percent EPT Richness	-0.26	0.53	-0.06	-0.13	0.31
Percent EPT Abundance	-0.01	0.80	-0.52	0.43	-0.04
Ephemeroptera Richness	-0.34	0.62	-0.21	-0.05	0.37
Trichoptera Richness	-0.49	0.21	-0.04	-0.37	0.68
Percent Chironomid Richness	0.42	-0.69	0.30	-0.03	-0.59
Percent Intolerant Taxa	0.30	0.29	-0.07	-0.03	-0.39
Percent Tolerant Taxa	0.37	0.17	-0.16	-0.10	-0.27
Percent Shredders	0.44	0.17	-0.11	0.03	-0.34
Percent Scrapers	0.40	0.14	-0.13	-0.05	-0.36
Percent Filterer-Collectors	-0.84	0.06	0.05	-0.30	0.52
Percent Gatherer-Collectors	0.71	-0.14	0.02	0.30	-0.40

Table 6.6. Pearson's coefficients for metrics and environmental variables for late summer. Values representing highly correlated relationships (r>|0.90|) between metrics and environmental variables are boxed and bold. Highly correlated relationships increase in number from mid summer to early fall. See table 6.1 for abbreviated variables.

	Discharge	DO	Overstory	TDP	SRP	TP
Abundance	-0.79	-0.73	0.48	0.51	0.68	0.58
Total Taxa	-0.61	-0.63	0.34	0.43	0.64	0.42
EPT Richness	-0.41	-0.53	0.88	-0.04	0.12	-0.11
EPT Abundance	-0.87	-0.82	0.41	0.57	0.73	0.66
Percent Dominant Taxa	0.39	0.49	-0.71	-0.32	-0.44	-0.18
Percent Non-insect Taxa	0.15	0.11	-0.64	0.39	0.48	0.26
Percent EPT Richness	-0.08	-0.27	**0.91**	-0.35	-0.28	-0.50
Percent EPT Abundance	0.22	0.32	-0.66	-0.25	-0.35	-0.05
Ephemeroptera Richness	-0.13	-0.39	0.77	-0.41	-0.25	-0.46
Plecoptera Richness	-0.69	-0.87	0.57	0.37	0.60	0.43
Trichoptera Richness	-0.30	-0.28	0.85	-0.05	0.03	-0.17
Percent Intolerant Taxa	**-0.91**	**-0.91**	0.45	0.45	0.57	0.63
Percent Tolerant Taxa	0.48	0.48	-0.62	0.15	0.18	0.01
Percent Shredders	**-0.92**	**-0.91**	0.40	0.49	0.61	0.68
Percent Scrapers	-0.87	-0.66	0.29	0.65	0.54	0.77
Percent Filterer-Collectors	-0.48	-0.49	0.83	0.16	0.22	0.09
Percent Gatherer-Collectors	0.57	0.59	-0.81	-0.22	-0.31	-0.21

Table 6.7. Pearson's coefficients for metrics and environmental variables for early fall. Values representing highly correlated relationships (r>|0.90|) between metrics and environmental variables are boxed and bold. Highly correlated relationships increase in number from mid summer to early fall. See table 6.1 for abbreviated variables.

	Discharge	Overstory	DO	TDP	TP	NH4	NO3
Abundance	0.42	0.82	-0.32	-0.53	-0.22	0.72	0.64
Total Taxa	0.06	0.86	-0.74	-0.62	0.04	0.32	0.52
EPT Richness	-0.16	0.76	-0.88	-0.54	0.10	0.03	0.40
EPT Abundance	0.06	**0.93**	-0.63	-0.76	-0.03	0.31	0.52
Diptera Richness	0.29	0.78	-0.37	-0.71	-0.19	0.41	0.56
Percent Dominant Taxa	-0.15	-0.80	0.51	0.46	-0.06	-0.57	-0.47
Percent Non-insect Taxa	0.49	-0.26	0.69	0.47	0.00	0.81	-0.02
Percent EPT Abundance	-0.69	-0.43	-0.07	0.08	0.37	**-0.96**	-0.59
Plecoptera Richness	**-0.95**	-0.22	-0.04	0.37	**0.98**	-0.40	-0.84
Trichoptera Richness	0.07	0.84	-0.89	-0.68	-0.13	0.11	0.61
Percent Intolerant Taxa	**-0.94**	0.04	-0.48	-0.07	0.74	-0.72	-0.55
Percent Tolerant Taxa	0.51	-0.23	0.70	0.47	-0.03	0.84	0.00
Percent Shredders	**-0.95**	-0.10	-0.20	0.21	**0.95**	-0.47	-0.74
Percent Filterer-Collectors	0.28	0.83	-0.70	-0.64	-0.46	0.24	0.75
Percent Gatherer-Collectors	0.23	-0.80	0.88	0.57	-0.05	0.04	-0.38
Biotic Index	0.68	0.03	0.53	0.26	-0.28	**0.97**	0.28

inter- and intra-region temporal variability of invertebrate assemblages in California streams. Maloney and Feminella (2006) found high seasonal variability in individual metrics when examining stream disturbance gradients and concluded that such metrics would not be appropriate to use alone. We found that in Kingston Creek, the relationship between environmental variables and invertebrate communities changed throughout the seasons and the reach differences were largest in mid summer when there is a mix of surface and groundwater.

Management Summary

These findings have important implications for managing aquatic resources in Kingston Creek and other Great Basin stream systems. The fact that the stream systems are incision prone makes establishing reference sites a formidable task. As a result, effective assessment and monitoring of these stream and meadow ecosystems require the following:

1. Locate monitoring sites for aquatic invertebrates based on an understanding of the past and present disturbance regime and of surface and groundwater dynamics. Because many Great Basin streams are incising, sites should be located in areas with minimal risk of incision (Chapters 3, 5, and 7). Also, to determine the relative influence of groundwater inputs on aquatic invertebrates, sites ideally would be paired and would include locations with and without groundwater inputs (Chapter 4). Finally, sites should be located in areas that are known to have perennial flow.

2. Replicate sites and include a minimum of three samples per site. Because watersheds differ both in the tendency to incise (Chapters 3, 4, and 5) and in water chemistry (Amacher and others 2004), sites should be replicated across watersheds. Spatial variability in groundwater inputs, even within seemingly similar stream reaches, necessitates multiple samples per site.

3. Collect data across multiple years and seasons. Stream flow is highly variable both among and within years in Great Basin watersheds. Our data show that aquatic invertebrates are highly responsive to the variability in stream flow. To ensure an accurate representation of the diversity and abundance of different taxa, it is necessary to sample aquatic invertebrates both among and within years.

4. Use multivariate tests such as MRPP or non-parametric MANOVA to ecologically and statistically validate multimetric index results. Multimetric and multivariate methods have different means of examining benthic communities. Since multimetric bioassessment methods can fail to recognize fundamental benthic community dynamics that are critical for informed managerial decisionmaking, multivariate testing provides a crucial technique for verifying multimetric results. Multimetric methods compare metrics that are commonly composed of groups of taxa while the multivariate method used in this study examines the entire population at greater resolution—taxon by taxon.

5. Generalized linear mixed models (GLMM) may offer another tool for describing population responses to environmental effects and for describing those population

USDA Forest Service Gen. Tech. Rep. RMRS-GTR-258. 2011.

93

distributions. GLMM could be used in place of the multiple ANOVAs and correlation calculations performed in this study and may not require distribution transformations.

References

Amacher, Michael C.; Kotuby-Amacher, Janice; Grossl, Paul R. 2004. Effects of natural and anthropogenic disturbances on water quality. In: Chambers, Jeanne C.; Miller, Jerry, R., eds. Great Basin Riparian Ecosystems—Ecology, Management and Restoration. Covello, CA: Island Press: 162-195.

Barbour, Michael T.; Gerritsen, Jeroen; Snyder, Blaine D.; Stribling, James B. 1999. Rapid bioassessment protocols for use in streams and wadeable rivers: periphyton, benthic macroinvertebrates and fish, 2nd ed. EPA 841-B-99-002: Washington, DC: U.S. Environmental Protection Agency, Office of Water.

Beche, Leah A.; Resh, Vincent H. 2007. Biological traits of benthic macroinvertebrates in California mediterranean-climate streams: long-term annual variability and trait diversity patterns. Fundamental and Applied Limnology. 169: 1-23.

Boulton, Andrew J.; Peterson, Christopher G.; Grimm, Nancy B.; Fisher, Stuart G. 1992. Stability of an aquatic macroinvertebrate community in a multiyear hydrologic disturbance regime. Ecology. 73: 2192-2207.

Burgherr, P.; Ward, J.V.; Robinson, C.T. 2002. Seasonal variation in zoobenthos across habitat gradients in an alpine glacial floodplain. Journal of the North American Benthological Society. 21: 561-575.

Chambers, Jeanne C.; Miller, Jerry R. 2004. Restoring and maintaining sustainable riparian ecosystems: the Great Basin ecosystem management project. In: Chambers, Jeanne C.; Miller, Jerry R., eds. Great Basin Riparian Ecosystems—Ecology, Management and Restoration. Covello, CA: Island Press: 1-23.

California Department of Fish and Game, Aquatic Bioassessment Laboratory, Water Pollution Control Laboratory [CA DFG]. 2003. California stream bioassessment procedures. Rancho Cordova, CA. 11 p.

Hannah, David; Brown, L.E.; Milner, A.M.; Gurnell, A.M.; McGregor, G.R.; Petts, G.E.; Smith, B.P.G.; Snook, D.L. 2007. Integrating climate-hydrology-ecology for alpine river systems. Aquatic Conservation: Marine and Freshwater Ecosystems. 17: 636-656.

Herbst, David B.; Silldorff, Erik L. 2006. Comparison of the performance of different bioassessment methods: similar evaluations of biotic integrity from separate programs and procedures. Journal of the North American Benthological Society. 25(2): 513-530.

Hubbard, J.P. 1977. Importance of riparian ecosystems: biotic considerations. In: Johnson, R.R.; Jones, D.A., eds. Importance, preservation, and management of riparian habitat: A symposium. Gen. Tech. Rep. RM-43. Fort Collins, CO: U.S. Department of Agriculture, Forest Service: 14-18.

Hunter, D.; Reuter, J.; Goldman, C.R. 1993. Lake Tahoe interagency monitoring program, draft standard operating procedures. University of California, Davis. 79 p.

Jenson, S.E.; Platts, W.S. 1990. Restoration of degraded riverine/riparian habitat in the Great Basin and Snake River regions. In: Kusler, J.A.; Kentula, M.E. eds. Wetland creation and restoration: the status of the science. Covello, CA: Island Press: 367-398.

Karr, James R.; Chu, Ellen W. 1999. Restoring life in running waters: better biological monitoring. Washington, DC: Island Press. 207 p.

Kennedy, Tom B.; Merenlender, A.M.; Vinyard, G.L. 2000. A comparison of riparian condition and aquatic invertebrate community indices in central Nevada. Western North American Naturalist. 60: 255-272.

Kerans, B.L.; Karr, J.R.; Ahlstedt, S.A. 1992. Aquatic invertebrate assemblages: spatial and temporal differences among sampling protocols. Journal of the North American Benthological Society. 11(4): 377-390.

Linke, Simon; Bailey, R.C.; Schwindt, J. 1999. Temporal variability of stream bioassessments using benthic macroinvertebrates. Freshwater Biology. 42: 575-584.

Maloney, Kelly O.; Feminella, Jack W. 2006. Evaluations of single- and multi-metric benthic macroinvertebrate indicators of catchment disturbance over time at the Fort Benning military installation, Georgia, USA. Ecological Indicators. 6: 469-484.

Mast, M.A.; Clow, D.W. 2000. Environmental characteristics and water quality of hydrologic benchmark network stations in the western United States. Circular 1173-D. U.S. Geological Survey. 114 p.

McCune, Bruce; Grace, J.B. 2002. Analysis of ecological communities. Gleneden Beach, OR: MjM Software Design. 300 p.

Merritt, Richard W.; Cummins, Kenneth W. 1996. An introduction to the aquatic insects of North America, 3rd ed. Dubuque, IA: Kendall/Hunt Publishing Co. 862 p.

Myers, Marilyn J.; Resh, Vincent. H. 2002. Trichoptera and other macroinvertebrates in springs of the great basin: species composition, richness, and distribution. Western North American Naturalist. 62: 1-13.

Parsons, M.; Norris, R.H. 1996. The effect of habitat-specific sampling on biological assessment of water quality using a predictive model. Freshwater Biology. 36: 419-434.

Post, D. 2005. Dytiscidae of California. Proceedings from CAMLnet taxonomy workshop. California State University, Chico.

Rehn, Andrew C.; Ode, Peter R.; Hawkins, Charles P. 2007. Comparisons of targeted-riffle and reach-wide benthic macroinvertebrate samples: implications for data sharing in stream-condition assessments. Journal North American Benthological Society. 26: 332-348.

Robinson, C.T.; Uehlinger, H.; Hieber, M. 2001. Spatio-temporal variation in macroinvertebrate assemblages of glacial streams in the Swiss Alps. Freshwater Biology. 46: 1663-1672.

Saab, V.; Groves, C. 1992. Idaho's migratory birds: description, habitats, and conservation. Nongame Wildlife Leaflet 10. Boise, ID: Idaho Department of Fish and Game. 16 p.

Sada, Donald W.; Fleishman, E.; Murphy, D.D. 2005. Associations among spring-dependent aquatic assemblages and environmental and land use gradients in a Mojave Desert mountain range. Diversity Distributions. 11: 91-99.

Sanders, Laura L. 1998. A manual of field hydrogeology. Upper Saddle River, NJ: Prentice-Hall Inc. 381 p.

Stewart, Kenneth W.; Stark, B.P. 2002. Nymphs of North American stonefly genera (Plecoptera), 2nd ed. Toronto, Canada: University of Toronto Press, Inc. 457 p.

Thorp, Jim H.; Covich, A.P. 1991. Ecology and classification of North American freshwater invertebrates. San Diego, CA: Academic Press, Inc. 911 p.

Wiggins, Glenn B. 1996. Larvae of the North American caddisfly genera (Trichoptera), 2nd ed. Columbus, OH: The Caddis Press. 457 p.

Yoder, Chris O.; Rankin, Edward T. 1998. The role of biological indicators in a state water quality management process. Environmental Monitoring and Assessment. 51: 61-88.

Zimmerman, Gregory M.; Goetz, Harold; Mielke, Paul W., Jr. 1985. Use of an improved statistical method for group comparisons to study effects of prairie fire. Ecology. 66(2): 606-611.

94

USDA Forest Service Gen. Tech. Rep. RMRS-GTR-258. 2011.

Chapter 7:   Charcterization of Meadow Ecosystems Based on Watershed and Valley Segment/Reach Scale Characteristics

Wendy Trowbridge, Jeanne C. Chambers, Dru Germanoski,
Mark L. Lord, Jerry R. Miller, and David G. Jewett

Introduction

Great Basin riparian meadows are highly sensitive to both natural and anthropogenic disturbance. As detailed in earlier chapters, streams in the central Great Basin have a natural tendency to incise due to their geomorphic history (Miller and others 2001, 2004). Anthropogenic disturbances, including overgrazing by livestock, mining activities, and roads in the valley bottoms, have increased both the rate and magnitude of incision (Miller and others 2004; Chambers and Miller 2004). Stream incision within meadow ecosystems alters channel structure and function and causes a decrease in the water table adjacent to the stream. Because meadow vegetation is closely related to groundwater depth (Allen-Diaz 1991; Castelli and others 2000; Chambers and others 2004a; Naumburg and others 2005; Dwire and others 2006; Loheide and Gorelick 2007), stream incision can result in changes in species composition and, following catastrophic incision, loss of the meadow ecosystem (Wright and Chambers 2002; Chambers and others 2004b). Wet and mesic meadow communities are particularly sensitive to lowered water tables (Castelli and others 2000) and typically decrease in extent following a drop in the water table. Decreases in groundwater levels also can lead to encroachment of upland vegetation and, ultimately, to conversion to *Artemisia* (sagebrush) dominated communities (Groeneveld and Or 1994; Wright and Chambers 2002; Darrouzet-Nardi and others 2006). Other disturbances such as small mammal burrowing (Berlow and others 2002) or overgrazing by livestock (Wright and Chambers 2002) can accelerate shrub encroachment. Once water tables have been lowered, the ecological potential to support a given meadow vegetation type changes and alternative management strategies must be considered (Chambers and Linnerooth 2001; Wright and Chambers 2002). An understanding of the vulnerability of different types of meadows to incision is necessary to prioritize restoration and management efforts.

There has been extensive work on the effects of reach-scale disturbances on meadow degradation—in particular on the impact of overgrazing by livestock on plant communities (Fleischner 1994; Green and Kaufffman 1995; Dobkin and others 1998; Martin and Chambers 2001; Kauffman and others 2004; Kluse and Allen-Diaz 2005; Jackson and Allen-Diaz 2006; Coles-Ritchie and others 2007) and on channel morphology (Fleischner 1994; Trimble and Mendel 1995; Sidle and Sharma 1996; Allen-Diaz and others 1998). There is considerably less information on the role that larger, watershed-scale processes play in governing reach-scale sensitivity to disturbance. Recent research in the Great Basin indicates that watersheds differ in their sensitivity to disturbance and that sensitivity is influenced by morphometry and geology (Germanoski and Miller 2004, Chapters 2 and 5). Drainage basins with morphologic characteristics that lead to rapid runoff are more sensitive to disturbance within the central Great Basin (Germanoski and Miller 2004). These same characteristics control the pattern and composition of riparian vegetation in the watersheds (Chambers and others 2004b). Similarly, research on process domains (Montgomery 1999) and river styles (Brierley and Fryirs 2000) demonstrates that, within watersheds, there are different zones that experience different stream power and that are dominated by different disturbance regimes and environmental characteristics. This prior work indicates that although all central Great Basin stream systems are prone to incision, they are not all equally vulnerable.

In this chapter, we expand on previous work to create a system for grouping meadows based on watershed-scale morphometric characteristics that are indicative of the rate and magnitude of runoff. Although stream gages are sparse in the Great Basin, prior research in the region indicated that it is possible to correlate discharge and watershed characteristics (Hess 2002). We had four main objectives: (1) develop a categorization of meadows within the central Great Basin based on both their watershed- and reach-scale characteristics; (2) sample and describe previously identified vegetation types and their species composition and relative abundance within the meadows; (3) determine how vegetation and other indicators of meadow degradation such as channel depth, number of knickpoints, and bank stability relate to the watershed and reach based categorization; and (4) provide managers with necessary information for analyzing meadows and for determining whether active management is needed.

Description of Study Meadows

The study area included 33 watersheds located in 6 mountain ranges in the central Great Basin (Shoshone, Toiyabe,

Toquima, Monitor, Roberts, and Hot Creek mountains), an area of 15,000 square km^2 (fig. 1.7). The whole watershed average annual precipitation ranged from 28 to 50 cm (Daly and Taylor 1998). Most of the precipitation falls as snow in the winter. Winter storms move from west to east across the study site, so larger, more western ranges tend to be wetter than small ranges farther east. The Toiyabes are the wettest and the Hot Creeks are the driest. In addition, west facing watersheds catch more precipitation than east facing watersheds. Summer precipitation is related to monsoonal moisture that moves north off of the Gulf of California. It is highly localized and variable. For both years of the study, precipitation at the Big Creek snow pack telemetry (SNOTEL) site located near the top of the watershed was near the long-term average—69.1 cm and 65.0 cm, respectively, compared to a 26-year average of 67.6 cm (NWCC 2007).

The 56 study meadows are montane meadows that are located in small upland watersheds. The watersheds range in size from 460 ha to 9500 ha and reach maximum elevations of 2275 to 3495 m. The size of the meadows range from 0.5 ha to 15 ha with a median of 2 ha, and elevations range from 2023 to 2631 m. Fifty-one of the meadows are on The Humboldt-Toiyabe National Forest. The remaining five are privately owned. The primary land use on all of these meadows is grazing of cattle and sheep. Not all meadows were grazed in the two years of the study, but all were intensively grazed at some point in the last 150 years of human habitation in the area (Jensen and Platts 1990). Some meadows are used sporadically for camping, hunting, and fishing, while others are rarely visited. There are existing roads to all but four of the meadows, but they are all unpaved and many are not maintained. The surrounding vegetation is primarily sagebrush steppe with pinyon and juniper woodlands in some watersheds. Mountain mahogany and limber pine occur at the highest elevations.

Methods

Meadows were selected to represent a range of current conditions, positions in the watersheds, size of watersheds, and land management types (from wilderness to privately owned). Some watersheds had multiple meadows (as many as five) while many had only one. Figure 1.7 shows the locations of the meadows. The variables measured describe the physical processes that control meadow characteristics, the biotic characteristics of the meadows, and the ecological condition of the meadows (table 7.1). Meadow condition variables were related to plant communities, knickpoints, and incision.

Table 7.1. List of the study variables and how they were measured and classified. The reach and watershed characteristics were used to create the meadow categorization.

Variable	Measurement method	Variable type
Meadow slope	long profile	reach characteristics
Number of knickpoints	long profile	reach characteristics
Knickpoint height	long profile	Indicators of meadow degradation
Knickpoint slope	long profile	Indicators of meadow degradation
Depth of channel in meadow	cross section	Indicators of meadow degradation
Percent vertical bank	long profile	Indicators of meadow degradation
Number of springs	count	reach characteristics
Sinuosity within the meadow	long profile	reach characteristics
Extent of each plant community	GPS	vegetation communities
Meadow size	GPS	reach characteristics
Length of channel in the meadow	long profile	reach characteristics
Total watershed area	GIS	watershed characteristics
Watershed area above meadow	GIS	watershed characteristics
Watershed area above 2743 m	GIS	watershed characteristics
Watershed area above 2438 m	GIS	watershed characteristics
Total channel length above meadow	GIS	watershed characteristics
Length of main channel above meadow	GIS	watershed characteristics
Length of the whole channel	GIS	watershed characteristics
Maximum watershed elevation	GIS	watershed characteristics
Elevation of top of main channel	GIS	watershed characteristics
Average precipitation	GIS (PRISM)	watershed characteristics
Meadow elevation	GIS	watershed characteristics
Mountain range	categorical variable	watershed characteristics
Watershed aspect (westness)	= Sin(aspect +180)	watershed characteristics
Watershed aspect (southness)	= Cos(aspect +180)	watershed characteristics
Relief	= Max watershed elevation—Meadow elevation	watershed characteristics
Channel relief	= Elevation of top of channel—Meadow elevation	watershed characteristics
Drainage density	= Total channel length above meadow / Area above meadow	watershed characteristics
Position	= Length of channel above meadow / Length of whole channel	watershed characteristics
Shape of the whole watershed	= Channel length above meadow^2/ Area above meadow	watershed characteristics
Shape of the watershed above meadow	= Total watershed area / length of whole channel	watershed characteristics
Total watershed precipitation	= Average precipitation X Watershed area above meadow	watershed characteristics

Data Collection

Field work was conducted over the course of two field seasons (2005 and 2006). For each meadow, a long profile of the stream channel and representative cross sections were surveyed. At each survey point along the long profile, bank stability (vertical versus continuous slope) was recorded. The maximum number of terraces was counted and knickpoints were identified and surveyed. Channel slope and sinuosity within the meadow were calculated from the survey data.

Three cross sections were surveyed in each meadow reach and in the reaches above and below the meadow. Points were surveyed or measured at breaks in slope, water surface, thalweg, and meadow surface on both sides of the channel. Channel depth was used as a measure of incision and was calculated by subtracting thalweg elevation from average meadow surface elevation.

A GPS unit was used to delineate plant communities and the meadow outline. The seven main plant communities were wet meadow (wet), mesic meadow (mesic), dry meadow (dry), dry shrub, willow, rose, and aspen (modified from Manning and Padgett 1995 and Weixelman and others 1996; Appendix 7.1). Areas were calculated for each plant community and the entire meadow. Plant community data are presented as a percentage of the total meadow area, excluding aspen, which is not strictly a meadow community. Plant communities were described using randomly located 0.25-m plots (between 15 and 20 per community, depending on community size). At each plot, aerial cover was estimated for all species using cover classes (trace, 1-5, 6-10, 11-25, 26-50, 51-75, 75-95, and 95-100 percent). Springs also were mapped using the GPS unit and were measured with a tape. Springs without geomorphic expression (localized and likely ephemeral wet spots) were mapped but not measured to minimize the effect of sampling date.

Watershed-level variables were measured using USGS topographic maps and DEMs in ArcGIS. Watersheds were delineated on 7.5-minute USGS topographic maps using ArcGIS software. Hawth's Analysis Tools (Beyer 2004) were used to measure total watershed area, watershed area above the meadow, watershed areas above the 2438-m and 2743-m contours and channel lengths. Relief and maximum elevations were determined by picking spot elevations from topographic maps. For this study, watersheds were defined as the catchment area above each meadow and the catchment area of the whole watershed above the terminal alluvial fan.

The Parameter-elevation Regressions on Independent Slopes Model (PRISM; a product of the Oregon Climate Service) was used to estimate average yearly precipitation throughout Nevada. This program models large-scale orographic and climatic processes and creates a map with isoclines of precipitation for the entire state. Total precipitation and watershed average precipitation were calculated by overlaying watershed area polygons on the PRISM map of annual precipitation.

Data Analysis

The raw data were transformed using a Box-Cox transformation. The resulting transformed data were then standardized and tested for normality using a Kolmogorov-Smirnov goodness-of-fit test. Principle Components Analysis (PCA) and Nonmetric Multidimensional Scaling (NMDS) were used to identify structure within watershed characteristics (see table 7.1 for watershed characteristics) and to create groupings of meadows with similar characteristics. We plotted PCA axis 1 versus 2 and 1 versus 3 and the two main nonmetric multidimensional scaling axes in order to visualize groupings based on the watershed characteristics. The plots were examined for natural groupings and breaks in the data that remained consistent across all three plots. Bar charts and one-way ANOVA analyses were used together with the eigenvectors to illustrate which variables were driving the groupings.

Vegetation communities and their characteristic species had been identified previously in this area (Manning and Padgett 1995; Weixelman and others 1996) and the vegetation mapping and sampling were based on these known community types (Appendix 7.1). To verify that these communities were distinct, we used MRPP using species cover values for all sampled plots. All analyses were carried out using PC-ORD (McCune and Mefford 1999). In addition, importance values for individual species within the community types were calculated using cover and presence absence data and add to 100 percent.

The groups that were created with the watershed characteristics were related to both the vegetation community types and physical indicators of meadow condition data (e.g., knickpoint slope and depth of channel) by calculating and graphing group averages and standard deviations. One-way ANOVAs were used to test for differences in watershed characteristics, vegetation, and meadow condition among the groupings.

The watershed and meadow geomorphic characteristics, the channel characteristics within the meadow, and the percentage of each vegetation type are summarized for each of the 56 study meadows in Appendices 7.2 through 7.5.

Results and Discussion

Watershed Characteristics

The meadows were divided into five groups based on measured watershed-and reach-level characteristics (table 7.2; fig. 7.1). These groups were selected based on the grouping of the meadows in both the PCA and NMDS diagrams (fig. 7.1). Groups 4 and 5 were distinct in all three projections. Groups 1 through 3 formed a continuum along axis 1 in the PCA and axis 2 in the NMDS. The PCA diagram of axis 1 versus axis 3 showed a better separation between these groups, and it led to the decision to create

USDA Forest Service Gen. Tech. Rep. RMRS-GTR-258. 2011.

97

Table 7.2. Categorization of the 56 meadows and group-averaged values for the most heavily weighted variables. Numbers in parentheses are standard deviations.

Variable	Group				
	1	2	3	4	5
	Birch 1	Lebeau	Corcoran 1	Meadow 1	Six Mile 1
	Birch 2	San Juan 2	Corcoran 2	Meadow 2	Six Mile 2
	Kingston 0	Green Monster	Corcoran 3	Birch Trib	Fandango 1
	Kingston 1	South Crane	Corcoran 4	Cahill 2	Fandango 2
	Kingston 3	San Juan 1	Corcoran 5	Cahill 3	East Dobbin
	Mosquito	Mohawk	Corcoran main 1	Emigrant 2	West Dobbin
	Barley 1	Danville	Corcoran main 2	Corral 2	Little Cow
	Indian Valley	Big Creek	Corcoran main 3	Johnson 2	Stargo
		Wadsworth 1	Round Mountain	Johnson 3	Wadsworth 2
		Cloverdale	Willow (Monitors)	Emigrant 1	Wadsworth 3
		Cottonwood	Barley Tributary	Red Canyon	Wadsworth 4
		Washington	West Northumberland	Johnson 1	
			Corral 1		
Watershed area above meadow (ha)	4421 (2676)	1381 (670)	631 (312)	294 (192)	129 (109)
Area above 2743 m (ha)	1356 (1505)	389 (199)	32.9 (21)	1.0 (2)	55.2 (51)
Length of channel above meadow (km)	11.84 (4.64)	6.63 (1.78)	4.25 (0.79)	2.63 (0.63)	1.75 (0.78)
Percent of channel above meadow	64.3% (0.19)	74.0% (0.19)	57.1% (0.13)	47.6% (0.22)	18.5% (0.08)
Watershed average precipitation (cm)	44.1 (7.5)	40.1 (6.7)	39.5 (4.9)	43.5 (3.9)	35.0 (4.7)
Relief (max elevation-meadow elevation) (m)	1090 (184)	957 (172)	591 (90)	366 (140)	409 (170)
Maximum watershed elevation (m)	3315 (187)	3208 (136)	2927 (93)	2595 (170)	2973 (178)
Meadow elevation (m)	2225 (68)	2250 (113)	2335 (61)	2229 (172)	2563 (50)
Meadow slope (%)	1.30% (0.01)	4.35% (0.01)	4.70% (0.01)	6.65% (0.05)	7.94% (0.03)
Meadow size (ha)	6.81 (4.38)	3.64 (2.63)	1.73 (0.97)	2.80 (1.41)	1.47 (1.00)
Meadow sinuosity	1.31 (0.20)	1.10 (0.06)	1.09 (0.04)	1.07 (0.04)	1.08 (0.03)
Number of springs per meadow	10.0 (8)	5.3 (4)	5.2 (6)	3.7 (3)	3.6 (4)

three groups. Figure 7.2 illustrates the relationship between the groups and the variables used to create them. Watershed area above the meadow was the most important driver of the groupings, but other variables were important for particular groups. For example, □st□□□tests showed that meadow elevation was not significantly different for Groups 1 through 4 but Group 5 meadows were at much higher elevations. Groups 1 through 3 represented a continuum from meadows at the bottom of large, high-elevation watersheds to meadows that were part of the way up smaller, lower-elevation watersheds rather than actual distinct groups. This was essentially a gradient of water capture. In the PCA analysis, these three groups lined up along the first axis (fig. 7.1). The eigenvectors of the first axis showed that the length of the main channel above the meadow, total channel length, total watershed precipitation, watershed area above the meadow, relief, area above 2743 m, and maximum watershed elevation were the variables that were most highly correlated with this axis (table 7.3). This axis

explained 37 percent of the total variability. These variables were all closely related to the watershed's ability to capture water and transport sediment.

The interpretation of the second PCA axis was more complicated. Group 5 was similar to Groups 3 and 4 with respect to axis 1, but it was distinct with respect to axis 2. Group 5 meadows were higher-elevation, steeper meadows at the top of their watersheds. They were also in the drier (less average precipitation) parts of the study area. Group 4 meadows were mostly in the northern Toiyabe Mountains, which were the wettest (highest average precipitation) area. As a result, these meadows were bigger than their axis 1 scores (water capture ability) suggested. Groups 4 and 5 represented more of a departure from the main discharge pattern and, thus, form more distinct groups. Table 7.3 and fig. 7.2 show that meadow elevation, mountain range, watershed shape, and position in watershed were the variables most highly correlated with this axis. This axis explained 14 percent of the total variability.

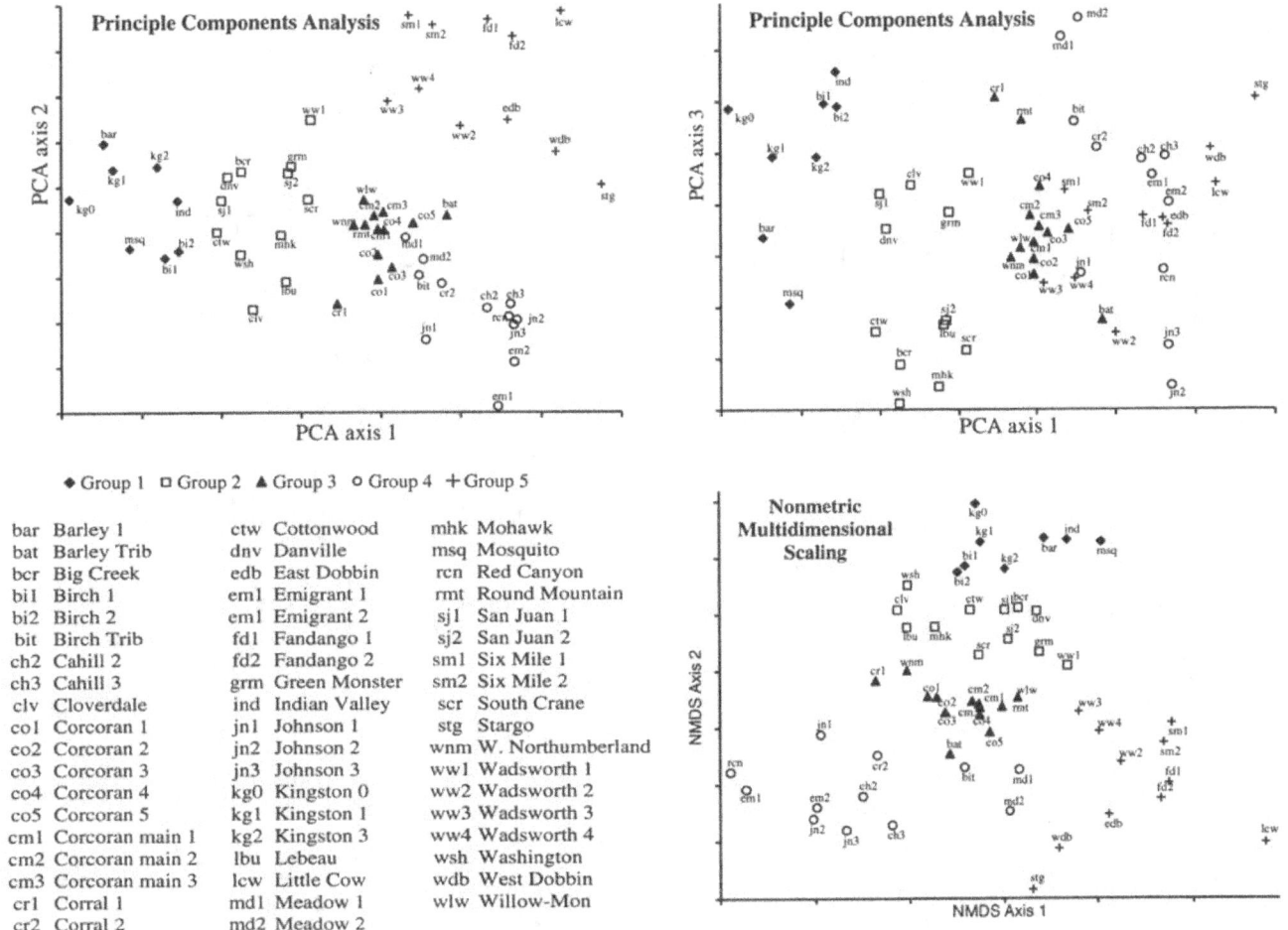

Figure 7.1. Diagrams of the first two PCA axes, the first and third axes for the NMDS, and the main axes for the NMDS. The final groups shown and the symbols are listed in the bottom left.

bar	Barley 1	ctw	Cottonwood	mhk	Mohawk
bat	Barley Trib	dnv	Danville	msq	Mosquito
bcr	Big Creek	edb	East Dobbin	rcn	Red Canyon
bi1	Birch 1	em1	Emigrant 1	rmt	Round Mountain
bi2	Birch 2	em1	Emigrant 2	sj1	San Juan 1
bit	Birch Trib	fd1	Fandango 1	sj2	San Juan 2
ch2	Cahill 2	fd2	Fandango 2	sm1	Six Mile 1
ch3	Cahill 3	grm	Green Monster	sm2	Six Mile 2
clv	Cloverdale	ind	Indian Valley	scr	South Crane
co1	Corcoran 1	jn1	Johnson 1	stg	Stargo
co2	Corcoran 2	jn2	Johnson 2	wnm	W. Northumberland
co3	Corcoran 3	jn3	Johnson 3	ww1	Wadsworth 1
co4	Corcoran 4	kg0	Kingston 0	ww2	Wadsworth 2
co5	Corcoran 5	kg1	Kingston 1	ww3	Wadsworth 3
cm1	Corcoran main 1	kg2	Kingston 3	ww4	Wadsworth 4
cm2	Corcoran main 2	lbu	Lebeau	wsh	Washington
cm3	Corcoran main 3	lcw	Little Cow	wdb	West Dobbin
cr1	Corral 1	md1	Meadow 1	wlw	Willow-Mon
cr2	Corral 2	md2	Meadow 2		

Meadow Group Characteristics

Group 1 meadows were located at or near the base of large wet watersheds with high maximum elevations and high relief. These were the highest discharge meadows, so it is not surprising that channel depths were greatest and percent vertical bank was highest in this group (fig. 7.5; table 7.3). These were large, flat meadows that tended to have numerous springs with deep channels, suggesting previous incision. Group 1 meadows had few knickpoints, which were not particularly large. This suggested that knickpoints move quickly through these meadows. Many of the Group 1 meadows had willows, but they were typically a small percentage (average 24 percent) of the overall cover (fig. 7.3). There was another group of even larger, flatter, lower-elevation meadows that were privately owned and actively managed. They were not included in this study because of management differences and permission issues.

Group 2 meadows also were located near the base of their watersheds, but these watersheds were smaller, lower relief, and drier than Group 1 watersheds. Many Group 2 meadows were still large, but there was more variability in this group. They were less flat, occurred at slightly higher elevations, and had fewer springs (table 7.3). Many of these meadows were dominated by willows (average 45 percent cover) and tended to have less wet meadow vegetation and more dry shrub vegetation (fig. 7.3). Many of these meadows also had deeper channels, although again there was more variability. Some meadows in this group were relatively unincised with water flowing in multiple channels across the surface while others had deeply incised channels. Group 2 meadows also had more knick points than Group 1 meadows.

Group 3 meadows were higher in their watersheds, and these watersheds had even lower maximum elevations and were smaller and slightly steeper than watersheds in the previous groups (fig. 7.2; table 7.3). These meadows were characterized primarily by substrates of volcanic origin, had relatively low discharge, and were dominated by a series of meadows in the Toquima Mountains (Appendices 7.2 and 7.3). Group 3 meadow plant communities were different from those in Groups 1 and 2. Willows were rare in this group (average 5 percent cover) and wet and mesic communities dominated (fig. 7.3). The stream channels within many of these meadows were completely unincised, and where incision had occurred, channel depths were small. In this respect, Group 3 was similar to Groups 4 and 5.

USDA Forest Service Gen. Tech. Rep. RMRS-GTR-258. 2011.

99

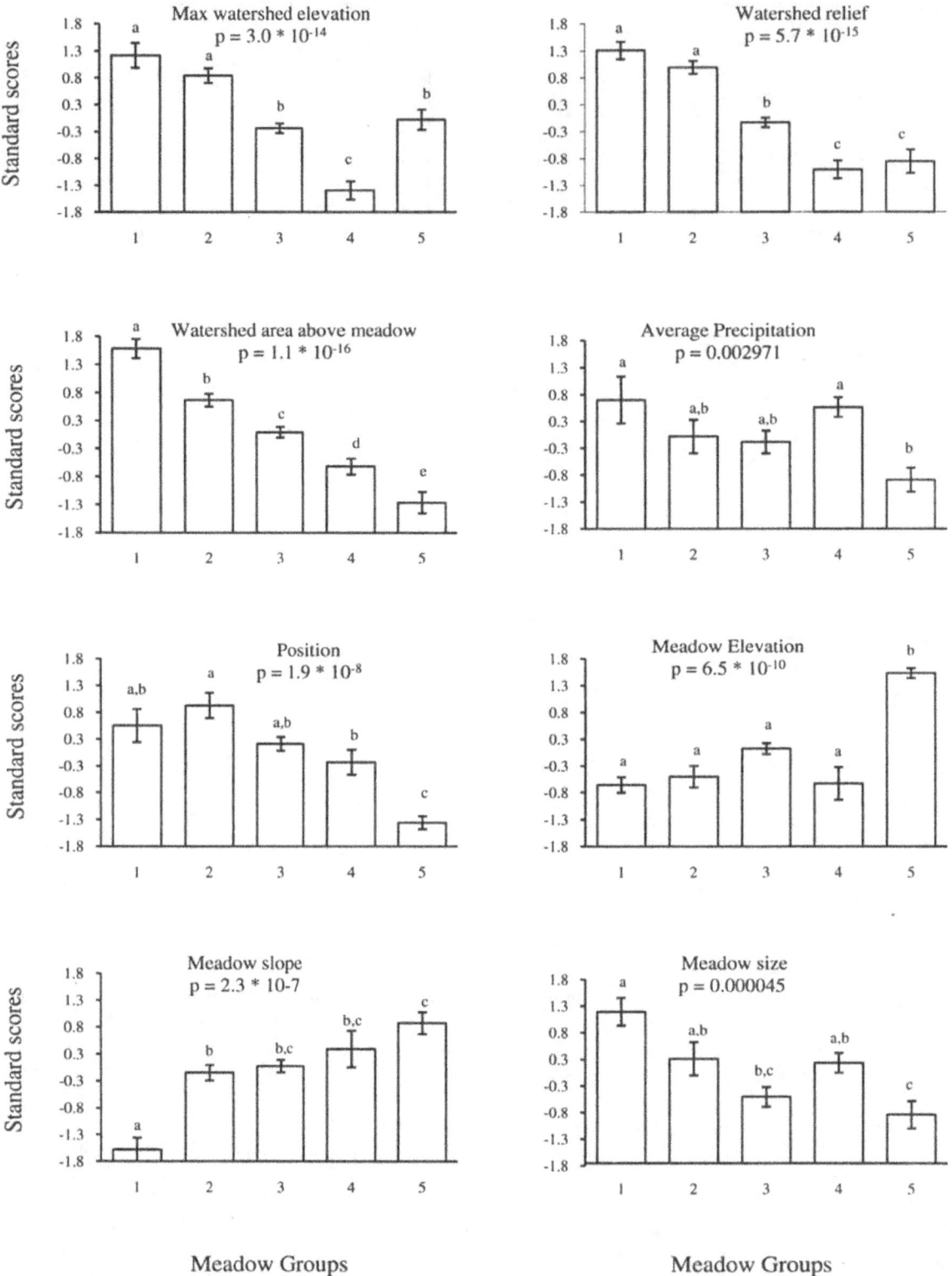

Figure 7.2. Mean and standard error for significant predictor variables by meadow group. Standardized values were used in these figures. P values show differences among groups from one-way ANOVAs. Groups with unlike letters are significantly different (p<0.05).

USDA Forest Service Gen. Tech. Rep. RMRS-GTR-258. 2011.

Table 7.3. The eigenvectors of the first four PCA axes that show which variables are most highly correlated with the different axes. Eigenvectors of greater than 0.24 or less than -0.24 are shaded for emphasis.

Variable	Eigenvectors			NDMS scores	
	1	2	3	1	2
Total watersed precipitation	-0.2847	-0.1220	0.0244	-0.0212	0.1511
Length of main channel above meadow	-0.2843	-0.1220	-0.0852	-0.0226	0.1541
Watershed area above meadow	-0.2828	-0.1063	0.0205	-0.0174	0.1509
Total channel length above meadow	-0.2805	-0.0561	0.0282	-0.0095	0.1512
Watershed area above 2438 m	-0.2802	0.0631	0.0373	0.0242	0.1449
Relief	-0.2732	0.0188	-0.2038	0.0067	0.1469
Channel relief	-0.2556	0.0364	-0.2448	0.0048	0.1385
Area of the whole watershed	-0.2035	0.1194	0.2072	0.0393	0.0998
Watershed area above 2743 m	-0.2597	0.2002	-0.1163	0.0457	0.1389
Maximum watershed elevation	-0.2392	0.2340	-0.1120	0.0535	0.1255
Elevation of top of main channel	-0.2037	0.2734	-0.1666	0.0557	0.1090
Drainage density	-0.0182	-0.2831	-0.0251	-0.0466	0.0022
Meadow elevation	0.1167	0.3889	0.1593	0.0840	-0.0656
Shape of the whole watershed	-0.0044	0.3083	-0.1034	0.0493	0.0140
Mountain range	0.1177	0.3236	0.0220	0.1123	-0.1065
Length of the whole main channel	-0.1992	0.2503	0.2047	0.0625	0.1006
Position	-0.1721	-0.2731	-0.2783	-0.0573	0.0991
Sinuosity within the meadow	-0.1755	0.1607	0.2790	0.0411	0.0830
Southness	-0.0737	-0.1827	0.2510	-0.0289	0.0264
Westness	-0.0448	0.1111	-0.2815	0.0134	0.0277
Meadow size	-0.1352	-0.1483	0.2626	-0.0184	0.0651
Length of channel in the meadow	-0.0830	-0.1646	0.2741	-0.0237	0.0359
Shape of the watershed above meadow	-0.0531	-0.0617	-0.3738	-0.0175	0.0371
Meadow slope	0.2045	0.0761	-0.2541	0.0139	-0.1081
Number of springs	-0.0983	0.0758	0.0505	0.0102	0.0447
Average precipitation	-0.0931	-0.1980	0.0269	-0.0452	0.0431
Hypsometric integral	-0.0040	-0.0636	0.1397	-0.0074	0.0058

Group 4 meadows were in small, low-elevation, low-relief watersheds. Their position in the watershed was similar to Group 3, but they were at lower elevations and tended to be larger than Group 3 meadows. Group 4 meadows mostly surrounded the town of Austin at the north end of the Toiyabe range, which, because of its proximity to Bunker Hill (3489 m), tends to have higher precipitation. Group 4 plant communities were drier than Group 3 meadows with more of the dry meadow community and less of the wet meadow community. These meadows were similar to those in Group 3 with respect to channel incision. Many Group 4 meadows were unincised or had unincised reaches, and where incision had occurred it was relatively shallow.

Group 5 meadows were small, high-elevation, high-slope meadows that were located near the top of their watersheds. We sampled these meadows in the Monitor and Hot Creek ranges, but this type of meadow existed throughout all five of the main mountain ranges. This was the most common meadow type in the central Great Basin. These meadows occur primarily in high-elevation watersheds around Bunker Hill, Little Table Mountain, Table Mountain, and in the Hot Creeks. Because of meadow position in the watershed, the capacity to capture water and deliver it to the meadow was limited. The meadows that we sampled in this group were the driest of the five groups. The mesic and dry shrub communities were dominant in these meadows with very little wet meadow and no willows. The average wet meadow cover was 10 percent and 5 of the 11 meadows in this group had no wet meadow component.

Plant Community Characteristics

Seven major plant communities were identified from the literature based on depth to groundwater and vegetation structure: wet meadow, mesic meadow, dry meadow, dry shrub, willow, rose, and aspen. Other authors (Manning and Padgett 1995; Weixelman and others 1996) have created more community groups based on species composition

USDA Forest Service Gen. Tech. Rep. RMRS-GTR-258. 2011.

101

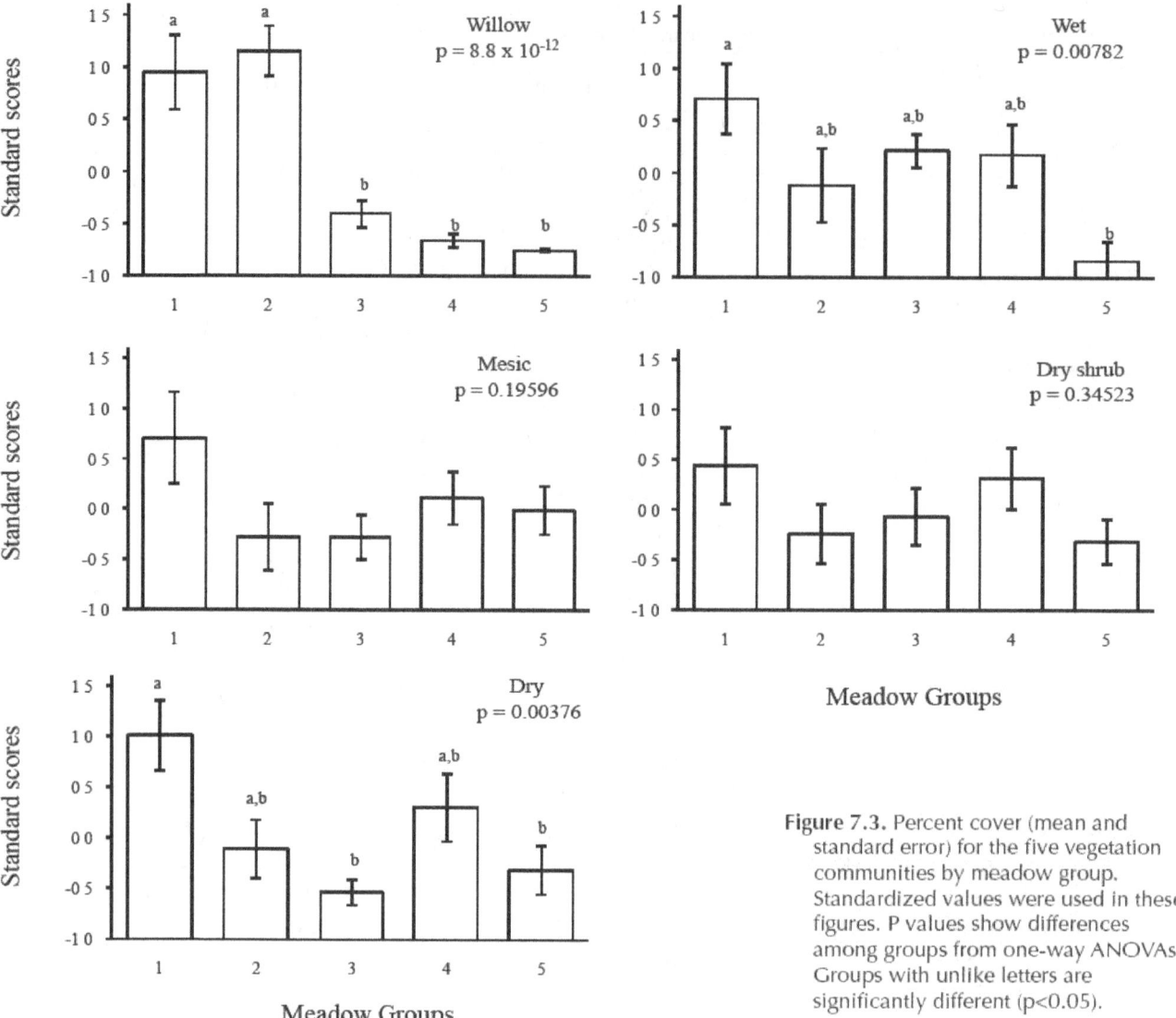

Figure 7.3. Percent cover (mean and standard error) for the five vegetation communities by meadow group. Standardized values were used in these figures. P values show differences among groups from one-way ANOVAs. Groups with unlike letters are significantly different (p<0.05).

and have related them to various physical characteristics like soils and elevation (Appendix 7.1). Because we were primarily interested in the relationship between vegetation and groundwater depth, we based our grouping on that used by Castelli and others (2000) who also studied this relationship. Results of the MRPP test show that there are significant differences among these groups based on species cover (p<0.0001, A = 0.168, and n = 3550). The large sample size was likely responsible for biasing the p-value downward, but the A statistic was typical of plant community data. The dry meadow and mesic meadow communities were the most similar based on their average distance.

Aspen groves were sometimes associated with meadows (14% of meadows), but we did not categorize them as a meadow community because they rely on different sources of water. Thus, aspen patches were mapped but not sampled. All of the meadows that were associated with aspen patches were in the northern Toiyabe Mountains.

The remaining six communities were found throughout all of the mountain ranges. The exact species composition changed from meadow to meadow across mountain ranges and with elevation, but the primary indicator species were consistent. Table 7.4 shows the average species cover and importance value of the main species in each community. Trends in life history groups also were important community indicators. As the plots became drier, rushes and sedges were replaced by forbs and then grasses. Finally, in the driest plots, shrubs dominated with dry meadow vegetation in the understory (fig. 7.4).

The wet meadow community occurred in areas that were supported by groundwater seeps or springs or at the bottom of meadows where water tables were highest. In these communities, groundwater is at or near the surface (typically within 30 cm) during June and July (Castelli and others 2000; Chambers and others 2004b). Eighty percent of the meadows that we sampled contained the wet meadow community. Rushes and sedges were the dominant life history

102

USDA Forest Service Gen. Tech. Rep. RMRS-GTR-258. 2011.

Table 7.4. The most common species in each vegetation community, sorted by importance value (a combination of cover and presence data). N = native, I = introduced.

Species	Mean cover ± S. E.	Importance value	Native/ Introduced	Life history category
Wet meadow				
Carex nebrascensis	42 ± 1.0	48%	N	rush/sedge
Juncus balticus	3 ± 0.2	10%	N	rush/sedge
Mesic meadow				
Juncus balticus	11 ± 0.4	18%	N	rush/sedge
Poa pratensis	5 ± 0.3	9%	I	grass
Carex nebrascensis	3 ± 0.3	6%	N	rush/sedge
Taraxacum officinale	2 ± 0.2	5%	I	forb
Iris missouriensis	3 ± 0.3	5%	N	forb
Achillea millefolium	2 ± 0.4	4%	N	forb
Poa secunda	2 ± 0.2	4%	N	grass
Symphyotrichum spathulatum	1 ± 0.1	3%	N	forb
Dry meadow				
Poa pratensis	4 ± 0.4	8%	I	grass
Poa secunda	3 ± 0.4	8%	N	grass
Juncus balticus	2 ± 0.3	7%	N	rush/sedge
Carex douglasii	3 ± 0.4	7%	N	rush/sedge
Pascopyrum smithii	3 ± 0.4	7%	N	grass
Iris missouriensis	3 ± 0.4	6%	N	forb
Taraxacum officinale	1 ± 0.2	4%	I	forb
Erigeron divergens	1 ± 0.3	4%	N	forb
Leymus cinereus	2 ± 0.5	3%	N	grass
Achillea millefolium	1 ± 0.2	3%	N	forb
Dry shrub meadow				
Artemisia tridentata	18 ± 0.8	24%	N	shrub
Chrysothamnus nauseosus	7 ± 0.6	8%	N	shrub
Chrysothamnus viscidiflorus	4 ± 0.4	7%	N	shrub
Juncus balticus	2 ± 0.2	5%	N	rush/sedge
Leymus triticoides	2 ± 0.2	4%	N	grass
Carex douglasii	2 ± 0.2	4%	N	rush/sedge
Poa pratensis	2 ± 0.2	4%	I	grass
Willow				
Salix exigua	23 ± 1.7	20%	N	shrub/tree
Salix lutea	16 ± 1.7	13%	N	shrub/tree
Rosa woodsii	9 ± 1.1	10%	N	shrub
Poa pratensis	2 ± 0.3	4%	I	grass
Betula occidentalis	5 ± 1.1	4%	N	shrub/tree
Carex nebrascensis	3 ± 0.5	4%	N	rush/sedge
Juncus balticus	1 ± 0.1	4%	N	rush/sedge

group (total importance value [IV] = 66%). *Carex* (IV = 53%) was the most common genus in this community type and *Carex nebraskensis* was the dominant species (IV = 48%). Forbs (IV = 21%) and grasses (IV = 12%) were comparatively minor constituents.

The mesic meadow community was one of the most common communities. It was present in 96% of the meadows that we sampled. Where it was found, it represented a relatively high percentage of the meadow cover (25%). Past research in this area indicated that water table depths for this community ranged from 30 to 80 cm (Chambers and others 2004b). *Juncus balticus* was the most common species in this community. It was found in 84% of plots, but because of its growth form it only represented an average of 11% of the cover. Although rushes and sedges were an important part

of this community, their importance value (IV = 33%) was less than that of the forbs (IV = 41%). Grasses also played a larger role in this community than in the wet meadow community (IV = 25%). The non-native grass *Poa pratensis* was largely responsible for this increase.

The dry meadow community was comparatively rare. Only 45% of meadows had this community, and where it was present, it was a relatively minor part of the total area (an average of 16%). Previous research indicated that this community occurred naturally on the landscape but increased in response to disturbances that resulted in lowered water tables (Wright and Chambers 2002). Water tables that can support this community under proper management range from about 80 to 120 cm (Wright and Chambers 2002). Grasses were the dominant growth form in this community

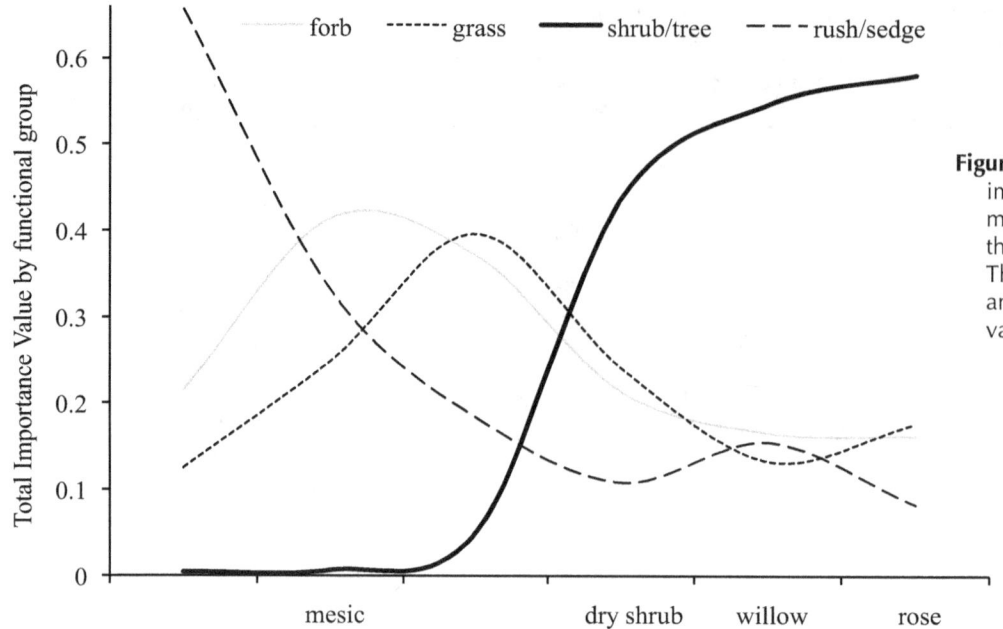

Figure 7.4. The change in the importance value of the four main life history groups across the six vegetation communities. The understory of the willow and rose communities are highly variable.

(IV = 40%). Non-native grasses were planted in some watersheds after fire and as forage. Consequently, these grasses were often a significant constituent of this community (IV = 13%). Native species that characterized this community type included *Poa secunda juncifolia*, *Pascopyrum smithii*, and *Leymus cinereus*, while introduced species included *Thinopyrum intermedium* and *Bromus inermis*. The species in this community were more variable from meadow to meadow than in other communities. As a result, there was no dominant species in this community. The ratio of grasses to sedges and rushes was the best descriptor, and it was significantly less in the wet meadow (0.19 to 1) and mesic meadow (0.75 to 1) than in the dry meadow community (2.13 to 1).

The dry shrub community had a shrub density similar to the surrounding upland community but had an understory of meadow species. This transitional community was present in 96% of meadows, and was one of the largest communities in most meadows (average 32% of total meadow area). *Artemisia tridentata* (subspecies *tridentata* and *vaseyana*) was the most common species in the community (IV = 18%), but *Chrysothamnus* species were also important (IV = 11%). The understory of this community was variable. Some patches were dominated by mesic meadow species, primarily *Juncus balticus*, and had fewer grasses. These patches also had more *Chrysothamnus* and *Rosa woodsii*. Other patches were more grass dominated with understory species similar to the dry meadow community. For the purposes of this report, these two patch types were lumped together as dry shrub.

The willow community was primarily found on terraces next to the stream channel. Overall, 54% of the meadows that we sampled had willows. Position in the watershed was an important predictor of willow presence. Of the meadows near the top of their watersheds (less than 45% of the stream length was above the meadow) only 20% had willows. The four meadows near the top of their watersheds

that had willows only had small patches, representing 2% or less of total meadow cover. In contrast, 72% of meadows at the bottom of their watersheds had willows and of those with willows, the average meadow cover was 33%. Elevation was collinear with watershed position, but since there were willows at high-elevation (both outside of meadows and in meadows that were at the bottom of high-elevation watersheds), there was clearly no physiological constraint. The actual willow cover in these communities was variable, but they were often quite dense with very limited understory. The willow communities along the channel tended to have understories similar to the wet meadow community, but patches away from the stream were much drier.

The rose community was the rarest community with only 14% of meadows having a distinct rose community. Rose patches in these meadows only made up 15% of the total cover. However, these statistics underestimated the importance of *Rosa woodsii* in these meadows because it was often a major constituent of the willow and dry shrub communities. Rose patches were often associated with the dry shrub community and had similar shrub and understory species to the dry shrub community. Overall, 57% of the meadows contained this species. In the patches where it was the dominant species, *Rosa woodsii* was quite dense (IV = 39%) and there was often limited understory. Rose generally is considered to be an indicator of disturbance in the Great Basin (Weixelman and others 1996; Chambers and others 2004a).

Indicators of Degradation

The relationships between the meadow groupings and the indicators of meadow degradation were complex (fig. 7.4). There were meadows with indicators of degradation in each group. The significant relationship between the knickpoint variables and the meadow groupings was driven by the comparative scarcity of knickpoints in Group 1 meadows.

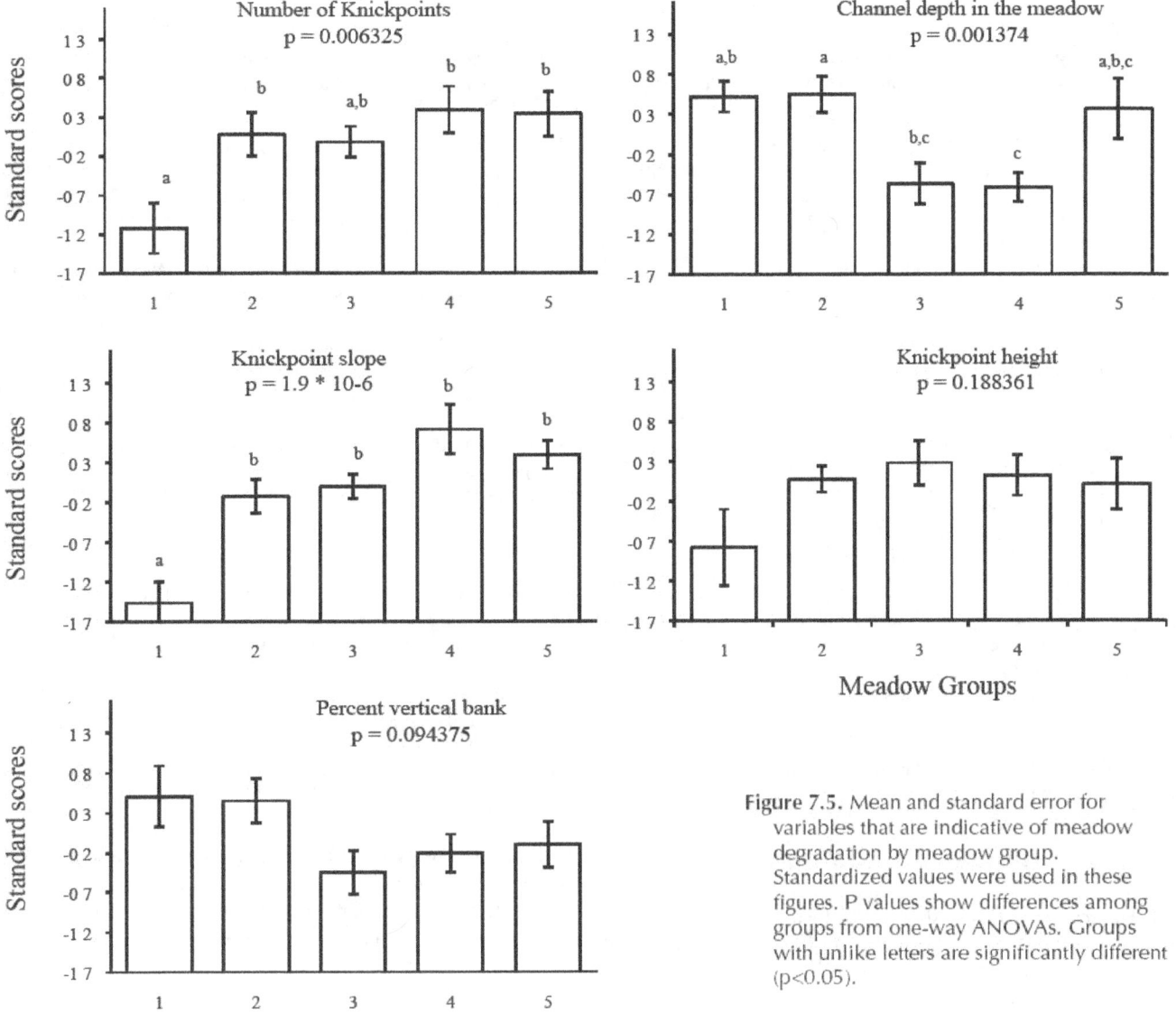

Figure 7.5. Mean and standard error for variables that are indicative of meadow degradation by meadow group. Standardized values were used in these figures. P values show differences among groups from one-way ANOVAs. Groups with unlike letters are significantly different (p<0.05).

Group 1 meadows tended to have fewer knickpoints than steep, low-discharge meadows. Knickpoint slopes were much steeper than the reach average slopes in this part of the system and, therefore, the disparity in stream power was much greater between the knickpoint and the surrounding channel gradients. This could cause knickpoint migration to occur more rapidly and, thus, fewer knickpoints to be observed. The difference in Group 1 knickpoints also could be related to differences in underlying sediment grain size.

Both depth of channel and percent of vertical bank generally increased with increasing discharge. As a result, Groups 1 and 2 had deeper channels and steeper banks than the other groups. Group 3 and 4 meadows had shallow channels with less steep banks. Group 5 meadows had mostly shallow channels, but a few exceptions skewed the average presented in fig. 7.5. The steepness of these meadows results in the potential for catastrophic incision.

There were significant differences in some of the vegetation communities across the meadow groups (ANOVA p

values ranged from less than 0.00001 to 0.345; fig. 7.5). The strongest patterns occurred in the willow and wet meadow plant communities. Groups 1 and 2 had substantial willow communities, primarily along the channel, while Groups 3 through 5 did not. The higher discharges that these meadows experienced during spring snowmelt were more likely to create the necessary conditions for willow establishment, including bare soils and inset terraces. Group 1 meadows had the most wet meadow community, while Group 5 meadows had very little of this plant community. This was likely the result of differences in groundwater discharge during the growing season. There were also significant differences in the dry meadow community across the meadow groups, but the pattern of the differences was similar to the pattern of meadow size across meadow groups. Since Group 1 meadows were bigger, they had more dry meadow community. A comparison of the percentage of the meadow complex that was dry meadow showed that there were no significant differences across groups (p = 0.067).

USDA Forest Service Gen. Tech. Rep. RMRS-GTR-258. 2011.

105

Table 7.5. Meadow groups and summary of geomorphic and vegetation characteristics.

Group	Watershed characteristics	Meadow characteristics	Discharge	Groundwater influence	Stream channel characteristics	Vegetation
1	Large, high elevation, high precipitation	Large watershed area above meadow, large size, very low meadow gradient	High to moderate	High; many springs and seeps, restrictive layers	Deep channels, high % vertical bank; few, small knickpoints	Wet, mesic, dry shrub and willow in similar abundance
2	Intermediate size and elevation, moderate precipitation	Moderate watershed area above meadow, moderate size and gradient	Moderate to high	Moderate; intermediate springs; restrictive layers	Variable, deeply incised channels to many surface channels; knickpoints intermediate	Willow dominate with lower amounts of wet, mesic, and dry shrub
3	Small, low elevation, high relief, moderate precipitation	Low to moderate area above meadow, small size, moderate gradient	Low	High; intermediate springs; strong, restrictive layers	Minimal incision, low channel depths; few knickpoints	Wet, mesic, and dry shrub dominate
4	Small, very low elevation and relief, high precipitation	Small area above meadow, small to intermediate size, high gradient	Low	High; few springs; strong, restrictive layers	Minimal incision, low channel depths; few knickpoints	Dry shrub, mesic, and wet dominate
5	Intermediate size and elevation, low precipitation	Very small area above meadow, very small size, very high gradient	Very low	Moderate, few springs; restrictive layers	Minimal incision, low channel depths; few knickpoints	Mesic and dry shrub dominate with lesser amounts of wet and dry

Management Summary

The results of this study indicate that the meadows in this region can be divided into groups based on their watershed size and elevation and their position in the watershed. These groups provide important information about what plant communities and channel shapes managers should expect to find and, thus, when active management is necessary to preserve meadow conditions (table 7.5). It is reasonable to expect that different groups will respond differently to stabilization efforts. In general, meadows that experience less discharge and that have lower slopes are likely to be the best candidates for stabilization. Stabilization of meadows with higher discharge and greater slopes requires a more detailed understanding of the meadow's geomorphic and hydrologic controls.

Table 7.5 provides a summary of the groups, and table 7.2 shows values for the watershed characteristics used to develop the groups. This information can be used by managers to make assessments of meadow conditions in the field. While it is not practical for managers to measure all of the variables used in this study, it is possible to quickly estimate many of the variables, such as relief and maximum elevation of the watershed and elevation and size of the meadow. This information can be used to determine the meadow group. Once the group is known, the meadow can be compared to other meadows with similar watershed characteristics to determine whether the channel is deeper than would be expected or if there is a larger willow community or smaller wet meadow community than would be expected. This approach allows managers to compare different meadows both within and across groups and to prioritize management and restoration activities accordingly. For example, a Group 1 meadow with large knickpoints and a small wet meadow community would be a higher priority for stabilization than a Group 5 meadow with similar conditions.

Acknowledgments

We thank Danielle Johnson, Rita Dodge, Jacob Miller, Anne Farady, and Dave Board for their hard work in the field.

References

Allen-Diaz, B.H. 1991. Water-table and plant-species relationships in Sierra-Nevada meadows. American Midland Naturalist. 126: 30-43.

Allen-Diaz, B.; Jackson, R.D.; Fehmi, J.S. 1998. Detecting channel morphology change in California's hardwood rangeland spring ecosystems. Journal of Range Management. 51: 514-518.

Berlow, E.L.; D'Antonio, C.M.; Reynolds, S.A. 2002. Shrub expansion in montane meadows: the interaction of local-scale disturbance and site aridity. Ecological Applications. 12: 1103-1118.

Beyer, H.L. 2004. Hawth's analysis tools for ArcGIS. Available: http://www.spatialecology.com/htools.

Brierley, G.J.; Fryirs, K. 2000. River styles, a geomorphic approach to catchment characterization: implications for river rehabilitation in Bega catchment, New South Wales, Australia. Environmental Management. 25: 661-679.

Castelli, R.M.; Chambers, J.C.; Tausch, R.J. 2000. Soil-plant relations along a soil-water gradient in great basin riparian meadows. Wetlands. 20: 251-266.

Chambers, J.C.; Linnerooth, A.R. 2001. Restoring riparian meadows currently dominated by *Artemisia* using alternative state concepts—the establishment component. Applied Vegetation Science. 4: 157-166.

Chambers, J.C.; Miller, J.R. 2004. Restoring and maintaining sustainable riparian ecosystems—the Great Basin Ecosystem Management Project. In: Chambers, J.C.; Miller, J.R., eds. Great Basin Riparian Ecosystems—Ecology, Management, and Restoration. Covelo, CA: Island Press: 1-24.

Chambers, J.C.; Miller, J.R.; Germanoski, D.; Weixelman, D.A. 2004b. Process based approaches for managing and restoring riparian ecosystems. In: Chambers, J.C.; Miller, J.R., eds. Great Basin Riparian Ecosystems—Ecology, Management, and Restoration. Covelo, CA: Island Press: 261-292.

Chambers, J.C.; Tausch, R.J.; Korfmacher, J.L.; Miller, J.R.; Jewett, D.G. 2004a. Effects of geomorphic processes and hydrologic regimes on riparian vegetation. In: Chambers, J.C.; Miller, J.R., eds. Great Basin Riparian Ecosystems—Ecology, Management, and Restoration. Covelo, CA: Island Press: 196-231.

Coles-Ritchie, M.C.; Roberts, D.W.; Kershner, J.L.; Henderson, R.C. 2007. Use of a wetland index to evaluate changes in riparian vegetation after livestock exclusion. Journal of the American Water Resources Association. 43: 731-743.

Daly, C.; Taylor, G. 1998. Annual precipitation (PRISM) 1961-1990. Water and Climate Center of the Natural Resources Conservation Service. Available: http://www.wcc.nrcs.usda. gov/. [18 Jan 2011].

Darrouzet-Nardi, A.; D'Antonio, C.M.; Dawson, T.E. 2006. Depth of water acquisition by invading shrubs and resident herbs in a Sierra Nevada meadow. Plant and Soil. 285: 31-43.

Dobkin, D.S.; Rich, A.C.; Pyle, W.H. 1998. Habitat and avifaunal recovery from livestock grazing in a riparian meadow system of the northwestern Great Basin. Conservation Biology. 12: 209-221.

Dwire, K.A.; Kauffman, J.B.; Baham, J.E. 2006. Plant species distribution in relation to water table depth and soil redox potential in Montane riparian meadows. Wetlands. 26: 131-146.

Fleischner, T.L. 1994. Ecological costs of livestock grazing in western North-America. Conservation Biology. 8: 629-644.

Germanoski, D.; Miller, J.R. 2004. Basin sensitivity to channel incision in response to natural and anthropogenic disturbance. In: Chambers, J.C.; Miller, J.R., eds. Great Basin Riparian Ecosystems—Ecology, Management, and Restoration. Covelo, CA: Island Press: 88-123.

Green, D.M.; Kauffman, J.B. 1995. Succession and livestock grazing in a northeastern Oregon riparian ecosystem. Journal of Range Management. 48: 307-313.

Groeneveld, D.P.; Or, D. 1994. Water-table induced shrub-herbaceous ecotone-hydrologic management implications. Water Resources Bulletin. 30: 911-920.

Hess, G.W. 2002. Updated techniques for estimating monthly streamflow-duration characteristics at ungaged and partial-record sites in central Nevada. Open-File Report 02-168. Carson City, NV: U.S. Geological Survey. 16 p.

Jackson, R.D.; Allen-Diaz, B. 2006. Spring-fed wetland and riparian plant communities respond differently to altered grazing intensity. Journal of Applied Ecology. 43: 485-498.

Jenson, S.E.; Platts, W.S. 1990. Restoration of degraded riverine/ riparian habitat in the Great Basin and Snake River regions. In: Kusler, J.A.; Kentula, M.E., eds. Wetland creation and restoration: the status of the science. Washington, DC: Island Press: 367-398.

Kauffman, J.B.; Thorpe, A.S.; Brookshire, E.N.J. 2004. Livestock exclusion and belowground ecosystem responses in riparian meadows of eastern Oregon. Ecological Applications. 14: 1671-1679.

Kluse, J.S.; Allen-Diaz, B. 2005. Importance of soil moisture and its interaction with competition and clipping for two montane meadow grasses. Plant Ecology. 176: 87-99.

Loheide, S.P.; Gorelick, S.M. 2007. Riparian hydroecology: a coupled model of the observed interactions between groundwater flow and meadow vegetation patterning. Water Resources Research. 43, W07414, doi: 10.1029/2006WR005233.

Manning, M.E.; Padgett, W.G. 1995. Riparian community type classification for Humboldt and Toiyabe National Forests, Nevada and eastern California. R4-Ecol-95-01. Ogden, UT: U.S. Department of Agriculture, Forest Service, Intermountain Region.

Martin, D.W.; Chambers, J.C. 2001. Restoring degraded riparian meadows: biomass and species responses. Journal of Range Management. 54: 284-291.

McCune, B.; Mefford, M.J. 1999. Multivariate Analysis of Ecological Data Version 4.25. Gleneden Beach, OR: MjM Software.

Miller, J.; Germanoski, D.; Waltman, K.; Tausch, R.; Chambers, J. 2001. Influence of late Holocene hillslope processes and landforms on modern channel dynamics in upland watersheds of central Nevada. Geomorphology. 38: 373-391.

Miller, J.R.; House, K.; Germanoski, D.; Tausch, R.; Chambers, J.C. 2004. Fluvial geomorphic responses to Holocene climate change. In: Chambers, J.C.; Miller, J.R., eds. Great Basin Riparian Ecosystems—Ecology, Management, and Restoration. Covelo, CA: Island Press: 49-87.

Montgomery, D.R. 1999. Process domains and the river continuum. Journal of the American Water Resources Association. 35: 397-410.

Naumburg, E.; Mata-Gonzalez, R.; Hunter, R.G.; Mclendon, T.; Martin, D.W. 2005. Phreatophytic vegetation and groundwater fluctuations: a review of current research and application of ecosystem response modeling with an emphasis on Great Basin vegetation. Environmental Management. 35: 726-740.

Sidle, R.C.; Sharma, A. 1996. Stream channel changes associated with mining and grazing in the Great Basin. Journal of Environmental Quality. 25: 1111-1121.

Trimble, S.W.; Mendel, A.C. 1995. The cow as a geomorphic agent—a critical review. Geomorphology. 13: 233-253.

U.S. Department of Agriculture, Natural Resources Conservation Service, National Weather and Climate Center [NWCC]. 2007. Historical accumulated precipitation (daily) for site 337 in the state of Nevada. Available: http://www.wcc.nrcs.usda. gov/snotel/snotelday2.pl?site=337&station=17k04s&state=n &report=precip_accum_hist. [15 September 2007].

Weixelman, D.A.; Zamudio, D.C.; Zamudio, K.A. 1996. Central Nevada riparian field guide. R4-Ecol-96-01. Ogden, UT: U.S. Department of Agriculture, Forest Service, Intermountain Region.

Wright, J.M.; Chambers, J.C. 2002. Restoring riparian meadows currently dominated by *Artemisa* using alternative state concepts—above-ground vegetation response. Applied Vegetation Science. 5: 237-24

Appendix 7.1. Meadow ecological types included in this study relative to those in prior studies by Manning and Padgett (1995) and Weixelman and others (1996).

	Wet meadow	Mesic meadow	Dry meadow	Dry shrub	Willow	Rose
Manning and Padgett (1995)	*Deschampsia caespitosa, Carex nebrascensis, Deschampsia caespitosa/Carex nebrascensis, Carex rostrata*	*Hordeum brachyantherum, Juncus balticus, Poa pratensis*	*Carex douglasii, Iris missouriensis/* Dry graminoid	not described	*Salix exigua/Rosa woodsii, Salix exigua/Mesic forb, Salix exigua/Bench, Salix lutea/Rosa woodsii, Salix lutea/Mesic forb, Salix lutea/Mesic graminoid, Salix lutea/Poa pratensis, Salix lutea/Bench*	*Rosa woodsii, Artemisia tridentata/Rosa woodsii*
Weixelman and others (1996)	*Deschampsia caespitosa, Carex nebrascensis*	Mesic graminoid	Dry graminoid	*Artemisia tridentata/ Leymus cinereus, Artemisia tridentata/ Poa secunda*	Warm willow/Mesic graminoid, Cold willow/Mesic graminoid, Warm willow/Mesic forb, Cold willow/ Mesic forb	not described

Appendix 7.2. Location and watershed characteristics of the 56 study meadows (ppt = precipitation).

Study meadow	Mountain range	UTM coordinates (zone 11, NAD83) X	Y	Watershed area above meadow (ha)	Average ppt above meadow (cm)	Total above meadow ppt (hectare meter)	Channel length above meadow (km)	Percent of channel above meadow
Barley 1	Monitor	529,295	4,276,464	7314	35.0	2559	19.65	84%
Barley Tributary	Monitor	526,723	4,274,294	378	27.9	105	3.73	76%
Big Creek	Toiyabe	489,606	4,353,018	1181	47.3	558	6.42	54%
Birch 1	Toiyabe	496,430	4,361,054	3548	48.7	1729	9.21	64%
Birch 2	Toiyabe	495,667	4,361,054	1967	49.1	966	8.53	60%
Birch Tributary	Toiyabe	495,974	4,363,926	293	48.3	141	2.61	23%
Cahill 2	Toiyabe	496,700	4,368,506	223	47.9	107	2.55	39%
Cahill 3	Toiyabe	496,069	4,368,479	143	47.7	68	2.04	31%
Cloverdale	Toiyabe	456,953	4,283,689	2617	31.6	827	9.61	92%
Corcoran 1	Toquima	515,000	4,282,390	687	37.3	256	4.94	74%
Corcoran 2	Toquima	514,653	4,282,279	649	37.5	244	4.51	67%
Corcoran 3	Toquima	514,007	4,282,497	498	38.9	194	3.86	57%
Corcoran 4	Toquima	513,540	4,282,488	438	39.4	173	3.30	49%
Corcoran 5	Toquima	513,193	4,282,706	200	41.4	83	3.03	45%
Corcoran main 1	Toquima	513,861	4,283,505	648	42.5	276	4.84	56%
Corcoran main 2	Toquima	513,635	4,283,634	583	43.1	251	4.38	51%
Corcoran main 3	Toquima	513,510	4,283,780	574	43.1	247	4.15	48%
Corral 1	Toquima	516,350	4,330,167	1482	46.6	691	5.79	76%
Corral 2	Toquima	514,558	4,331,776	738	45.3	334	3.20	42%
Cottonwood	Toiyabe	476,261	4,333,290	1859	47.1	877	8.16	87%
Danville	Monitor	541,631	4,291,374	1654	36.3	600	6.89	83%
East Dobbin	Monitor	542,226	4,309,058	124	33.0	41	1.45	29%
Emigrant 1	Toiyabe	497,845	4,374,140	346	43.7	151	2.87	56%
Emigrant 2	Toiyabe	497,728	4,373,870	171	43.2	74	2.42	47%
Fandango 1	Hot Creek	557,140	4,279,305	131	30.5	40	1.67	16%
Fandango 2	Hot Creek	557,029	4,279,484	104	30.5	32	1.45	14%
Green Monster	Monitor	540,510	4,288,100	862	35.3	304	4.81	55%
Indian Valley	Toiyabe	456,553	4,294,540	4195	32.8	1376	10.79	55%
Johnson 1	Toiyabe	491,499	4,364,700	320	45.5	146	2.97	77%
Johnson 2	Toiyabe	491,651	4,364,427	70	43.5	31	2.22	70%
Johnson 3	Toiyabe	491,775	4,364,160	61	43.6	27	2.01	64%
Kingston 0	Toiyabe	486,048	4,343,055	4146	49.7	2061	11.86	64%
Kingston 1	Toiyabe	485,696	4,344,852	2809	50.2	1412	9.49	51%
Kingston 3	Toiyabe	486,351	4,346,888	1885	49.5	933	6.91	37%
Lebeau	Shoshone	447,400	4,326,498	981	27.7	272	6.65	98%
Little Cow	Hot Creek	558,062	4,280,032	10	33.0	3	0.65	4%
Meadow 1	Toquima	506,930	4,282,767	327	38.9	127	2.46	22%
Meadow 2	Toquima	506,544	4,282,941	303	39.0	118	2.02	18%
Mohawk	Toiyabe	468,626	4,316,169	963	36.9	355	7.09	94%
Mosquito	Monitor	526,990	4,296,652	9503	38.0	3611	18.24	99%
Round Mountain	Toquima	509,254	4,281,450	501	40.7	204	3.34	36%
San Juan 1	Toiyabe	476,380	4,330,043	2296	40.2	922	6.52	63%
San Juan 2	Toiyabe	476,925	4,329,976	1077	43.0	463	5.86	57%
Six Mile 1	Hot Creek	560,532	4,281,282	361	32.8	118	2.50	18%
Six Mile 2	Hot Creek	560,435	4,281,069	289	33.0	95	2.29	17%
South Crane	Toiyabe	469,284	4,312,691	749	44.0	329	4.63	76%
Stargo	Monitor	543,507	4,311,320	33	33.0	11	0.71	14%
Wadsworth 1	Monitor	536,298	4,301,974	446	41.5	185	3.72	40%
Wadsworth 2	Monitor	536,347	4,301,500	41	43.2	18	2.20	25%
Wadsworth 3	Monitor	536,539	4,301,924	148	41.4	61	3.04	33%
Wadsworth 4	Monitor	537,125	4,301,385	126	42.0	53	2.25	24%
Washington	Toiyabe	477,281	4,334,192	1885	49.8	940	9.23	89%
West Dobbin	Monitor	541,312	4,311,707	46	33.0	15	0.98	10%
West Northumberland	Toquima	509,818	4,315,357	962	42.6	410	5.03	46%
Willow	Monitor	543,653	4,318,379	598	33.0	198	4.35	61%
Red Canyon	Roberts	550,627	4,415,250	529	36.0	190	4.23	82%

Appendix 7.3. Watershed and meadow geomorphic characteristics of the 56 study meadows.

Study meadow	Meadow elevation (m)	Area above 2743 m (ha)	Max watershed elevation (m)	Max relief (m)	Shape whole watershed	Area whole watershed (ha)	Length whole watershed (m)	Slope within meadow	Meadow size (ha)
Barley 1	2267	2978	3235	968	6.29	8645	23,320	1.4%	2.05
Barley Tributary	2271	0	2780	509	5.24	459	4907	6.7%	1.17
Big Creek	2168	403	3370	1202	4.16	3384	11,872	5.4%	0.64
Birch 1	2153	272	3287	1134	4.32	4722	14,284	2.1%	8.22
Birch 2	2179	245	3287	1108	4.32	4722	14,284	1.6%	9.32
Birch Tributary	2316	0	2749	433	2.06	4722	11,138	7.8%	1.72
Cahill 2	2304	0	2527	223	4.64	412	6537	2.5%	2.19
Cahill 3	2329	0	2527	198	4.64	412	6537	4.7%	3.15
Cloverdale	2157	41	2929	772	4.04	14,153	10,439	1.8%	4.45
Corcoran 1	2277	32	2974	697	3.84	695	6716	4.5%	1.14
Corcoran 2	2289	32	2974	685	3.84	695	6716	2.9%	0.81
Corcoran 3	2328	32	2974	645	3.84	695	6716	5.7%	1.94
Corcoran 4	2349	32	2974	625	3.84	695	6716	3.9%	1.68
Corcoran 5	2359	32	2974	614	3.84	695	6716	6.8%	1.52
Corcoran main 1	2365	41	2969	604	5.75	892	8671	3.9%	0.77
Corcoran main 2	2392	41	2969	577	5.75	892	8671	3.9%	1.31
Corcoran main 3	2403	41	2969	566	5.75	892	8671	5.2%	1.35
Corral 1	2373	0	2705	332	3.23	1786	7593	2.4%	2.25
Corral 2	2459	0	2705	245	3.23	1786	7593	4.0%	3.01
Cottonwood	2142	629	3343	1201	4.27	2045	9366	3.6%	1.36
Danville	2275	541	3301	1026	4.03	1694	8261	2.9%	4.46
East Dobbin	2537	15	2915	378	4.07	629	5062	13.7%	0.54
Emigrant 1	2094	0	2387	293	3.94	674	5153	2.0%	3.00
Emigrant 2	2108	0	2387	279	3.94	674	5153	3.0%	1.83
Fandango 1	2611	61	2928	317	10.11	1085	10,471	6.6%	0.88
Fandango 2	2631	53	2928	297	10.11	1085	10,471	6.8%	0.76
Green Monster	2342	377	3212	870	5.52	1386	8747	6.6%	4.27
Indian Valley	2244	249	2929	685	4.61	8485	19,786	0.4%	15.59
Johnson 1	2023	0	2648	624	3.22	459	3847	10.0%	4.46
Johnson 2	2098	0	2646	548	3.22	459	3166	15.6%	0.98
Johnson 3	2119	0	2646	527	3.22	459	3166	18.1%	1.86
Kingston 0	2239	1143	3489	1250	5.39	6361	18,524	0.2%	7.21
Kingston 1	2275	968	3489	1214	5.39	6361	18,524	0.9%	2.82
Kingston 3	2320	649	3463	1142	5.39	6361	18,524	1.4%	5.16
Lebeau	2134	82	3064	930	4.71	981	6799	6.2%	6.44
Little Cow	2611	2	2877	266	10.47	2544	16,317	10.6%	3.78
Meadow 1	2446	6	2786	340	1.82	6970	11,277	4.1%	3.92
Meadow 2	2473	6	2747	274	1.82	6970	11,277	5.1%	5.89
Mohawk	2259	418	3203	944	5.89	975	7579	3.5%	4.61
Mosquito	2129	4340	3321	1192	3.57	9509	18,418	2.2%	4.10
Round Mountain	2402	49	2972	570	3.03	6970	9304	4.4%	4.06
San Juan 1	2227	466	3110	884	3.82	2776	10,300	3.4%	3.67
San Juan 2	2254	367	3110	856	3.82	2776	10,300	4.3%	0.99
Six Mile 1	2530	141	2992	462	13.32	1427	13,788	4.0%	0.72
Six Mile 2	2545	110	2992	448	13.32	1427	13,788	4.8%	0.78
South Crane	2376	444	3261	886	3.99	922	6063	5.9%	1.21
Stargo	2585	0	2713	128	5.02	515	5081	6.4%	1.70
Wadsworth 1	2507	206	3189	682	4.74	1822	9294	3.6%	9.64
Wadsworth 2	2557	24	3032	475	4.15	1822	8696	11.5%	1.04
Wadsworth 3	2534	101	3189	655	4.15	1822	9294	7.3%	2.07
Wadsworth 4	2589	101	3189	600	4.15	1822	9294	10.1%	1.32
Washington	2178	698	3380	1202	5.46	2066	10,360	5.1%	1.98
West Dobbin	2464	0	2648	184	4.59	1990	9559	5.5%	2.58
West Northumberland	2192	12	2796	604	2.86	4185	10,931	5.7%	3.29
Willow	2403	83	2974	571	2.55	1994	7130	5.2%	1.25
Red Canyon	2024	0	2275	251	4.03	663	5171	2.8%	1.58

Appendix 7.4. Channel characteristics and number of springs of the 56 study meadows.

Study meadow	Sinuosity in meadow	Channel length in meadow (m)	Channel depth (m)	Number of knickpoints	Knickpoint height (m)	Knickpoint slope	Percent vertical bank	Number of springs
Barley 1	1.16	243	2.05	3	0.54	9%	39%	11
Barley Tributary	1.09	136	0.00	5	0.93	19%	0%	14
Big Creek	1.13	89	0.79	2	0.53	10%	75%	3
Birch 1	1.18	602	1.20	2	0.49	10%	56%	11
Birch 2	1.25	762	1.38	3	0.82	8%	67%	20
Birch Tributary	1.12	215	1.07	6	0.82	23%	22%	1
Cahill 2	1.07	370	0.43	5	0.70	28%	41%	0
Cahill 3	1.04	562	0.51	4	0.98	15%	36%	5
Cloverdale	1.03	451	0.19	3	0.65	14%	0%	2
Corcoran 1	1.05	266	0.00	4	1.26	13%	0%	0
Corcoran 2	1.06	136	0.00	3	0.86	24%	0%	0
Corcoran 3	1.07	263	0.12	3	1.29	15%	0%	0
Corcoran 4	1.14	168	0.26	2	0.71	13%	59%	0
Corcoran 5	1.12	360	0.00	6	0.29	25%	0%	0
Corcoran main 1	1.09	178	1.27	2	0.18	9%	56%	0
Corcoran main 2	1.07	129	1.10	2	0.82	14%	69%	5
Corcoran main 3	1.08	110	1.83	2	0.74	17%	51%	12
Corral 1	1.16	361	0.38	4	1.03	18%	8%	8
Corral 2	1.03	131	0.00	1	1.04	34%	0%	2
Cottonwood	1.09	188	1.95	4	1.02	16%	100%	1
Danville	1.12	204	1.29				81%	7
East Dobbin	1.10	80	2.13	6	1.56	32%	0%	12
Emigrant 1	1.01	370	0.40	4	0.44	24%	21%	0
Emigrant 2	1.07	149	0.72	6	0.32	14%	18%	1
Fandango 1	1.09	98	1.66	2	0.64	16%	22%	3
Fandango 2	1.08	143	1.24	6	0.50	24%	53%	2
Green Monster	1.17	228	1.11	5	0.66	28%	52%	13
Indian Valley	1.50	1093	0.51	2	1.57	11%	0%	0
Johnson 1	1.08	544	0.00	2	1.39	30%	0%	9
Johnson 2	1.06	201	0.00	2	1.00	49%	0%	5
Johnson 3	1.09	313	0.86	11	1.33	39%	17%	5
Kingston 0	1.60	732	0.97	0	0.00	0%	94%	18
Kingston 1	1.54	527	1.05	0	0.00	0%	0%	3
Kingston 3	1.19	373	1.54	0	0.00	0%	45%	17
Lebeau	1.09	806	0.75	9	1.00	19%	21%	5
Little Cow	1.05	190	0.00	5	0.97	26%	0%	2
Meadow 1	1.17	275	0.43	5	0.33	17%	40%	7
Meadow 2	1.12	475	0.87	7	0.51	15%	84%	9
Mohawk	1.07	94	0.52	6	0.69	12%	0%	0
Mosquito	1.08	192	1.22	3	0.26	9%	95%	0
Round Mountain	1.05	229	0.38	7	0.52	18%	0%	8
San Juan 1	1.20	555	1.65	4	0.55	7%	44%	6
San Juan 2	1.06	86	1.94	3	0.65	18%	48%	4
Six Mile 1	1.11	105	2.41	2	0.19	23%	15%	2
Six Mile 2	1.08	106	1.06	3	0.54	15%	41%	2
South Crane	1.09	98	2.04	2	0.40	13%	22%	3
Stargo	1.08	311	0.86	10	1.05	15%	24%	0
Wadsworth 1	1.16	677	1.54	5	1.08	24%	19%	12
Wadsworth 2	1.05	296	0.00	4	0.58	24%	0%	6
Wadsworth 3	1.12	230	2.61	7	0.41	15%	55%	4
Wadsworth 4	1.10	285	1.59	3	1.49	23%	92%	7
Washington	1.01	125	1.73	1	0.88	18%	100%	8
West Dobbin	1.03	216	0.00	3	0.26	17%	0%	0
West Northumberland	1.05	111	0.00	5	1.96	14%	0%	13
Willow	1.10	230	1.25	3	0.55	24%	0%	7
Red Canyon	1.04	218	0.00	5	0.44	11%	0%	0

USDA Forest Service Gen. Tech. Rep. RMRS-GTR-258. 2011.

111

Appendix 7.5. The percentage of eight vegetation types within the 56 study meadows.

Study meadow	Willow (%)	Wet meadow (%)	Mesic meadow (%)	Mesic shrub meadow (%)	Dry meadow (%)	Dry shrub meadow (%)	Aspen (%)	Rose (%)
Barley 1	41	13	0	36	0	10	0	0
Barley Tributary	7	28	10	7	15	33	0	0
Big Creek	49	10	9	0	0	32	0	0
Birch 1	4	50	18	0	16	13	0	0
Birch 2	25	11	33	0	14	10	7	0
Birch Tributary	1	25	18	0	0	0	45	11
Cahill 2	0	24	24	0	14	38	0	0
Cahill 3	0	10	6	0	35	33	15	0
Cloverdale	51	20	21	0	0	8	0	0
Corcoran 1	0	47	45	0	0	8	0	0
Corcoran 2	0	72	23	0	0	5	0	0
Corcoran 3	14	26	34	20	0	5	0	0
Corcoran 4	3	8	23	0	13	53	0	0
Corcoran 5	16	59	0	0	0	25	0	0
Corcoran main 1	0	18	33	0	0	49	0	0
Corcoran main 2	6	21	16	0	0	57	0	0
Corcoran main 3	0	27	15	0	0	58	0	0
Corral 1	0	34	22	7	0	36	0	0
Corral 2	0	10	8	0	14	68	0	0
Cottonwood	10	0	28	0	8	7	47	0
Danville	61	0	3	0	3	33	0	0
East Dobbin	0	14	41	0	0	45	0	0
Emigrant 1	0	0	31	0	22	47	0	0
Emigrant 2	0	0	15	0	36	49	0	0
Fandango 1	0	0	86	0	0	14	0	0
Fandango 2	0	0	39	0	0	61	0	0
Green Monster	46	14	11	11	0	18	0	0
Indian Valley	0	2	40	0	40	19	0	0
Johnson 1	2	60	12	0	0	25	0	0
Johnson 2	13	44	9	0	0	18	0	16
Johnson 3	0	29	15	2	0	11	20	22
Kingston 0	12	18	32	0	5	7	24	2
Kingston 1	58	8	11	0	6	17	0	0
Kingston 3	2	24	25	0	12	38	0	0
Lebeau	9	30	32	0	13	15	0	0
Little Cow	0	4	37	59	0	0	0	0
Meadow 1	0	29	27	0	0	43	0	0
Meadow 2	0	11	54	12	15	9	0	0
Mohawk	88	8	2	0	0	2	0	0
Mosquito	51	7	8	24	5	5	0	0
Round Mountain	0	4	51	0	3	42	0	0
San Juan 1	42	2	14	0	0	12	23	9
San Juan 2	52	1	18	0	0	29	0	0
Six Mile 1	0	0	38	2	11	49	0	0
Six Mile 2	0	21	29	0	0	49	0	0
South Crane	78	0	1	4	0	17	0	0
Stargo	0	0	35	31	0	34	0	0
Wadsworth 1	0	27	25	0	31	17	0	0
Wadsworth 2	2	61	7	0	1	29	0	0
Wadsworth 3	0	2	25	0	44	29	0	0
Wadsworth 4	1	9	26	0	20	44	0	0
Washington	49	12	3	0	10	0	11	16
West Dobbin	0	0	50	0	3	47	0	0
West Northumberland	1	15	12	0	0	55	0	17
Willow	16	26	24	0	0	11	0	23
Red Canyon	0	0	76	0	0	24	0	0

USDA Forest Service Gen. Tech. Rep. RMRS-GTR-258. 2011.

Chapter 8: Meadow Management and Treatment Options

Jeanne C. Chambers and Jerry R. Miller

Introduction

Restoration and management objectives and approaches are most effective when based on an understanding of ecosystem processes and the long- and short-term causes of disturbance (Wohl and others 2005). As detailed in previous chapters, several factors are critical in developing effective management strategies for streams and their associated meadow ecosystems in the central Great Basin. First, many streams and/or valley floors are still responding to a major drought that occurred almost 2000 years BP that stripped the hillslopes of available sediment and resulted in a natural tendency toward incision. Second, human disturbance has increased both the rate and magnitude of this incision. Since settlement of the Great Basin region in 1860, upland watersheds have undergone significant changes in land use, vegetation cover, and climate that have altered the hydrologic and sedimentologic regimes of the axial drainage system and its associated meadows. Many meadow complexes are at increased risk of incision because they often are located on valley floors with stepped profiles caused by side-valley alluvial fans in the longitudinal profile. While some of the stream systems and their associated meadow complexes have adjusted to the current hydrologic and sedimentologic regimes and are now in a quasi-equilibrium state, others are in a nonequilibrium state and are still actively incising. Consequently, return to pre-incision conditions is an unrealistic goal for these dynamic systems.

Chambers and others (2004a) defined the goal of restoration and management activities as re-establishing and maintaining sustainable fluvial systems and riparian ecosystems that exhibit both characteristic processes and related biological, chemical, and physical linkages among system components (modified from Natural Research Council 2002). In this context, sustainable stream systems and meadow complexes exhibit natural variability yet maintain characteristic processes, including rates and magnitudes of geomorphic activity, hydrologic flux and storage, biogeochemical cycling and storage, and biological activity and production (Christensen and others 1996; Wohl and others 2005). Management objectives and approaches for central Great Basin meadow complexes must acknowledge the dynamic character of these ecosystems and focus on the current potential to support a given set of geomorphic, hydrological, and ecological conditions over a reasonable period of time (Chambers and others 2004a). The primary management objective should be to maintain and enhance meadow complexes by preventing further incision and avulsion where possible and by improving ecological conditions.

The characterization of meadow complexes in the central Great Basin (Chapter 7) and discussion of basin sensitivity to disturbance (Chapter 5) illustrate that not all systems have responded similarly to natural and anthropogenic disturbance. Meadow ecosystems exhibit varying degrees of stream incision, groundwater lowering, and riparian vegetation degradation based on their geomorphic and hydrologic controls and disturbance history. Management plans must be based on careful assessment both of the dominant geomorphic and hydrologic controls and of the causes of disturbance at watershed, valley segment, and site scales. These plans also must consider the current magnitude of incision or degradation and the potential for stream stabilization and vegetation management. Important elements of meadow management are prioritizing which meadows to treat, establishing objectives on a meadow-by-meadow basis, identifying and selecting treatment options, evaluating success through monitoring, and using the results for adaptive management. Each of these tasks is briefly discussed below.

Prioritizing Meadow Management

This report provides insights into the geomorphic, hydrologic, and biological processes that function within meadow complexes in the central Great Basin. These include: (1) a basic understanding of the potential for future meadow degradation; (2) a description of the processes by which the meadows are degraded; and (3) a means of assessing the likelihood of success for various treatment options. At larger scales, stream incision and its effects on meadow ecosystems are influenced by their position in the watershed, the magnitude and rate of runoff, the geomorphic and hydrologic sensitivity of the meadow, and the linkages between the groundwater system and the stream channel. Chapter 7 provides a categorization of central Great Basin watersheds based on data collected from 56 meadows in upland watersheds in 2005 and 2006. A summary of the variables and methods of measurement are in table 7.1. The different meadow groups and their general characteristics are in table 7.5, and the averages for the most influential variables are in table 7.2. This information is a useful starting point for assessing current meadow conditions and the potential for future degradation. A metadata file and the data files for each meadow have been archived through the USDA Forest Service, Rocky Mountain Research Station and are available at: http://www.fs fed.us/rm/data_archive/dataaccess/Central_NV_Meadow_Characterization.shtml.

USDA Forest Service Gen. Tech. Rep. RMRS-GTR-258. 2011.

The files also can be accessed by following the links provided in the data archive: http://www.fs.fed.us/rm/data_archive. The central Nevada meadow characterization can be accessed by following the Data Access link. Prior to using these data, one must verify that the longitudinal and cross-sectional profiles and meadow characterizations are accurate because intervening high flows may result in knickpoint migration and other types of incision or avulsion. Also, inappropriate livestock use can influence meadow species composition.

Determining the likelihood of future meadow degradation and the potential for recovery requires an understanding of the geomorphic and hydrologic sensitivity of the meadows. The framework for understanding meadow sensitivity to disturbance is provided in Chapters 3 and 4, and its use is discussed in Chapter 5. Specifically, a set of factors is presented that can be used to determine the likelihood for geomorphic change and the probability that these alterations will result in significant declines in groundwater levels and, thus, changes in vegetation. Analysis of the sensitivity of individual meadows requires examining the factors discussed in table 5.1. This can be accomplished by using cartographic and remotely sensed data and by making field visits. Because meadow complexes are groundwater features that may or may not be closely tied to the surface channel system within the meadow complex, determining the linkages between the channel and groundwater flow system is of utmost importance in assessing the effect of channel incision on groundwater levels and vegetation types and distribution. A means of assessing surface water and groundwater interactions is described in Chapter 4 and examples are provided in table 4.2. This approach generally provides enough information to determine if major groundwater responses to incision (as well as various treatments) are likely.

Objectives and Design Criteria for Stream Stabilization and Meadow Vegetation Management

An understanding of the geomorphic, hydrologic, and biological processes within the meadows can be used to define a set of realistic management objectives for a given meadow. Developing these objectives is required to determine what constitutes project success, and it should be accomplished before any stream stabilization or vegetation management project is initiated. One must also formulate design or success criteria. Design (success) criteria are quantifiable benchmarks that specify how the various components of the work should perform and are used to ensure that the objectives of the project are met. Design criteria may include measurable limits to headcut or knickpoint advancement, bank stability, flood conveyance, and/or the aerial extent of specific meadow vegetation types (Skidmore and others 2001). Project success often depends on the effort that goes into developing design criteria because they are a guide to what needs to be accomplished for each component of the project (Miller and Orbock Miller 2007). Moreover, the process of constructing design criteria is likely to provide

important insights into whether a particular objective can be achieved given the biophysical processes operating at the site.

Identification and Selection of Treatment Options

Establishing a General Framework

In recent years, managers have increasingly relied on channel evolution models (CEM) (Schumm and others 1984; Simon and Hupp 1986; Simon 1989; Rosgen 1996, 2001, 2006) to evaluate the magnitude of incision and the evolutionary changes in channel morphology during the entrenchment process and to identify potential management options. These models, which portray a semi-systematic series of geomorphic events once incision has begun, are not always applicable to upland drainages in the central Great Basin. In these drainages, incision is often characterized by episodes of avulsion and/or cyclical periods of gully erosion and deposition. For management purposes, it is useful to first classify the drainages according to their morphologic characteristics and dominate erosional and depositional processes. A simplistic approach to classification is to separate basins into two groups: those that exhibit riparian corridors that possess a discontinuous drainage system and those that possess an integrated drainage network. In the former, the valley floor is usually characterized by short reaches of stream channel (tens to a few hundred meters) that are incised into the valley fill, separated by unincised reaches that are devoid of a recognizable channel system (fig. 8.1). The dominant processes that are operating in these areas (such as in Indian Valley) are gully development and headcut advancement (Chapter 3). In the latter, the riparian corridor contains a continuous channel network throughout the basin, although flow within the channel may be locally ephemeral, particularly during the late summer months. The integrated drainages may be further subdivided into those exhibiting (1) low to moderate depths of incision (zero to two times bankfull channel depths), (2) highly incised channels (more than two times bankfull channel depths), and (3) "fully" incised channels that are currently in a state of equilibrium. The separation of these channels on the basis of incision is arbitrary, but it provides a useful system to discuss potential management options that can be applied to maintain and/or improve meadow ecosystems.

Low to Moderately Incised Channels. If the stream exhibits a limited degree of incision, it may be possible to use in-stream structures and bank stabilization measures to stabilize the stream channel. Channels with minor incision occur within all meadow groups but are most common in the smaller stream channels that occur in meadow Groups 3, 4, and 5 (Chapter 7). Stabilizing channels and knickpoints when they first appear can prevent knickpoint migration and can minimize the effects of other factors that contribute to stream incision during episodic high flows. Channel stabilization is often sufficient to maintain meadow vegetation.

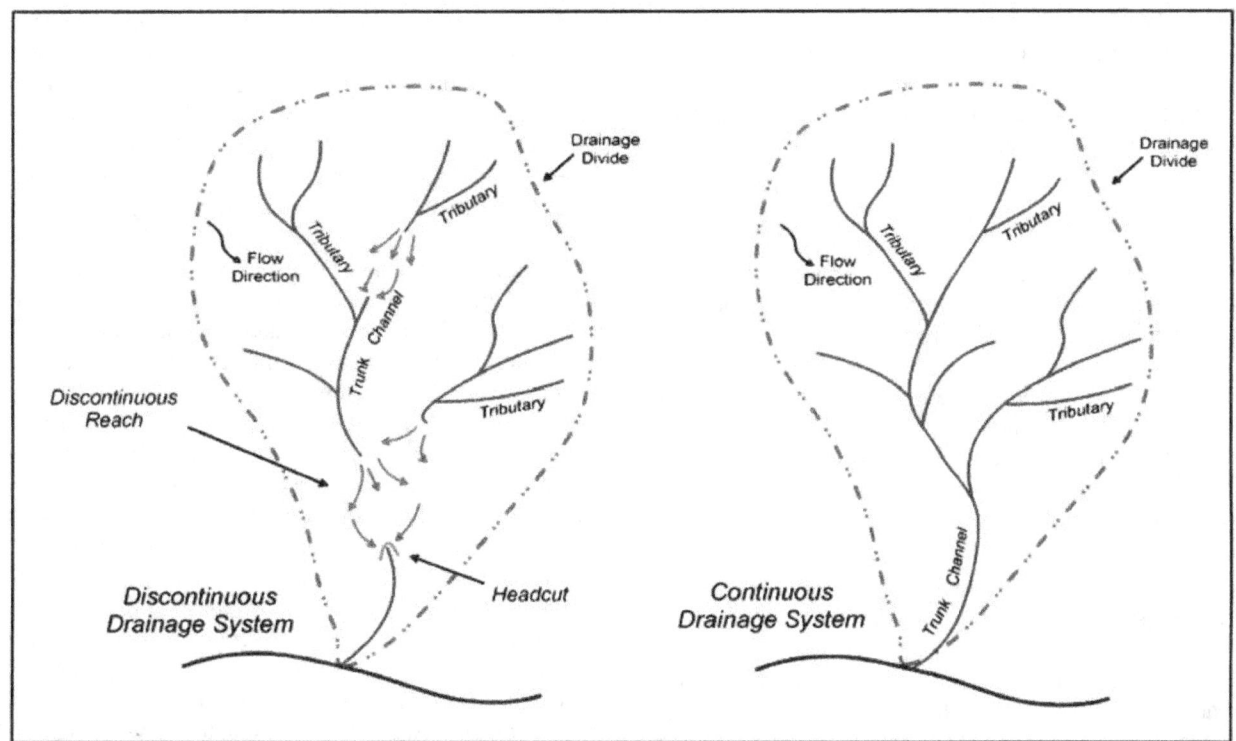

Figure 8.1. Schematic diagram of discontinuous (top) and continuous (bottom) drainage basins. Continuous drainages are thought to have had an integrated, axial drainage network throughout the late Holocene.

Highly Incised Channels. Highly incised channels are found in all meadow groups but are most pronounced in Groups 1 and 2 (Chapter 7). Stream stabilization measures are possible but must be based on careful assessment of (1) the geomorphic and hydrologic sensitivity both within and upstream of the meadow and of (2) the linkages between the groundwater system and stream channel. Structures should be designed to accommodate geomorphic irregularities, like side-valley alluvial fans, episodic high flows, and the predominantly high gradients that occur in these systems. The primary objective of installing in-stream structures is to prevent or minimize further incision of the main channel, prevent incision of spring channels, and maintain existing springs and seeps. In some cases, it may be possible to stabilize the stream banks with plugs or transplants of meadow vegetation. The net effect of stabilizing stream channels can be to maintain or improve existing meadow vegetation if a progressive decrease in water tables can be halted. Once incision has been stopped, active vegetation management can be used to improve ecological conditions.

Fully Incised Channels. In cases where stream channels are fully incised and are now in a state of equilibrium, as sometimes occurs in Group 1 and 2 meadows (Chapter 7), the stream channel typically has reached a stable configuration, although minor adjustments may occur as the stream works to expand its floodplain. It is seldom ecologically or economically feasible to reconstruct or elevate these streams. If groundwater tables have dropped, as indicated by shrub encroachment and drier vegetation types, it may be possible to actively manage the area to maintain meadow vegetation based on understanding the relationships between groundwater tables and riparian vegetation, as described below. It may not be possible to return these areas to the large, meadow complexes they once supported but, if water tables are sufficiently high, active vegetation management can be used to maintain them as smaller meadow complexes or dry meadows. Maintaining meadow vegetation within riparian corridors allows a mosaic of shrub- or tree-dominated areas and meadow complexes that more closely resembles predisturbance conditions and that provides important wildlife habitat.

General Considerations for Stream Stabilization

The approaches used for stabilizing minimally incised and highly incised streams must be aligned with the dominant mechanisms of incision. These mechanisms can vary among meadows, or even among areas within a given meadow. In some cases, incision may involve the grain-by-grain entrainment of channel bed sediment; in other instances, incision may be related to upstream migration of knickpoints generated by a lowering of the base level. Incision also may occur by means of groundwater sapping and headcut retreat. Areas affected by these different incision processes require their own set of objectives, design criteria, and treatment strategies.

While incision is likely to be the predominant problem of concern, it also is important to recognize that meadow

USDA Forest Service Gen. Tech. Rep. RMRS-GTR-258. 2011.

115

complexes are groundwater features, and other geomorphic and hydrologic processes that operate in these environments must be considered in project design. The most important of those processes are: avulsion, breaching of confining units, and erosion by groundwater processes.

Avulsion

Although a stream may be incised, the instantaneous influx of coarse sediment to the meadow from upstream areas may lead to channel avulsion and entrenchment of a new stream segment in a completely different part of the meadow complex. In-stream structures and changes in riparian vegetation alter flow resistance and transport processes and may increase the potential for channel aggradation and avulsion. Thus, the sensitivity of the meadow to avulsion processes should be considered at every site where biophysical treatments are applied.

Breaching of Confining Units

Hydrologic data from instrumented meadows demonstrate that fine-grained (silt and clay-rich), confining units are an essential component of meadow development. Breaching of these units has the potential to result in major changes in the subsurface flow system and drainage of the meadow complex. Thus, management strategies must consider how any treatment will affect surface and subsurface flow systems and their interactions. Approaches like channel reconstruction or plug and pond methods that require excavation of alluvial materials are probably not appropriate for most central Nevada meadow systems and should be applied with extreme care.

Erosion by Groundwater Processes

Groundwater sapping (seepage erosion) has been observed to dramatically affect the riparian corridor of these upland catchments where there is ample water and the alluvial valley fill is composed of highly permeable sand or grus-sized sediment. Even minor modifications to these systems may lead to unexpected, deleterious consequences such as formation of deep gullies.

In-Stream Structures and Aquatic Habitat Enhancement Devices

In-stream structures and other aquatic enhancement devices were initially used at least a century ago to improve fish habitat in the United States (Beschta and others 1992; Thompson 2005). Since then, Federal agencies have relied heavily on the use of these structures to improve aquatic and riparian habitat (Frissell and Nawa 1992; Thompson 2005).

These devices fall into four broad categories (which are not mutually exclusive): grade control devices, habitat cover structures, bank protection devices, and flow deflectors or concentrators (Miller and Kochel 2008, 2010). Grade control

structures are perhaps the most widely used and are intended to maintain the bed of the channel at its present elevation. These devices are typically composed of logs or large boulders and are installed within the channel in such a way as to inhibit channel bed erosion. Historically, these structures included various types of dams and/or weirs, including check dams, K-dams, jack dams, wedge dams, log or rock sills, and log drop structures (Seehorn 1992). Cover structures are intended to provide or improve aquatic habitat, particularly for fish. They include a wide range of devices, the most common of which are bank lunkers or cribs, raft and boom covers, log-and-brush shelters, and felled trees. Bank protection devices are designed to reduce the magnitude and rate of bank erosion. Until recently, these devices lined part or all channel margins with some form of erosionally resistant material and include A-Jacks, dirt or rock filled gabions, rock or crib walls, and rip-rap and stone toe revetments. Most flow deflection devices protrude out from the stream bank and are intended to narrow the channel, protect banks from erosion, or create pools (and pool habitats) through redirection and concentration of flow. The most common types are single or double wing deflectors and spurs. Flow deflectors also include various types of boulder placements, a practice that involves placing large boulders along the banks or within the channel to create localized zones of scour.

Since the early 1990s, there has been an attempt to restore or rehabilitate at least part of the structure, function, and diversity of the historic river (Riley 1998). Many projects use extensively hardened habitat improvement devices, including a new generation of rock or log structures that are endorsed by Rosgen and his colleagues (Rosgen 2001, 2006), including cross-vanes, J-hooks, rock (or single arm) vanes, and W-weirs. These newly designed in-stream structures are intended to decrease near-bank velocities and shear stress by redirecting flow away from banks. Thus, their purpose is to reduce bank erosion and improve aquatic habitat by creating localized zones of channel bed scour and pool formation.

The uses, design, and installation of older habitat improvement devices, which are used extensively, have been thoroughly described in a number of manuals, including Arthur (1936), USDA Forest Service (1952), and Seehorn (1985, 1992). Use and design of more recently developed in-stream rock and log structures are described in Rosgen (2001, 2006). These manuals should be consulted to gain additional information on these structures.

Use of In-Stream Structures

A review of the past performance of in-stream and other improvement structures, combined with an understanding of erosion processes in Great Basin meadows, indicates that stream stabilization methods must be tailored to the specific characteristics of the system. As indicated in previous chapters, meadows often are located upstream of side-valley fans and are characterized by convexities in long channel/valley profiles. Where this occurs, installing grade control structures at the toe of the fan may effectively stabilize the

116

USDA Forest Service Gen. Tech. Rep. RMRS-GTR-258. 2011.

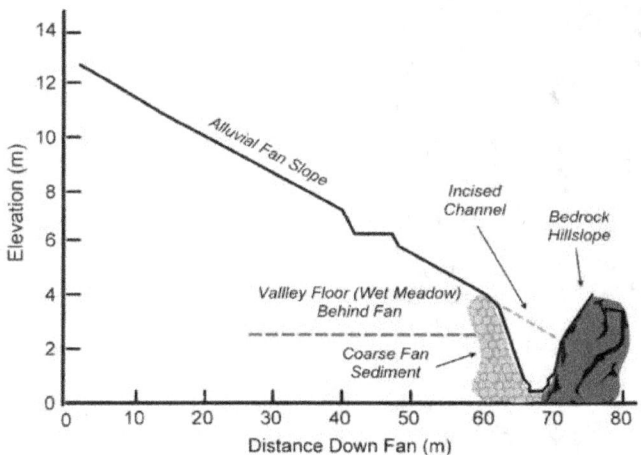

Figure 8.2. Radial fan profile near Kingston 3 meadow in Kingston Canyon. Erosion around structures within and immediately upstream of the fans is limited by coarse fan sediments and bedrock beneath the hillslope, which reduces the probability of failure.

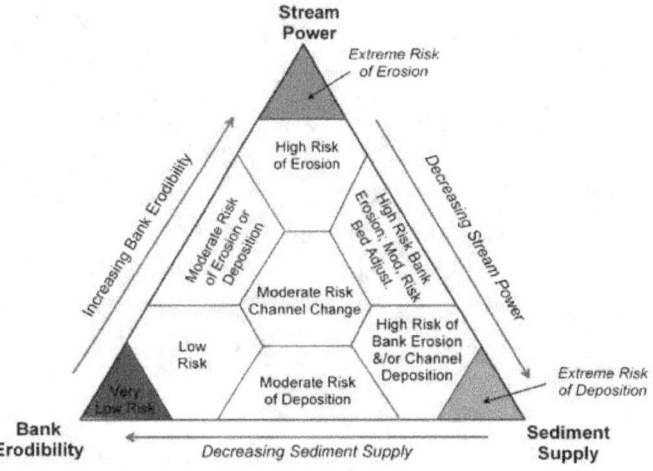

Figure 8.3. Ternary diagram showing the likelihood that instream structures will fail. The diagram is based on detailed assessments of structures in North Carolina and, to a lesser degree, in Virginia and shows that the probability of failure is related to stream power, sediment supply, and bank erodibility (from Miller and Kochel 2008, 2010).

channel. These stream reaches are important local, base-level controls that dictate the magnitude of upstream incision. Inhibiting incision at the toe of the fan, which is generally co-located with a convexity in the longitudinal profile, will limit the amount of future erosion that can occur within the meadow. Erosion around these structures is more difficult as erosion in these reaches often requires the removal of bedrock or coarse-grained colluvial and alluvial fan sediments (fig. 8.2).

The use of in-stream structures and other devices throughout the meadow and upstream of side-valley fans should be used with more caution, particularly where there is evidence of past channel avulsions. Although structures such as rock vortex weirs and cross-vanes are intended to maintain sediment transport through the reach (Rosgen 2001), post-project evaluations in numerous regions of North America (such as British Columbia, California, and North Carolina) have shown that these structures often lead to in-channel deposition (Miller and Kochel 2008, 2010). Along meadow reaches where avulsions occur frequently, use of such structures may lead to channel deposition and flood flows over the meadow surface. This may cause subsequent incision or new channel formation and meadow degradation along a new part of the valley floor.

It also is important to recognize that post-project evaluations have shown that performance of in-stream structures and other habitat improvement devices varies dramatically from site to site (Miller and Kochel 2008, 2010). Variations in performance appear to be partially related to stream channel dynamics. Effectiveness is greatly reduced along channels that are characterized by high stream power, large sediment supplies, and erodible banks (fig. 8.3; Miller and Kochel 2008, 2010). Performance also tends to be much lower along unstable channels that experience changes in channel dimensions or incision. Use of rock gabions to halt

ongoing incision in the Hot Creek Mountains resulted in the stream cutting around the structures (fig. 8.4a). Use of log cross-vanes in San Juan Creek resulted in the stream cutting under the structures (fig. 8.4b). Many investigators have noted that in-stream devices will require continued maintenance to prolong effectiveness (Frissell and Nawa 1992; Miller and Orbock Miller 2007). One cannot simply install these devices and expect them to function for long periods of time (multiple years to decades). They will need to be continually inspected and repaired. Given the inherent instability of most upland channels in the central Great Basin, continued maintenance will be particularly important to ensure device effectiveness in meadow complexes.

Use of Headcut and Gully Stabilization Measures

A common form of meadow degradation is development of gullies and upvalley migration of associated headcuts. Gullies are particularly common along relatively steep and narrow reaches of the valley floor, which often characterize downstream areas of meadow complexes. As a result, upvalley gully propagation, primarily by means of headcut advancement, is an especially important management issue. Unfortunately, gullies represent a particularly difficult form of degradation to treat, and it can be argued that effective management strategies have yet to be developed for these systems. Gullies are not only the product of surface flows but they result from the combined effects of both surface- and groundwater (seepage) erosion associated with shallow groundwater levels and layered stratigraphy. Thus, gully treatment must include measures to deal with multiple mechanisms of erosion that may occur at different times

(a)

(b)

Figure 8.4. (a) Stream avulsion around a rock gabion structure in the Hot Creek Mountains. (b) Incision under an X-vein structure in San Juan meadow. Photos by J. Chambers.

and under different hydrologic conditions. Complicating the problem further, data with which to evaluate the effectiveness of headcut and gully mitigation strategies in meadow complexes in the region are limited.

In general, commonly utilized treatment strategies fall into four categories: (1) using in-stream check dams and weirs to stabilize the base level and to retain sediment; (2) regrading and vegetating the gully banks and headcut to increase channel cross-sectional areas, reduce shear stress, and inhibit bank failure by mass wasting processes; (3) lining the headcut and banks with rock or other erosionally resistant material; and (4) spreading and/or diverting surface flows to reduce the amount of water entering the gully and to limit the concentration and erosive forces of surface flows on the valley floor. Exactly which method is most appropriate

depends on the gully's current morphology, its hydrologic and geologic setting, its position and integration within the drainage network, and the mechanisms responsible for headcut migration. Thus, selection of the stabilization approach must be based on a sound understanding of the gully or gully system to be treated.

Some of the most intensively treated gullies to date are located in Indian Valley at the southern end of the Toiyabe Range. Near the mouth of Indian Valley, a number of shallow, discontinuous gullies that terminate upstream in headcuts have entrenched the valley fill within a wide, low-gradient meadow complex. Treatment of these shallow gullies relied primarily on a combination of headcut and bank regrading, followed by placement of large rocks over the regraded area. Treatment likely began following major

　　　　USDA Forest Service Gen. Tech. Rep. RMRS-GTR-258. 2011.

flood events in the early 1980s, and vegetation associated with the regraded area suggests that the rock has been in place for at least a decade. When used on gullies with limited groundwater seepage and groundwater erosion, we observed that the structures were not affected by any erosion, although it is unclear whether they had been subjected to significant overland flow events. In some locations, however, seepage erosion had undermined the rock, leaving a disorganized array of boulders in the channel bed, while the headcut continued to migrate upvalley. Our qualitative observations suggest that where groundwater seepage is not important, gully regrading combined with localized "rip-rap" may be effective. This approach will be only marginally effective for reducing groundwater erosion and will require repeated maintenance to be effective against surface flows.

Large gullies in Indian Valley often were treated by constructing linear ridges across the valley floor, starting in the mouth of the gully. The intent was to spread surface flows over a larger area, thereby reducing erosive potential. Examination of sequential aerial photographs revealed that the approach was often successful at reducing erosion immediately downstream of the captured gully (i.e., the gully dammed by the earthen ridge) but usually resulted in development of new gully systems on another part of the valley floor (fig. 3.17). In fact, field observations revealed that even minor flow diversions within the meadow complexes could lead to unintended flow concentrations and gully formation elsewhere. Despite the meadows' low gradients and extreme widths, they are extremely sensitive to erosion, and even minor changes in overland flow routes or depths can negatively affects meadow integrity. The difficulty of treating these gullies where both groundwater and surface water erosion are important stresses the need to manage the meadows such that gullies do not form in the first place. Once they establish, there may be little that can be done to rehabilitate the site.

However, not all gully and headcut systems are like those of the stream in Indian Valley. Many tend to be restricted to narrow, steeper reaches of the valley floor. Headcuts in these areas also are likely to be formed by a combination of surface- and groundwater erosion processes. However, in contrast to Indian Valley, where a very large supply of groundwater is continuously available and surface water flows can be enormous, the upstream supply of water to the site in these areas is more variable. Thus, the potential to reduce the rates of headcut advancement may be higher and more closely linked to factors such as upstream water supply, valley width, valley slope, and sediment composition of the valley fill. In very general terms, more water; narrow, steep valley floors; and permeable, non-cohesive sediments will increase the likelihood of headcut advancement as well as the difficulty of treating the problem.

Use of Biotechnical Methods

Stream bank stabilization within meadow complexes can be facilitated using biotechnical methods that focus on the use of live plant materials. Methods for biotechnical streambank stabilization are diverse and typically include the use of living plant material (tree or shrub stems and grass, sedge and rush plugs, or transplants) and inert erosion control materials (natural and synthetic geotextiles, rock rip-rap, log cribs, or coconut fiber rolls). The root systems of living plants increase streambank stability by providing resistance to shallow mass movement. Plant roots can reinforce the soil through tensile fibers in the root mass and anchor the slope through deep root penetration into more stable strata (Gray and Sotir 1996). Actively growing riparian vegetation can increase shear strength by reducing poor pressure (Gray and Sotir 1996). Also, foliage and stems of shrubs and trees on streambanks can decrease flow velocities and dissipate energy by redistributing flow patterns and directions (Li and Eddleman 2002).

A review of biotechnical streambank stabilization methods and their properties and applications is found in Li and Eddleman (2002). The stream environment is often complex, and different types of stabilization may be required for the zones associated with various stream stages. For example, more intensive measures may be required in the zone between average flows and typical high flows and in zones characterized by groundwater sapping. Combining different biotechnical methods, like inert erosion control materials and living plant material, is often most effective. In Kingston 3 meadow, placing coconut fiber rolls in the zone between average flows and typical high flows and planting deep-rooted meadow species effectively stabilized a bare streambank that exhibited groundwater sapping (figs. 8.5a and b).

Information on harvesting, propogating, and planting wetland species that is appropriate for Great Basin meadow complexes is provided in Hoag (2003). Individual riparian species occur within well-defined water table regimes and depths to saturation (Chambers and others 2004b). Success of transplanting "wildlings" or plant materials harvested from the site or propagated in the greenhouse depends on matching water requirements of the species with the period of saturation and available soil water of the stream bank. Plantings are most vulnerable during the first two years of establishment and may require maintenance if high flows occur during the establishment period. Deferring grazing use for two years after bank stabilization is necessary to ensure success of the project.

General Considerations for Vegetation Management

The methods used for vegetation management within meadow complexes depend on the water table regime and the composition of meadow vegetation, as influenced by the disturbance history of the site. As discussed in Chapter 2, the hydrologic regime is the primary determinant of soil characteristics, plant community composition, and dynamics of riparian meadow complexes (Chambers and others 1999; Castelli and others 2000; Martin and Chambers 2001a, 2001b, 2002). A classification of riparian ecological types in the central Great Basin based on climate, landforms, soils,

(a)

(b)

Figure 8.5. Bank stabilization of an area in Kingston 3 meadow using coconut fiber rolls and graminoid plugs from the meadow (a) immediately after installation and (b) three years later. Photos by J. Chambers.

and vegetation identified five meadow ecological types (Weixelman and others 1996). Three of the meadow ecological types are characterized by similar, high water tables and are differentiated based on elevation and soil texture. They are aquatic sedge (*Carex aquatilis*; high elevations), tufted hairgrass (*Deschampsia ceaspitosa*; coarser textured soils), and Nebraska sedge (*Carex nebraskensis*; mid to low elevations and fine textured soils). The remaining two types occur over a gradient of decreasing water table depth and are the mesic (mesic graminoid) and dry (dry graminoid) meadow types. An additional ecological type often occurs at the periphery of graminoid meadow complexes and is characterized by lower water tables: sage meadow (basin big sagebrush/Great Basin wildrye; *Artemisia tridentata* ssp. *tridentata*/*Leymus cinereus*). At higher elevations, a similar ecological type occurs that is dominated by mountain big sagebrush (*A. tridentata* ssp. *vaseyana*) and Great Basin wildrye. "Average" water table depth and relative variability have been determined for the wet (*Carex nebraskensis*), mesic, dry, and sage meadow ecological types (fig. 8.6; Chambers and others 2004b). Wet and mesic meadows have the highest water table requirements and tolerate the least variability in water table depth (Castelli and others 2000). Stream incision within meadow complexes has the potential to lower the base level of groundwater discharge into the stream (depending on the hydrologic setting), cause lowered water tables, and result in a change in the composition of meadow vegetation in areas affected by lower water tables (Chambers and others 2004a, 2004b). As a result, big sagebrush and other upland species can encroach and eventually dominate in areas formerly characterized by meadow vegetation (Chambers and Linnerooth 2001; Wright and Chambers 2002).

120

USDA Forest Service Gen. Tech. Rep. RMRS-GTR-258. 2011.

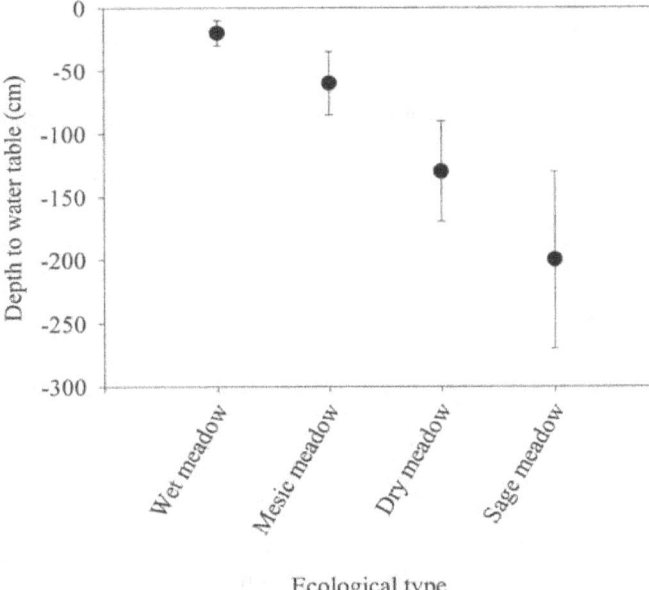

-50
-100
-150
-200
-250
-300

Figure 8.6. The water table depths (means ± S.E.) for meadow ecological types typical of intermediate elevations in the central Great Basin (from Chambers and others 2004b).

An understanding of the factors that differentiate ecological types and of the potential states and transitions within ecological types can be used to design effective strategies for restoring and managing meadow complexes. A model state and transition diagram that illustrates the relationships among the wet, mesic, and dry meadow ecological types and that shows potential alternative states and transitions within each ecological type is shown in fig. 8.7. The diagram illustrates that meadow ecological types occur along water table gradients and are characterized by unique vegetation communities. Abiotic thresholds exist among the different ecological types that are determined by water table depth. Thresholds can be defined based on the parameters that determine the limits of natural variability (Ritter and others 1999) for each ecological type. Threshold crossings occur when a system does not return via natural processes to the original state following disturbance (Laycock 1991; Ritter and others 1999).

Alternative vegetation states within each ecological type typically occur along anthropogenic disturbance gradients (fig. 8.7). Biotic threshold crossings to new alternative states can result from either internal interactions, like competition, or from external factors, like inappropriate livestock use or species invasions. If an ecological threshold to an alternative state has been crossed, management intervention typically is required to return the system to the former state (Wright and Chambers 2002; Chambers and others 2004a). Large changes in either biotic or abiotic conditions and, consequently, ecosystem processes can result in new ecological types with different sets of restoration potentials. For example, a lowering of the water table by as little as 30 cm can result in an abiotic threshold crossing from a wet meadow to a mesic meadow (fig. 8.6).

Use of Vegetation Management

Minor stream incision can result in transitions to drier vegetation communities within meadow ecological types. Management options include stabilizing the stream system and stream banks, as described above, and managing the meadow complex to prevent overgrazing by livestock and invasion of weedy species. Monitoring grazing use, ensuring that utilization guidelines are met, and treating weedy species as soon as they appear can prevent transitions to undesirable states.

Incision that causes a significant drop in the water table may cause all or part of the meadow to transition to a new ecological type with a new site potential. The change in the stream system and groundwater table may occur during one or multiple events. In those cases where it is not ecologically or economically feasible to stabilize the stream system, it may be necessary to wait until the stream has obtained a new base level or is at grade before initiating active vegetation management. In meadows with active springs or seeps that are not adjacent to the stream, portions of the meadow may remain relatively wet.

The first step in determining the potential of a site to support a given ecological type is to monitor the depth to saturation or the water table. This can be accomplished by using soil augers, digging soil pits to evaluate depth to saturation, or installing groundwater wells to measure water table depths. Because water table depths are highly variable both among and within years in mesic, dry, and sage meadow ecological types (Castelli and others 2000; Martin and Chambers 2002), monitoring should be conducted several times during the growing season and for at least two years prior to project initiation (Chambers and others 2004b). The water table depths shown in fig. 8.6 can be used to evaluate site potential. Plant species composition also can be used as an indicator of site potential with the caveat that riparian obligate and facultative species are often long-lived and significant lag times can occur during transition to new ecological states. Establishment and persistence of upland species like the shrubs, big sagebrush (*A. tridentata* ssp. *tridentata*, *A. tridentata* ssp. *vaseyana*), or rabbitbrush (*Chyrsothamnus* species), are strong indicators that site potential has transitioned to sage meadow.

Sites that have maintained their potential to support wet or mesic meadow types may exhibit slight changes in species composition and may only require stabilization of spring channels or stream banks. However, sites that have transitioned rapidly from wet or mesic meadow types to sites with the potential to support dry or sage meadows may exhibit weedy species invasions or undesirable species compositions (Wright and Chambers 2002). Active management that includes prescribed fire to remove upland shrubs and revegetation can be used to improve the ecological condition of these sites and to maintain them as dry or shrub meadows.

The dry meadow type, as originally described, is dominated by grasses and sedges and has relatively shallow water table depths and depths to saturation (-70 to -100 cm in June

USDA Forest Service Gen. Tech. Rep. RMRS-GTR-258. 2011.

121

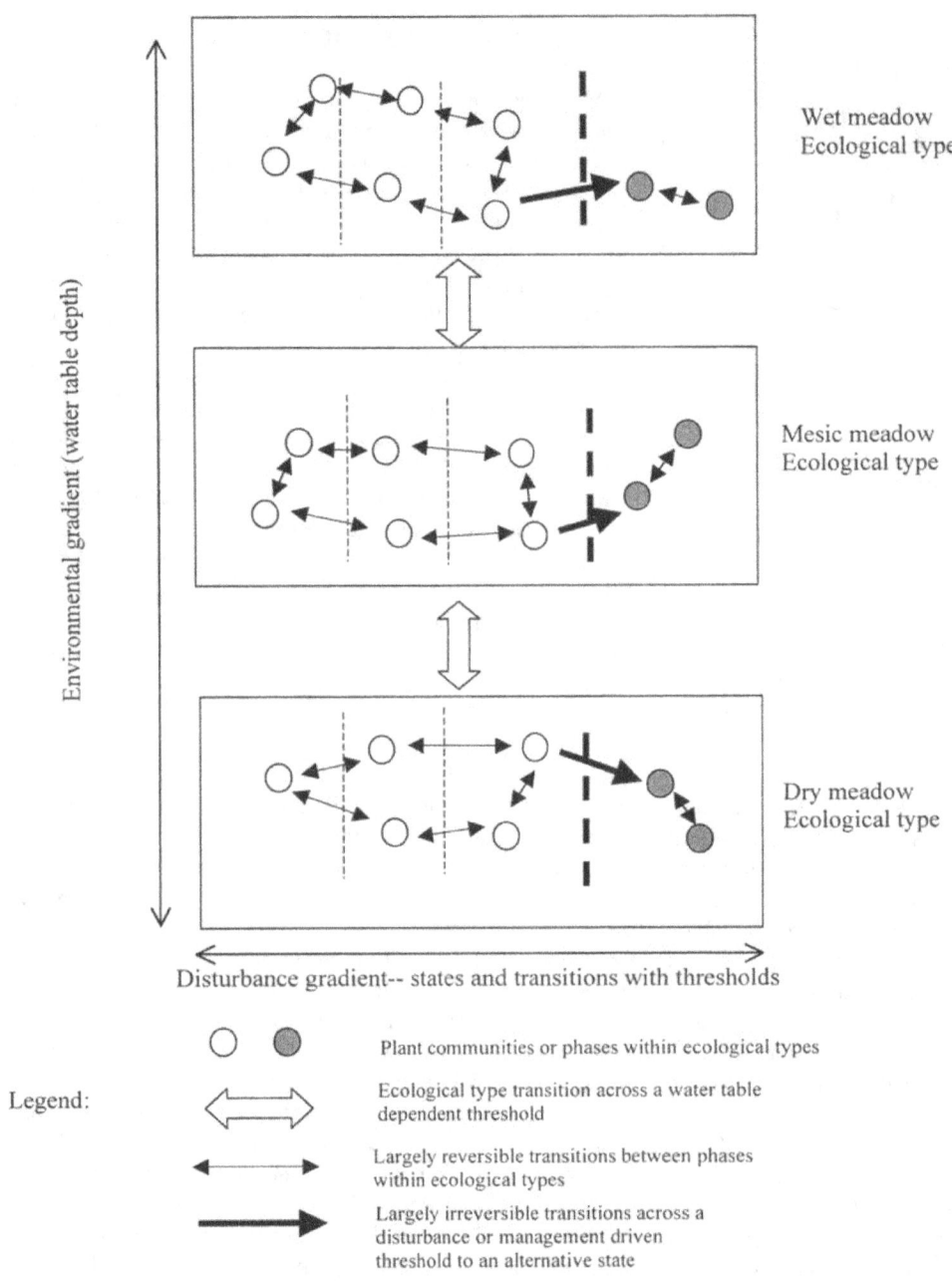

Environmental gradient (water table depth)

Wet meadow
Ecological type

Mesic meadow
Ecological type

Dry meadow
Ecological type

Figure 8.7. Hypothetical state and transition models for the wet, mesic, and dry meadow ecological types. Differences among ecological types are largely dependent on water table depths; differences among states are largely dependent on disturbance and management history (from Chambers and others 2004b).

Disturbance gradient-- states and transitions with thresholds

Legend:

○ ●   Plant communities or phases within ecological types

⇔   Ecological type transition across a water table dependent threshold

↔   Largely reversible transitions between phases within ecological types

➔   Largely irreversible transitions across a disturbance or management driven threshold to an alternative state

and July) (Weixelman and others 1996). These water table depths facilitate establishment and persistence of typical dry meadow species such as Nevada bluegrass (*P. secunda* ssp. *juncifolia*). Saturated rooting zones during the spring and early summer prevent establishment and persistence of big sagebrush and other shrubs (Ganskopp 1986). Overgrazing and other perturbations can alter species composition but will not result in shrub encroachment unless the water table drops. Sites with slightly lower water tables (-150 to -250 cm) are characterized by dry meadow species but are susceptible to sagebrush encroachment. Dry meadow species persist because occasional high water tables and favorable environmental conditions facilitate episodic establishment (Chambers and Linnerooth 2001). However, water tables are sufficiently low that basin big sagebrush also can establish

and persist (Wright and Chambers 2002). Inappropriate livestock use increases sagebrush establishment by reducing competition from herbaceous species (see Belsky and others 1999). Designation of sites with lower water tables (-150 to -250 cm) as alternative states of the dry meadow ecological type depends on the interpretation of the "range of natural variability" within an ecological type. If the range is considered sufficiently broad to include sites with slightly lower water tables that can exhibit sagebrush encroachment, then these sites represent alternative states of the dry meadow ecological type. Regardless, sites that exhibit sagebrush encroachment but that have typical dry meadow species in the understory can be maintained as dry meadows with prescribed fire and proper livestock grazing (Wright and Chambers 2002).

Sites with deeper water tables (-250 to >-300 cm) are dominated by sagebrush with a minor component of dry meadow species. These sites have crossed abiotic thresholds and no longer have the potential to support the dry meadow ecological type. The failure of typical dry meadow species to establish (Chambers and Linnerooth 2001) indicates that any dry meadow species that occur on the sites are probably remnants of what existed prior to stream incision and lowered water tables. These sites are unstable and can exhibit several different pathways depending on the disturbance regime and initial species composition. In the worst case scenario, they can transition to sagebrush dominance with an understory of upland herbaceous or invasive species. Past research shows that at low to intermediate elevations within the watersheds, basin big sagebrush and Great Basin wildrye can establish on these sites (Wright and Chambers 2002). Thus, the potential exists for at least the more xeric species that characterize the basin big sagebrush/Great Basin wildrye ecological type to also establish (Weixelman and others 1996). Prescribed fire can be used to remove the sagebrush overstory on these sites. Because the herbaceous understory species that characterize the basin big sagebrush/Great Basin wildrye ecological type are almost nonexistent, they must be seeded onto the site. Fire alone can convert these sites to annual forbs and grasses, especially if the fire-adapted, exotic grass cheatgrass (*Bromus tectorum*) or annual mustards exist in the understory (Wright and Chambers 2002).

Methods for successfully revegetating these types of sites can be found in Whisenant (1999) and Monsen and others (2004). Native species that have been successfully established on these sites and that are commercially available include the grasses—Great Basin wildrye (*L. cinereus*), western wheatgrass (*Pascopyrum smithii*), and creeping wildrye (*Elymus triticoides*)—and forbs—yarrow (*Achillia millifolium*) and blue flax (*Linum lewissii*) (Wright and Chambers 2002). Ample sources of sagebrush seeds typically exist adjacent to meadow complexes, and sagebrush usually establishes on its own. If rabbitbrush occurs on the site, it will re-sprout following fire and may preempt the site unless the herbaceous species establish rapidly. Maintenance of these sites requires preventing inappropriate livestock use and invasion of non-native species.

Other Management Considerations

The degree of stream incision and current ecological conditions of meadow complexes in Great Basin watersheds are affected significantly by anthropogenic disturbance. Ongoing studies provide direct evidence that roads have increased the rate and magnitude of stream incision. Several cases of "road captures" have been documented and many others have been observed where streams have been diverted onto road surfaces during high flows (Lahde 2003). These diversions onto road surfaces increase shear stress and stream power and, ultimately, stream incision (Lahde 2003). Once initiated, stream incision can propagate through large portions of the system as a result of knickpoint migration. Active management of roads is needed to minimize the

potential for stream diversion onto roads during high flows. This includes minimizing new road crossings and maintaining road conditions that decrease the likelihood of avulsion and stream diversion during high flows. It also includes long-term management that is aimed at relocating existing roads and positioning new roads out of the valley bottoms.

Inappropriate livestock use and other types of disturbance like off-road vehicle use and camping activities can alter physiolological responses and competitive interactions of meadow species (Martin and Chambers 2001a, 2002) and, thus, community composition and ecological condition of meadow ecological types (Martin and Chambers 2001b). These disturbances can increase the effects of changes in water tables resulting from stream incision. For example, inappropriate livestock use (timing, season, or duration) of riparian meadows often compacts soils and decreases infiltration capacity (Weixelman and others 1997) and alters plant physiological processes and population and community dynamics through vegetation removal and nitrogen deposition (Martin and Chambers 2001a, 2001b). Inappropriate livestock use also can decrease stream channel stability by removing stream bank vegetation, decreasing bank undercuts, and increasing bank erosion (NRC 2002). Informal fall monitoring of several riparian meadows in the central Great Basin by Chambers over multiple years indicated that repeated overuse by livestock (60 to 80% utilization) likely affects streambank stability and ecological conditions in many of these meadows. Proactive management of livestock use and other anthropogenic disturbances is essential to maintain and improve the ecological conditions of these meadows and to ensure that stream stabilization and vegetation management projects succeed.

Post-Project Evaluation, Monitoring and Adaptive Management

Until recently, evaluations, or post-project appraisals (PPA), of most stream and meadow restoration/stabilization projects were limited to qualitative assessments, if they were conducted at all. The potential benefits of such appraisals have received considerable attention in recent years, and it is apparent that PPAs are essential for developing sound management strategies. Several advantages exist for systematically collecting post-project data for stream stabilization/restoration projects (Downs and Kondolf 2002) that are applicable to meadow complexes in the central Great Basin. These advantages are: determining (1) if the treatment was carried out or constructed as originally planned; (2) whether the treatment accomplished the project's objectives or success criteria; (3) if the project resulted in unexpected, negative effects; (4) if the project could be altered to improve future treatments; and (5) whether the treatment proved to be an effective use of limited resources.

It is important to note that the development of a PPA does not start after the project has been implemented. Rather, it begins at the onset of the project with the creation of one or more explicit statements that define success criteria. As

USDA Forest Service Gen. Tech. Rep. RMRS-GTR-258. 2011.

123

previously stated, success criteria are quantitative objectives against which post-project data can be compared to evaluate the performance of a specific approach. A PPA also requires collection of pre-project baseline data and post-project monitoring data, which can be compared to quantitatively determine how a system changes through time.

Many investigators and land managers now argue that PPAs should be combined with an adaptive management strategy (Walters 1986, 1997; Downs and Kondolf 2002). Halbert and Lee (1991) define adaptive management as an approach that:

> …treats management programs as experiments. Rather than assuming that we understand the system that we are attempting to manage, adaptive management allows management to proceed in the face of uncertainty. Adaptive management uses each step of a management program as an information-gathering exercise whose results are then used to modify or design the next state in the management program.

Adaptive management is not the same as management by trial and error. Rather, adaptive management involves systematic collection and analysis of data through sound ecosystem monitoring and subsequent revision of a management approach on the basis of the collected scientific information. The primary advantage of this approach is that it allows management decisions to be revised as new information is obtained on how the system functions (Wieringa and Morton 1996).

It may not seem necessary to expend the time and effort to develop detailed design criteria and post-project appraisals for relatively small meadow treatments. However, given the importance of meadow ecosystems to the region and the limited quantitative data regarding the performance of meadow treatments, we believe that PPAs coupled with adaptive management strategies should be used in the Great Basin.

References

Arthur, M.B. 1936. Fish stream improvement handbook. Washington, DC: U.S. Department of Agriculture, Forest Service. 33 p.

Belsky, A.J.; Matzke, A.; Uselman, S. 1999. Survey of livestock influences on stream and riparian ecosystems in the western United States. Journal of Soil and Water Conservation. 51: 419-431.

Beschta, R.L.; Platts, W.S.; Kauffman, J.B. 1992. Field review of fish habitat improvement projects in the Grande Ronde and John Day River basins of eastern Oregon. Portland, OR: U.S. Department of Energy, Bonneville Power Administration, DOE/BP-21943-1, February 1992. 53 p.

Castelli, R.M.; Chambers, J.C.; Tausch, R.J. 2000. Soil-plant relations along a soil-water gradient in Great Basin riparian meadows. Wetlands. 20: 251-266.

Chambers, J.C.; Blank, R.R.; Zamudio, D.C; Tausch, R.J. 1999. Central Nevada riparian areas: physical and chemical properties of meadow soils. Journal of Range Management. 52: 92-99.

Chambers, J.C.; Linnerooth, A.R. 2001. Restoring riparian meadows currently dominated by *Artemisia* using alternative state concepts—the establishment component. Applied Vegetation Science. 4: 157-166.

Chambers, J.C.; Miller, J.R.; Germanoski, D.; Weixelman, D.A. 2004a. Process based approaches for managing and restoring riparian ecosystems. In: Chambers, J.C.; Miller, J.R., eds. Great Basin Riparian Ecosystems—Ecology, Management and Restoration. Covelo, CA: Island Press: 261-292.

Chambers, J.C.; Tausch, R.J.; Korfmacher, J.L.; Miller, J.R.; Jewett, D.G. 2004b. Effects of geomorphic processes and hydrologic regimes on riparian vegetation. In: Chambers, J.C.; Miller, J.R., eds. Great Basin Riparian Ecosystems—Ecology, Management and Restoration. Covelo, CA: Island Press: 196-231.

Christensen, N.L.; Bartuska, A.M.; Brown, J.H.; Carpenter, S.; D'Antonio, C.; Francis, R.; Franklin, J.F.; MacMahon, J.A.; Noss, R.F.; Parsons, D.J.; Peterson, C.H.; Turner, M.G.; Woodmansee, R.G. 1996. The report of the Ecological Society of America Committee on the scientific basis for ecosystem management. Ecological Applications. 6: 665-691.

Downs, P.W.; Kondolf, M.G. 2002. Post-project appraisals in adaptive management of river channel restoration. Environmental Management. 29: 477-496.

Frissell, C.A.; Nawa, R.K. 1992. Incidence and causes of physical failure of artificial habitat structures in streams of western Oregon and Washington. North American Journal of Fisheries Management. 12: 182-197.

Ganskopp, D.C. 1986. Tolerances of sagebrush, rabbitbrush, and greasewood to elevated water tables. Journal of Range Management. 39: 334-337.

Gray, D.H.; Sotir, R.B. 1996. Biotechnical and Soil Bioengineering Slope Stabilization. A Practical Guide for Erosion Control. New York, NY: Wiley. 378 p.

Halbert, C.L.; Lee, K.N. 1991. Implementing adaptive management. The Northwest Environmental Journal. 7: 136-150.

Hoag, J.C. 2003. Harvesting, propagating and planting wetland plants. Tech. Note. Plant Materials No. 13. Boise, ID: U.S. Department of Agriculture, Natural Resources Conservation Service. 11 p.

Lahde, D. 2003. The influence of secondary roads on stream incision in watersheds of the central Great Basin. Natural Resources and Environmental Sciences, University of Nevada, Reno. Thesis. 103 p.

Laycock, W.A. 1991. Stable states and thresholds of range condition on North American rangelands: a viewpoint. Journal of Range Management. 44: 427-433.

Li, M.; Eddleman, K.E. 2002. Biotechnical engineering as an alternative to traditional engineering methods. A biotechnical streambank stabilization design approach. Landscape and Urban Planning. 60: 225-242.

Martin, D.W.; Chambers, J.C. 2001a. Restoring degraded riparian meadows: biomass and species responses. Journal of Range Management. 54: 284-291.

Martin, D.W.; Chambers, J.C. 2001b. Effects of water table, clipping, and species interactions on *Carex nebrascensis* and *Poa pratensis* in riparian meadows. Wetlands. 21: 422-430.

Martin, D.W.; Chambers, J.C. 2002. Restoration of riparian meadows degraded by livestock grazing: above- and below-ground responses. Plant Ecology. 163: 77-91.

Miller, J.R.; Kochel, R.C. 2008. Characterization and evaluation of stream restoration projects in North Carolina. Final Report to the North Carolina Clean Water Management Trust Fund, CWMTF. Project No. 2002B-805. 109 p.

Miller, J.R.; Kochel, R.C. 2010. Assessment of channel dynamics, in-stream structures and post-project channel adjustments in North Carolina and its implications to effective stream restoration. Environmental Earth Sciences. 59: 1681-1692.

124

USDA Forest Service Gen. Tech. Rep. RMRS-GTR-258. 2011.

Miller, J.R.; Orbock Miller, S.M. 2007. Contaminated Rivers: A Geomorphological-Geochemical Approach to Site Assessment and Remediation. Berlin, Germany: Springer. 418 p.

Monsen, S.B.; Stevens, R.; Shaw, N.L., comps. 2004. Restoring western rangelands and wildlands. Gen. Tech. Rep. RMRS-GTR-136-vol-1. Fort Collins, CO: U.S. Department of Agriculture, Forest Service, Rocky Mountain Research Station. 294 p.

National Research Council [NRC]. 2002. Riparian Areas: Functions and Strategies for Management. Washington, DC: National Academy Press. 428 p.

Riley, A.L. 1998. Restoring Streams in Cities. Washington, DC: Island Press. 423 p.

Ritter, D.F.; Kochel, R.C.; Miller, J.R. 1999. The disruption of Grassy Creek: implications concerning catastrophic events and thresholds. Geomorphology. 29: 323-338.

Rosgen, D.L. 1996. Applied River Morphology. Pagosa Springs, CO: Wildland Hydrology, Inc. 390 p.

Rosgen, D.L. 2001. The cross-vane, w-weir, and j-hook vane structures. Their description, design and application for stream stabilization and river restoration. Proceedings of ASCE Conference on Wetlands Engineering and River Restoration: 27-31 August 2001; Reno, NV. Reston, VA: 1-22.

Rosgen, D. 2006. The cross-vane, w-weir, and j-hook vane structures (Updated 2006). Description, design and application for stream stabilization and river restoration. Wildland Hydrology, Inc. Available: http://www.wildlandhydrology.com.

Schumm, S.A.; Watson, C.; Harvey, M. 1984. Incised channels: morphology, dynamics and control. Littleton, CO: Water Resources Publications.

Seehorn, M.E. 1985. Fish habitat improvement handbook. Technical Publication R8-TP 7. Atlanta, GA: U.S. Forest Service, Southern Region. 30 p.

Seehorn, M.E. 1992. Stream habitat improvement handbook. Technical Publication R8-TP 16. Atlanta, GA: U.S. Forest Service, Southern Region. 30 p.

Simon, A. 1989. The discharge of sediment in channelized alluvial streams. Water Resources Research Bulletin. 25: 1177-88.

Simon, A.; Hupp, C.R. 1986. Channel evolution in modified Tennessee channels. Proceedings of the Fourth Federal Interagency Sedimentation Conference. 24-27 March 1986; Las Vegas, NV; in two volumes: 5.71-5.82.

Skidmore, P.B.; Shields, F.D.; Doyle, M.W.; Miller, D.E. 2001. A categorization of approaches to natural channel design. In: Hayes, D.F., ed. Proceedings of the 2001 wetlands engineering and river restoration conference. Reston, VA: American Society of Civil Engineers. CD-ROM.

Thompson, D.M. 2005. The history of the use and effectiveness of instream structures in the United States. Geological Society of America. Reviews in Engineering Geology. Vol. XVI: 35-50.

USDA Forest Service. 1952. Fish stream improvement handbook. Washington, DC.

Walters, C.J. 1986. Adaptive Management of Renewable Resources. New York, NY: Macmillan Pub. Co. 374 p.

Walters, C.J. 1997. Challenges in adaptive management of riparian and coastal ecosystems. Conservation Ecology [online]. 1(2):1. Available: http://www.consecol.org/vol1/iss2/art1/.

Weixelman, D.; Zamudio, D.; Zamudio, K.; Heise, K. 1996. Ecological type identification and ecological status determination. R4-ECOL-96-01. Ogden, UT: U.S. Department of Agriculture, Forest Service, Region 4.

Weixelman, D.; Zamudio, D.C.; Zamudio, K.A.; Tausch, R.J. 1997. Classifying ecological types and evaluating site degradation. Journal of Range Management. 50: 315-321.

Whisenant, S.G. 1999. Restoring Damaged Wildlands. A Process-Oriented, Landscape-Scale Approach. Cambridge, United Kingdom: Cambridge University Press. 312 p.

Wieringa, M.J.; Morton, A.G. 1996. Hydropower, adaptive management and biodiversity. Environmental Management. 20: 831-840.

Wohl, E.; Angermeier, P.L.; Bledsoe, B.; Kondolf, G.M.; MacDonnell, L.; Merritt, D.M.; Palmer, M.A.; Poff, N.L.; Tarboton, D. 2005. River restoration. Water Resources Research. Vol. 41: W10301.

Wright, M.J.; Chambers, J.C. 2002. Restoring riparian meadows currently dominated by *Artemisia* using threshold and alternative state concepts—aboveground vegetation response. Applied Vegetation Science. 5: 237-246.

USDA Forest Service Gen. Tech. Rep. RMRS-GTR-258. 2011.

125